THE REPAIR & RESTORATION OF
WOODEN BOATS

THE REPAIR & RESTORATION OF
WOODEN BOATS

Mike Harper & Dave Johnston

Charles Scribner's Sons New York

We should like to thank Mustafa Sami for his fine artwork, and also our wives, Sarah Johnston and Diana Harper for all their help.

First published 1980
© Mike Harper and Dave Johnston 1980
First U.S. edition published by Charles Scribner's Sons, 1980

1 3 5 7 9 11 13 15 17 19 I/C 18 16 14 12 10 8 6 4 2
Printed in Great Britain.
Library of Congress Catalog Card Number 80-65288
ISBN: 0-684-16632-1

Contents

Why this book?

Despite—some might say because of—the fibre glass invasion of boat building and the subsequent increase in interest in steel, aluminium and ferro-cement construction, there are still a very large number of wooden boats about. This book attempts to assist the owners of these boats to maintain, improve, restore and renovate their craft.

An investment in a boat is not one which should be written off just because time has passed. If most of a boat is sound, there should be no reason why time and effort, not to mention money, should not be put into it to protect that investment. At the same time, there is no sense in pouring cash into a vessel whose end has come. Again, this book attempts to enable readers to make a reasonable appraisal of what is involved in keeping an ageing lady afloat and in service, so that they can judge when the point has been reached when the work is beyond their capabilities and the cost would be too much to justify offering the work to a boatyard.

The number of skilled craftsmen in boatbuilding is not increasing, not least because youngsters do not wish to follow a long and arduous and ill-paid apprenticeship, not least because a skilled boat-builder can often earn more doing rough carpentry on a building site or relatively unskilled and less satisfying work with shopfitters or exhibition contractors. Hence the possibility of finding a yard which is able and willing to do a decent boatbuilding job on a wooden vessel is diminishing. We hope, therefore, that this book will encourage owners to get around the problem by tackling work themselves.

Dave Johnston is a boatyard owner who 'did his time', as they say, as a shipwright, and who has a real and genuine love of wooden boats. Mike Harper is a professional journalist whose first wooden craft was afloat over thirty-five years ago and who has never lost a deep feeling for wooden craft.

Together we have tried to offer hard practical advice for those fortunate enough to own a boat built of wood.

We should like to thank the editor and publishers of BOAT, in whose pages much of this work appeared for the first time.

Chapter 1
From basics

If you are going to have anything to do with boats of any size it is a good idea to have the proper terms at your fingertips, to enable you to talk about the job or understand any professional advice you may get.

It may be enough simply to take a car to the garage saying "it's broken", but it can save money and time (and dignity) to be able to say "the clutch is slipping", or whatever.

A shipwright may well guess what is wrong if you say, for example, that water is coming in the bottom of your boat, but if you tell him you think the garboard is leaking midships he will know where to look and what sort of repair would be needed (and so, incidentally, will you).

So, to start off on the right foot, here are some explanations of those mysterious-sounding and commonly-heard terms.

Types of planking and categories of hull:

Carvel
One of the oldest and most common forms of planking, carvel construction has longitudinal planks running from stem to stern, each one individually cut to shape to produce a fair line as near as possible to parallel with the sheer line, and butting on to each other. This form of planking is caulked to make the joint watertight.

Clinker
Commonly found in traditional beach and estuary boats, clinker planking is easily spotted by its overlapping planks, each one overlapping the one below.

Diagonal carvel
Exactly what the name implies. Instead of the planking being parallel to the sheer, it runs approximately 30° diagonally to the horizontal, and the planks are caulked as in carvel planking.

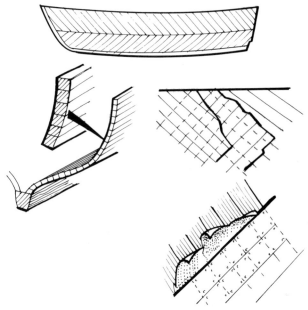

Fig. 1b At top is an example of diagonal chine construction and below to the left is an example of strip planking. To the right of that is cold moulded construction and at the bottom is double diagonal with calico between the layers

Strip planking
This is a form of carvel planking where the planks are not shaped because they are narrow strips (e.g. 1in × 1in) which easily take the shape of the hull. These are generally glued and nailed to each other, and there is no caulking.

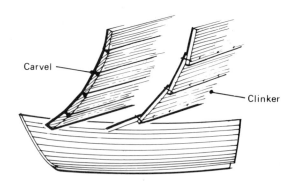

Carvel

Clinker

Fig. 1a,

9

Photo 1 An example of carvel construction in an older boat

Photo 2 Clinker construction on a Norwegian-built boat seen at an Earls Court boat show.

Photo 3 Hard chine hull built of plywood

Double diagonal

This type of planking is made from two thin skins of diagonal carvel with a layer of oiled calico between, each skin's diagonal running in the opposite direction for strength. This does not need caulking.

Cold moulded

Cold moulded construction is a diagonal construction except that there are three or more skins which are glued to each other as though making a sheet of plywood.

Round bilge construction (Fig. 2a)

As the name implies, this type of hull has a rounded shape under the water and no sharp changes of shape. This is the traditional hull shape.

Hard chine (Fig. 2b)

This is easy to recognise by its definite changes in hull shape which produce a distinct line where the underwater section meets the topsides.

Multi-chine (Fig. 2c)

This is a progression from the hard chine shape in which there are three or four or even more distinct angular changes in hull shape. These hard chine constructions have developed with the introduction of plywoods and diagonal techniques of planking.

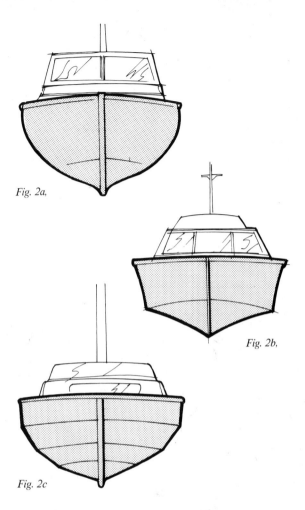

Fig. 2a,

Fig. 2b,

Fig. 2c

Anatomy of the boat

1 *Stem*

The very front of the boat, and part of its backbone. The front end of the planking is fastened into it.

2 *Forefoot*

The forward part of the underwater section of the stem.

3 *Apron*

The inside of the stem to which the planking is fastened.

4 *Deadwood*

The inside of the forefoot to which the planking is fastened—it is shown scarphed on to the apron.

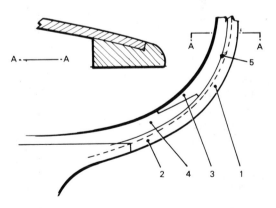

Fig. 3 This is the way the stem of a conventionally built yacht is put together. The numbers are fully explained in the text. The inset half-drawing shows in plan view how a plank is rebated into one side of the stem

11

5 *Rebate line*

(You will sometimes hear this referred to as the 'rabbit line'). It is where the planking is inset (rebated) into the keel, forefoot, stem, etc. The planks are rebated or shouldered into the timber to protect their end-grain and to ensure a nice 'fair line' plus a watertight joint. In the illustration, the dotted line is the rebate line.

6 *Keel*

This is the outside of the backbone. It's the long length of timber you see sticking below the planking on the bottom. It helps to boat to keep a straight course, and to prevent it 'sheering' (turning right or left of its own accord when under way).

7 *Hog*

Only found in timber boats and is the length of wood to which the planking is fastened along the keel (which is its backbone). The hog forms the rabbit (rebate), like the stem and apron do.

8 *Keelson*

Again, only in some wooden boats, not in GRP (Glass Reinforced Plastic) craft. It's a second hog, but it runs over the top of the frames and timbers. It ties all the frames, timbers and the hog together when bolted through the keel.

9 *Bilgekeels*

These are lengths of wood which are bolted outside the hull (like the keel)—but they are fitted, one each side, just on the turn of the bilge. They serve to help the keel in steerage, slowing down the roll of the boat, add strength longitudinally, and they also help when the boat has its own weight on one side when laying on its side. Bilgekeels are often fitted to glass boats for the added protection they give the gelcoat on the hull's bilge, afloat or on the hard.

10 *Buttblocks*

Pieces of timber which cover the seam where two planks meet end on. The butt-block is usually about 2in wider than the planks' width square and is fastened to the planks' joint to hold them *in situ*.

11 *Sheer*

It's the line produced where the planking joins the deck. For example, on a house the sheer

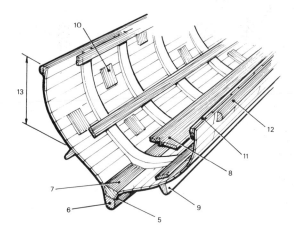

Fig. 4 This cross-section shows conventional construction of a wooden boat. The numbers indicate the different structural members and are fully described in the text

would be the line of the guttering.

12 *Rubbers*

Lengths of timber which run from stem to stern along the sheer. They serve, as the name implies, to protect the hull's top planking from chafing.

13 *Topsides*

Term used for the planking from the waterline up to the sheer.

14 *Half beams*

These are the small deck beams lying athwartships along the side decks.

15 *Carlings*

Lengths of timber which run fore and aft along the inside of the side decks, engine hatches, and any other hatch openings. Their purpose is to receive the ends of the half-beams. In wooden boats, all carlings and deck beams should be dovetail jointed. In GRP the term carlings is still used to indicate the same areas.

16 *Cab-sides*

Pieces of wood that usually cover the carlings around the cockpit and hatch openings.

17 *Coamings*

They are the sides of the superstructure, and run from the carlings up to the cab shelf. You could be excused for calling them cabin sides.

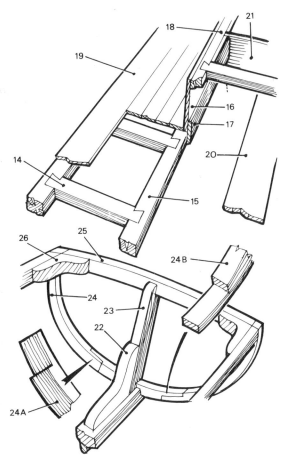

21 *Bulkheads*
These are partions which go across the boat at right-angles to the centre-line, and are of great importance for strength.

From deck-level, let's go aft to the transom and surrounding area. Principally, this will apply more to wooden craft than others—and more particularly to round-bilge boats which are more complicated to construct in many cases than the flat (planing or hard-chine) hull.

22 *Stern knee*
This is like all other knees and is found where the hog joins the stern post. It forms a strong corner-bracket to the transom.

23 *Stern post*
This is a post which goes from the hog or keel up to the underside of the deck at the centre of the transom. It is like a continuation of the backbone and, as stated earlier, the stern knee is fastened through it.

24 *Fashion pieces*
These are the outside framework of the transom. They are usually cut out of solid timber and halving-jointed together.

25 *Transom beam*
This is a continuation of the fashion pieces, and is usually the same thickness.

26 *Quarter knees*
These join the gunwales to the transom, and tie in the transom, like the stern knee.

Main frame parts

27 *Frames*
These perform rather the same function as your ribs, except that they run plumb (vertical) to the waterline. They will determine the shape of the boat before it is built.

28 *Ribs or timbers*
These are like frames, but they are usually smaller in 'scantlings' (measurements) than the frames—and are usually steamed into shape. Frames are usually cut to shape.

Fig. 5 Here we continue describing the parts of a boat, dealing now with transom, deck and superstructure. The explanation of the different numbered parts is continued in the text. This drawing should be studied in conjunction with fig. 3 and fig. 4.

18 *Cab-shelf*
In its way, it performs the same kind of job as the ship's gunwale but it runs along the top of the cab-side on the inside. It takes the ends of the cabin's beams.

19 *Covering board*
This is the wide deck-plank which runs around the outside just above the gunwale. It is usually about two or three times wider than its deck planks.

20 *King plank*
Again, this is a wide deck plank, usually four or five times the width of the deck planks, which runs right down the centre-line of the boat.

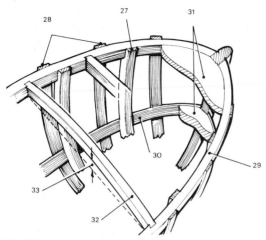

Fig. 6 These are the main structural members of a boat. Their description is continued in the text

29 *Gunwale*

This is the timber which runs the whole length of the boat around the inside at the top of the hull just under the deck at the side, *into* which the deck beams are jointed.

(*Shelf.* This is also a gunwale but is so named because the deck beams sit *on* the shelf; so the shelf will be the thickness of beam below the deck. You only have one or the other—shelf or gunwale.)

30 *Bilge stringer*

A length of timber which runs the full length of the boat around the inside of the hull, just on the turn of the bilge, or close to the water line.

31 *Breasthook*

A lump of wood cut into a wedge shape to fit snugly between the gunwales or the bilge-stringers at the apron.

32 *Deckbeams*

The timbers which span across the boat from gunwale to gunwale; they are usually cambered.

33 *Camber*

The name for the radius of the deck over the deck-beams.

Here are three general descriptive terms you will hear bandied about, so it's as well to know what they mean.

1 *Tumble home*

This is where the hull's topsides (the topsides are the sides on top of the waterline) turn *inwards* on some craft, so that the sheer (top arrow) is narrower than the beam (lower arrow) at that point.

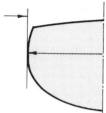

Fig. 7a,

2 *Flare*

That is where the hull's shape reverses *outwards* in a concave form—and of course you can have flare below the water line as well as above—as indicated by the arrows.

Fig. 7b,

3 *Tuck*

Well, of course, as everyone knows, the tuck of a boat could be classed as the stern's outboard deadwood. Too complicated? Right then—the tuck is where the planking runs into the stern and ends up vertical, forming a sort of knife point (arrowed).

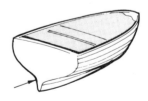

Fig. 7c,

4 *A fair-line*

You will notice that we will frequently refer to a *fair line*. This means that if you are drawing any line (such as around the boat for example) or between two or more points (such as when spiling a plank) on a piece of wood or template, the line you draw must be a good smooth even shape. (A). Or, if it starts as a straight line and then curves, it must flow nice and evenly. There should not be any kinks in it, or bumps and hollows (B).

Fig. 7d

In other words, the line, when drawn, should be pleasing to the eye.

Old Dave Johnston proverb—if it looks right, it is right.

5 *Hogging (Fig. 8, top illustration)*
This is where the boat has altered its shape lengthwise. If you look along the bottom of the keel, it will look as if the stern and stem have dropped—or as if the midships have lifted. This causes straining on the planking and longitudinals on wood boats, and possibly permanent distortion of a GRP boat.

This can be caused by bad slipping or laying-up, and results from too much weight being taken amidships, and with the fore and aft overhang being unsupported.

6 *Sagging (Fig. 8, bottom illustration)*
This is another example of the keel being distorted but in this case it is in the opposite direction to hogging. The stem and stern have lifted, or the midship section has dropped.

It is obvious that the craft has had too much support at the fore and aft extremities and too little (if any) amidships. In my experience, *sagging* is not so common as *hogging*.

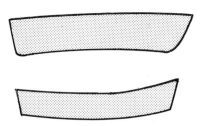

Fig. 8 Hogging and sagging

There is one final point, relating to taking boats from the water—one is often dismayed how many boatyards lift craft in a cradle, *but without a top spreader frame*. Frankly, I would never take a boat near such a place for lifting. The rings at the ends of the cradle straps are simply attached to the hook on the crane—with the result that as the boat is lifted, a crushing force is exerted against the hull sides—and I have known of craft caving in under the strain!

The sling I have illustrated here is a large wire, nylon or fibre webbing designed to go under the boat in a U—usually in pairs connected to a cross-frame, which prevents much of the crushing effect. It is a quick, efficient way of landing a boat but, as you can see, great care is necessary to prevent hogging or sagging during the operation.

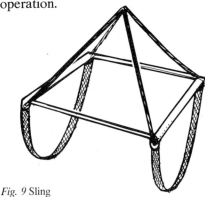

Fig. 9 Sling

Cradling

To finish dry berthing, here are the terms for laying-up craft and an illustration of how a boat should be supported, plus an explanation of the terms used for various aspects of cradling—it sounds more like a boat zoo, with its dogs and foxes!

1 *Shores*
Props which help to hold up the boat when it is on dry land. They usually go up under the gunwale.

2 *Toms*
They are also props. These go under the boat around the turn of the bilge, or along the chine. They help to support the hull, and take off some of the strain caused by internal weight on the heel.

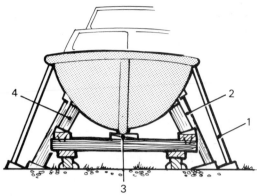

Fig. 10 Chocking up a boat. The numbers are explained in the text

3 Fox wedges

A pair of long, tapered timber wedges which, when held together, form a rectangle. They are normally used for chocking up under the keel when a boat is laid up, or having work done on a slip.

4 Keel blocks

Generally pieces of softwood timber about 12in square by 3ft or 4ft long. They are put under the keel of a boat, again when she is on the slip or being laid up to prevent hogging or sagging, and the space under the keel (if any) is taken up by fox wedges.

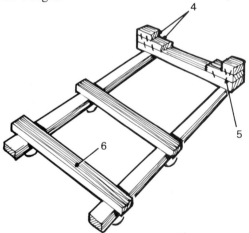

Fig. 11 Details of a cradle for housing a boat on dry land. The numbers are explained in the text

5 Dogs

Big iron staples, about 18in long of ¾in or 1in iron bar, and the two teeth or spikes are about 6in long. They are used to hold together two or more keel blocks on top of each other—the dog being driven in to the keel blocks, spanning as many as it can to hold them together in the manner of a cramp.

6 Cradle

A big trolley, usually on old railway lines, or a greased runway. A cradle is used for slipping a boat. It is operated by a winch, which pulls it down under the boat when she is floating and then cradle and boat are winched up the slip together. Just before the boat is losing buoyancy it is chocked to the cradle, which prevents the boat rolling sideways as they both come out of the water.

Joints

Joints which are used in boatbuilding, could be put into two categories: longitudinal strength (keeping a fair line) and locking joints.

Here are some of the more important types:

Scarph joint
This is used a great deal in boatbuilding. There are four types of scarph joint in general use in boatbuilding, which join timber lengthwise in a 'fair line'. A good point to remember about scarph joints is that their length should be about six times the thickness of the timber. For example, for a 2in × 1in timber, the scarph will be 6in long.

1 Splice—a straight diagonal cut which is glued.

2 Single-lip scarph—it is also used as a glueing joint. This has a lip at one end, and can be screwed as well.

3 Double-lip scarph—used as a dry joint (a term used when the joint is painted or bedded and is then bolted or riveted).

4 Locking scarph—also a dry joint, generally used in big timber like a keel. It is the hardest of all scarphs to do.

5 Dovetail joints—interlocking joints which should always be used on any beams or carlings. Any ordinary joint, such as a halving joint, would soon pull out with the movements of the boat. There are several ways of doing dovetails, two of which are shown here.

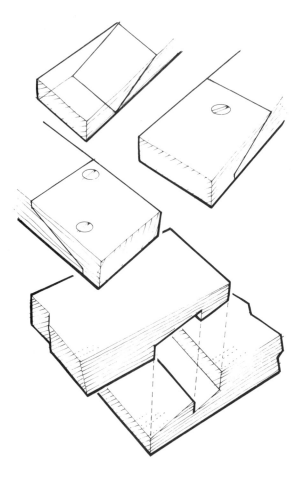

Fig. 12 Four types of scarph joints

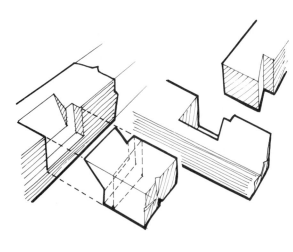

Fig. 13 Dovetails into beams etc.

Tools

What sort of tool kit should you have? Boat building is basically carpentry, except for certain extra skills, which will become apparent as time goes on. So the basic tools are:

1 Claw hammer
2 Tenon saw
3 Panel saw
4 Smoothing plane
5 Set of chisels (¼in, ½in, ¾in, 1in)
6 Brace and bits—also ranging from a ¼in up to 1in.
7 Set or a collection of high speed drill bits, ranging from $\frac{1}{16}$in up to ⅜in.
8 A square
9 A bevel.
10 A boat or building level.
11 A rule or tape-measure.
12 Oil stone.
13 Screwdriver.

I have made a lot of my own tools, as I have gone along. I will mention a few which can be easily made, but first, do you know how to sharpen what tools you have and use them correctly?

Sharpen it!
Half the battle when working in wood is to use tools that are sharp and properly sharpened!

Before you dive for a chisel, grab the oil-stone first and let's get that chisel sharp. An oil-stone (A), for its own protection, should be in a box (B). Take a set-square (C) or steel rule and lay it on the oil-stone lengthways, and then hold it up to the light. Look for any hollow (D) in the stone surface. Now put the square or rule across the stone and look for a hollow (E) in that aspect.

If there is, you must get the stone flat before using it to sharpen tools.

Find an old pane of thick glass or mirror and a handful of fine sand. Sprinkle the sand on the glass, add a drop of water, lay the oil-stone face down on top of the sand and run it around in circular motion—and keep this up till the stone is nice and flat once again.

Now to the chisel. The tapered bit should be a ground bevel of about 22° (F) from the back or bottom. Put a drop of light oil on the stone, lay the chisel flat down on it, and rub it up and down a few times. Wipe the oil off the chisel, turn it up and examine it closely. You can see where the

17

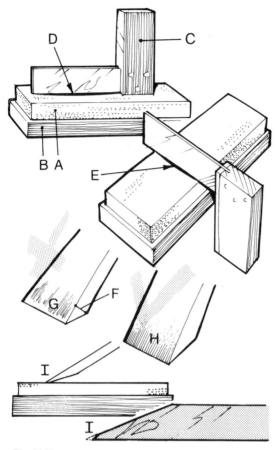

Fig. 14 Sharpening tools

stone has rubbed on the back of the chisel by the smooth matt surface (G).

Ideally, this smooth surface should appear all the way across the back of the chisel, and about 1in up. In the sketch the unshaded bits (G) are those which are being missed by the oil stone. The object is to make the whole of the back of the blade flat (H).

Flattening the back of the chisel can be a very slow job—but it must be done for a perfectly sharp sharpening. When you have succeeded in flattening the back, turn it over and lay the chisel's ground bevel fully on the stone. Then tip the chisel up a few more degrees—so that you are now able to make a new bevel (I) at about 35°.

Rub the chisel up and down the whole length of the stone, working across from left to right and back again, keeping the chisel at the same sharpening angle.

Now that you have put this sharpening bevel on the chisel, turn it over and rub the back or flat side of the chisel up and down the stone a few times. Then wipe the dirt off the chisel and gently strop it up and down the heel of the palm of your hand. If you have done the sharpening properly, when you strop it, a very fine sliver of steel should break away from the point.

So much for the chisel. Now you can sharpen your plane and spokeshave blades the same way. (And don't be tempted to open tins of paint with your chisel—or use it as a screwdriver or lever!)

Now let's have a look at planes in general—and the jobs that each particular type will do.

1 *Smoothing plane*
This is the one automatically used by many people. It should be used on timber which is near the stage of painting. Don't use it on long lengths if they are to be straight, as the plane will follow each hollow and bump. It should be used as its names implies—to smooth the surface.

2 *Shooting planes*
(Whilst we are still with the steel planes.) Sometimes they are known as 'forward joiners'. These range from about 12in up to 18in long, and are for use on straight or flat runs—for example the edge of a door, or a work surface.

3 *Rebate plane*
And it is used for cutting rebates or shoulders The blade is the same width as the plane, and can be moved forward to the nose of the plane. If needed, some of them have an attachment which governs the depth and width of cut.

4 *Bullnose plane*
Like a rebate plane, but without any attachments. They do, though, come in several widths and lengths. They are used for small joinery work, such as cutting shoulders on mortice joints. Never use them on wide surfaces.

5 *Combination plane*
This, as the name implies, is a combination of planes—mainly moulding planes. The plane has usually about 10 to 20 different size and shape cutting blades, which can be interchanged. This plane is mainly used in joinery for making mouldings.

6 *Block plane (wood)*
About the same size as a steel smoother, and was the forerunner of the smoothing plane. Its throat is wider than the steel plane so be careful, when using it, that it does not tear or judder.

7 *Try-plane*
(One of which I have) is about 2ft long. You can get steel try-planes as well. These are used for very long and straight runs. I use mine for 'shooting-up' my planking.

I also have several small block planes which vary from concave to convex in the shape of their bottoms. These I made myself, or converted old ones for a job; I had bought them from a junk (sorry, an 'antique') shop.

I have a useful habit of buying old moulding planes (wooden ones, the forerunners of the combination plane), and reshaping them to suit a particular job I might be doing, which needs a certain shaped plane.

8 *Compass plane*
Made of wood or steel, and has an adjustable bottom which can be altered to suit any size circumference—hence the name.

9 *Spoke shaves*
(Which I class as planes—and of which you can get flat-bottomed and round-bottomed ones.) These are used for curves—the flat-bottomed ones for outside curves and the round-bottomed variety for inside curves.

So, as you may see, when it comes to the most suitable tool for the job, it's not always plain sailing—or plain planing!

Now, how many times have you persuaded yourself you don't need to use that panel saw, or tried to work a job so that you won't need to use that particular one—because the so-and-so has a mind of its own and just won't cut where you want!

Well, why won't it? Let us take a look at the saw first. Is it sharp? If not, get it sharpened—which will save you effort and timber. How do you know if it is blunt enough to need sharpening? If it is blunt, the teeth are flattened along the top as in Fig. 15b. It should resemble 15a.

When the saw has been sharpened, take a look at the 'set' on the saw (15c). Look along the top of the saw from the handle and you will see that the

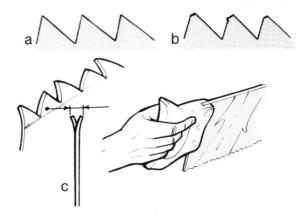

Fig. 15 Saw sharpening

teeth lean out to the side of the saw—which is what we call the 'set'. The set should be wider than the saw's thickness, which stops the saw sticking as you are sawing and helps to clear the sawdust out of the cut. It also helps you turn the saw a little to follow a line when cutting. So, when you take your saw to be sharpened, ask for it to be set as well.

Of course, everybody can cut a bit of wood with a saw. It's child's play! But what comes naturally is not necessarily the most effective, so here are a few instructions. Take the saw in your hand—and make it feel comfortable. Get used to it, and its weight. Let your index finger lie along the outside of the handle, as if you are pointing at something (see above).

Now to cut. The wrist, forearm, elbow, upper arm and shoulder should all be in line, so that you operate like a piston. Don't let your elbow flap about when cutting—keep in line with the saw. All this may come to you slowly, as bad habits are hard to lose.

One more point: when cutting try to keep the saw at a 30° angle of cut, and make a slow fore-and-aft rocking movement with the saw as you cut, like (if you will forgive me) a seesaw!

In the tool list I mentioned a bevel, which leads me into a yarn where I nearly put my foot in it when the man at the bus-stop said to his friend, with an air of much authority, ". . . and boat-builders never use a square." However, before I had time to butt in, wounded by this affront to my profession, he saved the day with ". . . they always use a bevel instead."

In fact, we do use both—but perhaps a bevel more often. For example, in fitting a screen we

19

would use a bevel as a guide for drilling holes underneath the deck-head to line up with the lower frame of a screen.

Here, you will see just how it is used. (A) The bevel was laid on the cab roof and the blade angled to the screen and clamped with the pinch-bolt in this position; then in to the cabin where the through-holes had been drilled in the cab roof for the screws. (B) Laying the bevel against the underside of the cab roof you will be able to line up the hand-drill with the blade. Thus the pilot holes, when drilled, will go straight into the bottom screen frame dead centre.

That is just an example of how a bevel can be put to use and while on the subject of bevels, here is how you can make one, either in wood or metal: get a piece of hardwood 18in long of ½in × 1in and cut it into three 6in lengths. Lay them together and cramp them (A) making sure that they are flush all around.

Drill one ¼in hole (1) about ½in from one end, and fit a ¼in machine screw (2) with a wing-nut. Now drill a ¼in hole (3) a ½in from the other end.

Let the cramp off and pivot the centre piece of wood out and cut 1¼in off the end (4) at an angle.

Put some wood glue on the two sides of the little angled piece you have just cut off, and put it back between (5) the two outside bits of wood and tap a ¼in dowel down through the hole, with a bit of glue on it. You can use either dowelling bought at a DIY shop or make your own. Here is how. Drill a hole of the size of the dowelling you require—in our case ¼in — in a piece of stout steel. Then cut a piece of wood just a bit bigger than the hole. Taper off one end and then hit the wood through the metal with a mallet. This works for sizes up to about ½in.

Now put the cramp on the glued end, making sure the edges are all flush and let dry.

Finally sand off any excess dried glue, and there is your bevel (B) ready for use. If you make it in metal, just use a copper nail and rivet it instead of using dowels.

Let us drift into something for a while which I feel is important, and that is screws.

It is not surprising that the uninitiated look blank when they go to their local store and ask for a box of 1½in screws, let's say, and the man says "Yes sir—what size?" Well, the size he is talking about is the gauge of the screw and nobody need by ashamed of not knowing.

Really it is quite simple. What you do is to

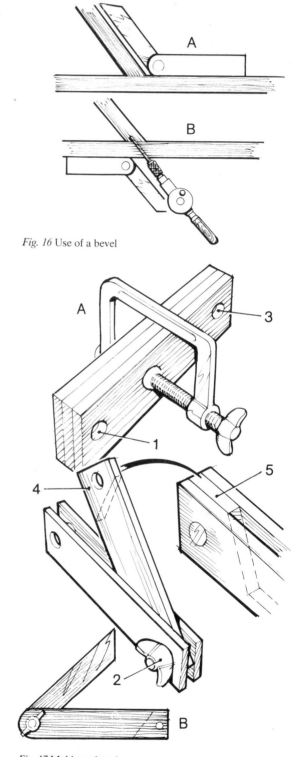

Fig. 16 Use of a bevel

Fig. 17 Making a bevel

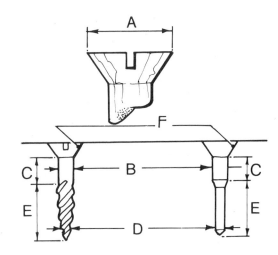

Fig. 18 Hammering through a dowel rod

Fig. 19 Measuring a screw

measure across the head of the screw (A) in sixteenths. Let's say that this (A) is $^7/_{16}$in. You double that—then subtract $^2/_{16}$in. Thus it is $^7/_{16}$in plus $^7/_{16}$in, which equals $^{14}/_{16}$in, less $^2/_{16}$in, which leaves $^{12}/_{16}$in. The screw you need is a 12 gauge.

Remember—the bigger the gauge number of the screw, the bigger the diameter of the screw.

But, just to confuse you completely, this is reversed when it comes to nails. A 2-gauge nail is one of the thickest and a 12-gauge nail is very thin!

How to screw

Now, let's to this job properly and we won't have any more of those screws that either won't go fully home (or break off when you are trying to get them home)—or which, sooner or later, pull loose.

Measure the shank (B) where there is no thread and drill a hole of the same width to the length (C) of the shank. Then measure the solid part of the thread at the bottom (D) and drill a hole of that diameter, the same length (E) as the thread. (F) is the countersink.

How to drill

A big question that confronts many people is how to prevent a drill going further into the wood than is intended. Obviously, if the drill of the same diameter as the shank is allowed to drill

down deeply, it ruins that screwing position for all intents and purposes.

The answer is quite simple—you can use a stop-collar. It is best made of softwood. For example, if the hole required is $^1/_2$in deep, and your drill is $1^1/_2$in long, you can cut a 1in length of softwood dowel, drill through the middle of this, and slip it over the drill shank. Thus, when you have drilled to a depth of $^1/_2$in, the collar stops the drill from going further. A rather more trouble-some method is, of course, to reduce the length of the drill bit to the appropriate length and resharpen it—which might be appropriate if you had dozens of such holes to drill. The problem here is that the chuck segments can gouge the surface of the wood, whereas the piece of softwood dowel will not.

Talking about drilling holes, brings to mind this story. Some time ago, when I was working for a boatyard, the situation arose where an apprentice was standing and moaning about there being no tools to do the jobs, and so on.

"What's the problem?", I asked. He grumbled that he had to cut a 2 $^3/_{16}$in dia. hole up tight against the bulkhead and deckhead—and that there was not one drill in the yard the right size to do the job. When I said I had a drill that would do the job, he looked considerably relieved. He followed me like a dog with two tails to my tools, where I handed him a $^3/_{16}$in drill.

He looked at it and then me—and said, "That won't do!" So I offered him a $^1/_8$in drill. He looked at me again and said in some choice words what I

could do with my drills. I offered him again the
³/₁₆in drill to cut his 2 ³/₁₆in dia. hole. Again, he
called me some sort of idiot. So I made him take
the ⅛in drill—and go away and think about it. I
must explain, of course, that it was our responsibility to instruct apprentices.

About an hour later he returned me my drill,
and apologised.

So—what's the secret of cutting out a bigger
hole with a small drill? Quite simple, you mark
your hole out, and then drill just inside the
outline of the larger hole, many small holes, as
close together as possible. Then very carefully
chop out with a sharp chisel and there is your
hole. Any smoothing you may find necessary can
be done with a half-round wood file, or an
abrasive flap-wheel.

Enough of tools for now. We will come on to
them again later.

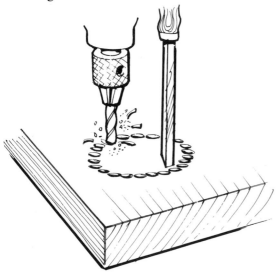

Fig. 20 Cutting a large hole

Wood

Nowadays, with hardwoods being so expensive,
softwoods are being used more frequently.

Drying wood

Although it is almost impossible for anyone not
connected with the wood or joinery industry to
know what '17% moisture content' or suchlike
represents, it is fair to say that for many practical
purposes, so long as the timber is properly dry, it
can be glued; more so, of course, if it is fully-
seasoned timber that has been in use, and which
you are repairing.

Now in order for timber to dry out, it must be
bare timber! If there is something like paint
residue in the grain, it will retard or prevent
drying out.

Incidentally, it is not widely realised that in the
case of a marine or exterior-grade plywood, it is
usually only the outer lamination that is wet, as
the wet has almost certainly not penetrated the
inter-layer resin so long as the wood is good.

Plywood rots, certainly, but you will usually
find that it does so at the edges, where water can
penetrate to a considerable depth to all laminations, if the medium at that point has become
defective.

Another point to bear in mind is that softwoods
such as pine, etc. have big pores and will dry
quickly—but hard-woods have smaller pores
and dry slowly. If you are going to apply GRP or
varnish to wood, it must be very dry! If there is a
high moisture content, these will simply lift off,
as the damp will prevent these agents from
penetrating the surface and 'keying' themselves
in.

Joinery timber is usually kept inside, so can be
used as it is—so long as it is not then exposed to
the elements beforehand. If using timber that
has been stored outside (or indeed, if working on
anything made of timber that has been exposed
to normal exterior atmosphere) I like to move it
into a warm shed two to three days before
working with it—or using resins, paints or
varnishes on it. 16°C (60°F) or above is a good
drying temperature—inside. Make sure your
timber is dry (and clean) before working with or
on it!

Also, when working with wood, you have got
to preserve it. If you don't the answer is quite
simple—it will probably rot very much more
quickly than expected.

In the case of new timber it is fairly straightforward. In the case of old timber, you may have
to determine if there is worm or rot, what kind of
rot, and deal with whatever the problem in the
appropriate manner.

To preserve new timber the simple rule is to
cover it all with paint or some other sort of
sealing solution. Do it like this.

1 Coat the timber with a well-known preservative
such as Cuprinol or Worminol—which can be
obtained in green, brown, or colourless form.

These mixtures are poisons which kill worm or dry rot. However, they do not stop wet rot.

2 After delivering a death blow to the woodworm, add an extra protection by giving your paintwork a sound base—apply a primer paint. This again should cover all the surfaces if possible.

3 On top of the primer, yet another protective layer goes on—this time it is undercoat.

4 Fill all the cracks and splits with a filler such as trowel cement, P38 filler, or Poly-filler (used inside).

5 When the filler has hardened, rub it and the undercoat back to a smooth finish, trying not to break through to the bare wood. If this should happen, you must touch up again with primer and undercoat.

6 Next apply what we call 'half and half'—which is, as the name may suggest, half undercoat and half gloss. Mix it thoroughly.

7 Gently rub the dried half and half with a fine paper (grade 100 to 150) to get rid of the slightly rough surface.

8 Apply the finishing coat of gloss.

Old timber requires the same treatment, but with the following preliminaries: If there is a bit of rot there already, you may be able to see what looks like a fine network of veins or roots in the timber, where it is wet or decaying. This would indicate dry rot.

If these are not visible, it may be advisable to get an expert's advice, as dry rot and wet rot appear superficially the same. The importance of finding which it is lies in the fact that dry rot can travel extensively through timber in search of moisture.

Dry rot
There is only one sure way of killing off dry rot, and that is to burn around the infested area with a blow lamp, burning the spores and veins of the rot.

First dig out the soft rotted wood, making sure none of it falls in the bilge or is left in the boat, as this can cause re-infestation. Then burn around the area inside and out with the blow-lamp, being very careful not to set the boat on fire, especially if it is caulked with cotton or oakum!

Wet rot
This is caused by constant dripping, or water being trapped in or on timber. Dig out the wet rot until you come back to hard timber—and try to trace the course of the rot, to determine its cause. For example, an old screw hole, split timber, water traps such as corner posts, leaking windows and so on.

Once all the damp timber is removed and the cause of the dampness eliminated, you should have no further trouble from wet rot.

Make sure the timber you have disturbed and new surfaces exposed get protective coats of paint.

Woodworm
If it is in the timber, it is very difficult to kill it. All you can hope to do is to prevent its re-cycle, which is done by giving the timber a very good soaking of wood preservative. This should prevent more worm re-entering, although the worm that is in there will have to come out in its own good time. If you see a few worm holes, there is no harm in giving them an extra dose of killer to give the worm a nasty half hour!

If the timber is really infested with worm, then it is advisable for structural safety to replace the timber concerned. And carefully inspect nearby timber for any sign of worm holes!

Even GRP boats go through what you could call 'a rotting stage'. (That has knocked the smile off a few GRP owners' faces!)

But here I will deal with timber; it has been a growing plant, and had to carry its food (sap) up to its branches, etc. So, basically the structure of a tree is like thousands of drinking straws, all stuck together. Being a plant, it will decay in time if left exposed to air. Therefore if the end-grain is not sealed off, moisture can travel up its pores, which in turn will make the wood expand as it absorbs the moisture. The outside surface of the wood (the paint or varnish) cannot stretch, so it cracks and lifts off, exposing the bare surface of yet more timber. This in turn, being exposed to air, is susceptible to rot spores and worm. All your troubles can start with your underwood inside of joints' hidden timber, parts of the wood one cannot see. The old saying 'What the eye doesn't see, the heart won't grieve at' should in boatbuilding be 'What the eyes don't see the mind should worry about'. So, paint all the timber you put in your boat, whether seen or not—as rot usually starts where one cannot easily see it or get at it.

Photo 4 A classic example of travelling dry rot

Photo 5 below Wet rot

Back to wood—soft wood in particular

Well, let's face it, at about £1.50 per foot for a hardwood plank, you've got to do a bit of thinking beforehand, haven't you? Especially when a good quality softwood might do the job equally well at a fraction of the cost! And cost, of course, is only one of the factors involved when using wood in boat construction or repair.

Have you ever done a job in timber and wondered—Have I used the right wood? Will it be strong enough? Will it last long before it rots? And so on. Treatment with paint and wood preservatives sometimes is not enough. The wood might not stand up to the task it has been given. Some timbers bend easily. One wood might glue better than some others. Some like to be immersed in water, while others prefer to be kept dry. The list goes on and on.

As a guide, I have compiled a list of timbers which are common in the UK and I have listed their accepted uses in the boatbuilding trade. But please don't follow it absolutely religiously! Use it as a general guide—and if you cannot follow it exactly, it should at least help you choose a good substitute for your job.

A few points which cannot be put into the list are:

1 When buying your timber, try to choose it yourself. See that there are not any splits, and that the timber is not warped. If it is wet, stack it properly, which is on little sticks along its length, between each plank—as you see in timber yards. And try to keep all timber out of hot sun. If you cannot keep it out of the sun, cover it with a canvas or something to slow its drying down. If it drys too rapidly, it will split. Or if it gets soaked and dried rapidly, the same will happen.

2 If using softwoods, always try to use preservatives on them as well as paint. This will prevent worm and fungus infestation.

3 If the timber is greasy or oily use an oil-based paint—which will stay on the timber longer than two-pot mixes or polyurethane paints, which have been known to bubble, blister, peel or otherwise part company with the timber underneath.

4 Glueing can be a problem if the timber is greasy or oily, as the glue might not take. If you know you will be glueing, for example, a gunwale scarph, it might be an idea not to use a greasy timber like pitch pine—instead use Oregon pine.

Teak is a particularly notorious culprit in this respect, and I must admit I have not yet found a glue which has stood the test 100%. In fact, I am still working through various glues every time my teak coffee table falls apart!

5 The choice of timber is important with joinery or superstructures. Is it to be glued? Will it be varnished or painted? You can often use softwood in joinery, but it should be what we call No 2 Clear and Better. This is the best quality, and there are not any (or very few) small knots in it. If you are using redwoods, like mahoganies, keep your eye open for what we call thunder shakes. These look like little cracks or fractures which run across the grain. They are caused by the tree falling across another when it is felled or dropped. If the timber shake is not spotted before you make and varnish your joinery, it will stand out then all too well—so beware! Also, if you are going to bend the timber it will break like a carrot where the shake is.

Now a word about plywood. The most common type of marine plywoods are mahogany, utile, sapele, gaboon and makore. These are a marine ply made in the UK to BS 1088. They are a superior grade wood and are usually 5 or 7 ply (laminations), and the glue is a marine glue which will stand up to salt (or fresh) water. Remember, they will still rot or delaminate if unprotected. So, if you use ply, make sure the edges are well sealed with paint or varnish.

There is an exterior ply which is not to BS 1088 which can be used inside your boat, but it is not advisable to use it below the floor. It can be used safely in joinery or partitions. This ply is usually of poorer grade timber lamination than marine ply, and the glue is not up to BS 1088 quality. Also the outside veneer may not be of hardwood. Avoid 'interior-grade' plywood in boats for any job at all. Also remember, when using plywood of any kind, that it is the facing plies which are the best quality wood, and the inner plies may be of inferior timber—so don't be tempted to sand away the outer layer or you may provide future problems.

Now, where can you get your wood? Obviously, you first think of your nearest timber merchant or perhaps a DIY wood stockist.

But there can be problems. For example, big timber merchants may not stock hardwoods at all or may supply only whole lengths of timber or

Timber	rot resistance	soft or hard wood	lbs weight per cu. ft	good points	bad points	where to use	other comments
Pitch pine	Quite good	S/W	41	Very good, hard-wearing. pockets. Texture greasy.	Occasional gum Any longitudinals Not recommended for glueing.	Planking. Decking. Care necessary e.g. bilge stringers.	Can split at ends. when painting (greasy).
Parana pine	Bad	S/W	36	Straight grain. Dry timber. Glues well.	Splits easily and warps. Very soft. Rots easily if not protected.	Chines or stringers (not often used).	Needs a lot of protection.
Oregon pine	Bad	S/W	33	Quite a durable timber. Glues well. Can be very straight grain.	Occasional gum and chalk pockets. Can split easily at ends.	Planking. Keel. Stem. Stringers. Gunwales. Deck-beams. Carlings. Spars.	If used in any superstructure Protect well.
Sitka spruce	Bad	S/W	28	Light and straight grain very small knots. Very flexible. Glues very well.	Soft timber. Splits easily.	Spars. Gunwales. Stringers. Deckbeams.	—
Larch	Fair	S/W	38	Durable timber. Gets quite hard when dry.	Can be very knotty. Splits easily.	Planking. Decks. Deckbeams. Gun-wales. Stringers.	Can rot quickly in fresh water. Not good for joinery.
Western red Cedar	Quite good	S/W	27	Very light. Glues well.	Soft. Bruises easily.	Planking. Super-structure. Very good for fast boats. Joinery.	Paints well.
English Oak	Good	H/W	48	Very hard. Contains an acid. Glues quite well, but better in large lumps.	Can destroy iron fastenings very quickly. Splits when dry.	Stem and Keel Frames. Gunwales. Deckbeams. Steamed timbers. Rubbers.	—
Iroko	Good	H/W	42	Very similar to oak, but no acid in timber.		Same as oak. Also Decking. Planking and Sawn Frames.	A slightly greasy timber.
Teak	Very good	H/W	42	Very oily.	There can be problems with glueing due to oil.	Where not to use it— Spars, Gunwales, Stringers, Timbers.	Teak does rot, don't forget.
Afromosia	Good	H/W	44	Oily like teak. Hardwearing.	Glueing can be a bit like teak. Grain a bit awk-ward to work.	Can look nice in joinery. Used as imitation for teak.	—
Utile	Fair	H/W	38	Dry timber in texture. Glues well.	Can warp. Prone to thunder shakes.	Joinery. Planking. Superstructure.	Used as substi-tute for mahogany.
African Mahogany	Fair	H/W	31	Dry in texture, but can have silky feel.	Prone to thunder shakes.	As above.	•see No. 5 on choice of timber.
Rock elm	Good	H/W	48	Nice hard timber. Glues very well. Very good in steaming.	Can rot quickly if damp.	Steamed timbers.	—

Timber	rot resistance	soft or hard wood	lbs weight per cu. ft	good points	bad points	where to use	other comments
English elm	Good	H/W	35	Very hard when dry. (Grain very whorled).	Splits when dry.	Keel. Deadwood.	Keep either totally immersed in water or completely dry.
Wych elm	Good	H/W	48	Easy to work when wet. Dries quite hard.	Grain very whorled. Not very good in glueing.	Planking for clinker boats.	—
Ash	Bad	H/W	44	Very good for steaming. Glues well.	If not treated with preservatives will rot.	Steamed timbers in small boats.	—

Fig. 21 Get the right wood for every purpose

sheets of plywood, not less. They may not be able, or be prepared, to cut to the lengths or shapes you may want. And it is often not possible to walk around and choose the particular timber you want, so you may get a proportion that's useless for boatbuilding.

At your local DIY wood stockist you may not find hardwood in sufficient size or quantity for your job—simply because the man just cannot afford to stock it in a large range or quantity! But he is more likely to sell you part of a sheet of plywood or cut things to size or perhaps shape.

You will often find, too, that in many wood-yards large or small, they may not be prepared to advise you on what wood is suitable for a particular boatbuilding job, either because they sell more to the house and garden market, or because they do not want to be blamed for a faulty recommendation.

But, of course, you cannot buy timber today in feet and inches in the UK. Just to confuse you, it is sold now in metric measure.

Basically, one metre is 3.2808ft—about 4in more than a yard. 1ft of timber is 0.3048 of a metre. There is such a thing as a metric 'unit'—which is 300mm and about as near to 1ft as you can get.

Incidentally, it is worth bearing in mind that sawn timber is a true size, whereas planed timber is nominal size, that is to say it is about $\frac{1}{8}$in less per planed face than the stated size—so allow for this when making measurements.

As a rough guide, base your calculations for timber on 1in=25mm. But 1in is fractionally more, so that there are actually 305mm (within a tiny fraction) to 1ft.

To take a few typical sizes—if for example you want some 1in × 2in, you would ask for 25 × 50. 2in × 3in is 50 × 75. 2in × 4in is 50 × 100—and a 1in thick × 6ins wide plank would be 25 × 100 × the length you want of course, in metres. Just a few more useful incidentals—$\frac{1}{4}$in is 7mm, $\frac{1}{2}$in is 13mm, $\frac{5}{8}$in is 16mm, $\frac{3}{4}$in is 19mm and $\frac{7}{8}$in is 22mm—at least, that is as close as you will get.

Chapter 2
What place for GRP?

The basic technique for using GRP is simple. Resin is mixed with a hardener and possibly an accelerator, which does exactly what its name implies, and the mixture is well stirred. It is then immediately worked into a layer of glassfibre material, and when the mixture has finally 'cured' the result is a rigid structure with much greater strength than many materials of the same thickness. It is made watertight and given a smooth shiny surface by using a special resin called gelcoat, without which a glassfibre structure will allow water to permeate it with disastrous results.

Hulls, and deck and coachroof structures, are made by laying up the GRP in a mould. A release agent is applied first to the mould surface so that the moulding can be released when it has cured. The mould is then available to make another hull, or whatever.

The cost of the mould is considerable, because it must be as nearly perfect as possible so that the number of imperfections which will be faithfully reproduced in the moulding are so few as to be undetectable. The mould cost can be amortised against all the boats built from it, so that if a large number of boats is built the cost of the mould per boat is low.

Relatively unskilled labour can be used in the manufacture of GRP boats. Skilled labour is needed to make the moulds and to do the joinery and wood trimming, and competent, experienced, people employed to supervise the mixing of the chemicals, because if this is not done properly the results can be pretty disastrous. Proper supervision of the actual laying up is also essential because 'cowboy' labour can produce results which are equally unacceptable if not watched.

But it follows that if unskilled labour can be used to make GRP hulls equally unskilled labour can use the same material to repair them or repair wooden boats, and GRP has a place in the inventory of any one reading this book.

The actual use of GRP materials can be learnt from the many good books available, and it is noteworthy that the leading manufacturers have seen clearly that it is in their interests to educate their customers so that they achieve satisfactory results. Some of these manufacturers run classes

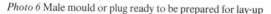

Photo 6 Male mould or plug ready to be prepared for lay-up

in which they demonstrate the use of their products, while many of them either give away, or sell at low cost, handbooks of their own.

It is most unwise to mix different products from different manufacturers, or to use glass from one firm and resin and chemicals from another. If you do this you could well wind up using materials which are not compatible.

Where GRP is invaluable for readers of this book is for sheathing (or skinning) hulls and decks, making hatches, and for repairing or reinforcing original structures.

The first step when using GRP for the first time is to select a manufacturer and get his literature and handbooks, and then study it. This should enable you to decide whether your particular application is a good one for GRP. It may also set your mind running along fresh tracks. Jobs which sounded difficult and time-consuming in wood or other materials can sometimes be quite simple in GRP.

There are two kinds of cold-curing plastics on the market, both in general use: polyester resin systems and epoxy resin systems. The one most widely offered to the DIY man is polyester, because it is cheaper. Its other properties include shrinking between 5 and 8% on maturing, which can be an asset at times, and a poor adhesion to other materials compared to epoxy resin. Poly-ester resins react to all fuels other than diesel oil and should not therefore be used for fuel tanks, and without a gelcoat should not be used for water tanks. Even then there are problems of getting rid of the taste and the slight contamin-ation which accompanies it.

Epoxy resins are used in some paint systems or in applications where good adhesion is important.

Just to complicate matters, it should not be forgotten that GRP structures burn well, and it is therefore often important to specify fire retardant or self-extinguishing resins.

The resins commonly used all give off unplea-sant and even toxic fumes while gelling, and in a confined space these can be dangerous. The answer is either to ensure that there is additional ventilation by using fans or else to restrict your fibreglassing to relatively small sessions.

There is no problem in building up a thick layer, by making several stabs at a job.

Fibreglass is available as a mat, as a cloth, as a tape, or as a tissue. In the mat the fibres are laid in a random formation and in the cloth they are woven in a regular pattern. The two types have different applications and the way they are used can have a major influence on the strength of a structure. Mat is sold in different weights, the most common being 1oz, 1½oz and 2oz. Heavier weights are seldom required for the purposes discussed in this book. Tape is usually used to reinforce seams.

Tissue is generally used as a strengthening layer between gelcoat and the actual structural laminate, and it also increases adhesion between them.

The interaction between the glassfibre and the resin is for the former to provide the tensile strength, while the latter provides the rigidity and stiffness.

Gelcoat resins are thixotropic, which means that they will not 'curtain' when applied to vertical surfaces, whereas resin will run.

Different colours can be achieved by mixing pigments with the resin or the gelcoat. Usually the gelcoat only is pigmented. Several firms make pigments, and colour charts are obtainable just as with ordinary paint. A little pigment goes a long way.

GRP can be painted, but advice should be sought first from a major manufacturer of marine paints to make sure that the paint you buy is compatible. Normally Polyurethane paint works well.

The secrets of successful GRP work are to get the proportions of resin, hardner (and accelerator if using one) correct by careful measurement, to saturate the glass thoroughly with the resin before it starts to go off, to make sure that any structure you are making is in a mould—a point we shall return to later, and to watch the temperature and humidity to ensure that con-ditions are right when you start work. A high temperature speeds up the chemical reaction and a low one slows it down, and the ideal temperature is about 10°C (50°F). Temperatures can rise noticably in the mixing pot, though this is much less noticeable in the laminate.

The actual going off splits itself into three phases—the initial gelling, which normally takes about 40 minutes, with the peak of the chemical reaction in the first 15-20 minutes, followed by the hardening time, which means the time before the material is hard enough to withdraw from the mould. Disturbing a laminate before it has hardened sufficiently can cause problems, such as distortion, because the hardening mixture is no longer supported. Finally, there is the maturing time, which can vary from hours to weeks, depending on the proportion of hardner to resin, the type of resin, and the chemical curing properties of the system. The application of heat after an interval of 24 hours or so will accelerate maturing. The longer the maturing period before the laminate meets water the more water resistant it will be.

If you are going to use a proper mould, which would be the case if you wanted to make hatch covers, for example, you must apply the release agent to the mould before you start to lay up. Sometimes this involves polishing the mould with a special silicone-free wax to achieve a high gloss and allowing it to harden, before spraying the surface with a film of Polyvinyl Alcohol.

Whatever system your supplier operates, it is important to start gelcoating as soon as possible to prevent dust, grit and other particles getting into the mould. The gelcoat itself requires careful application with a brush to make sure it is even and consistent in thickness. Once applied it should not be touched again until it is dry enough for the finger to come away clean when touched. Normally the gelcoat will remain tacky as part of its function of bonding to the next layer of resin.

Too thin a coat will result in wrinkling as well as allowing the weave of the glassfibre to show through.

Too thick a gelcoat may produce cracks or crazing, and an uneven coat is also likely to crack or craze because the different thicknesses will dry at different rates and set up stresses in the gelcoat itself.

For best results a layer of tissue is applied next, with a thin layer of laminating resin brushed on and stippled or rolled to make sure it thoroughly impregnates the glass.

The next layer would normally be a lightweight mat which will conform easily to the shape of the mould and reduce the possibility of voids between the laminates. The technique is to lay the mat onto a layer of resin and then apply more resin with a brush or lambswool roller to make sure that the material is thoroughly wetted. Avoid trapping air, which can be detected in unpigmented resin by its milky appearance.

It is very difficult to deal with large areas of mat in one operation, and at least one authority says that a piece of mat about 18in square is all you can hope to handle in one unit. Overlapping two separate pieces of mat about 2in ensures that there is unity in the structure, but the places where the overlaps occur should be different in each layer. If you are making something with sudden curves or abrupt changes in direction within the mould it is easy to shape the mat with sharp scissors, and perhaps cut in a few 'darts', like a tailor making a jacket. When the mat is thoroughly wet it is relatively easy to make it conform to the mould with the brush. The mat itself is made with a binding agent in it to ensure that the fibres stay in position in the mat, but this dissolves when the resin is applied, and ham-fisted action with the brush leads to the fibres bunching together. Many people find a roller easier to work with for this reason.

You can then either lay up the next coat or wait until the curing process is well advanced before you carry on. Too much work at one time leads to the production of excess heat, which can damage the gel coat, so little and often is a good motto. Four layers of 1½oz glass is normally enough before allowing the initial gelling to be completed.

A structure can be stiffened by local thickening (although this must be done with circumspection), or by laminating—in PVC tube, paper rope, cardboard, or the special foams which have been developed for sandwich construction,

When making such stiffenings it should be remembered that a GRP structure is more flexible than most other materials of similar thickness, so that if one section is absolutely rigid where it is stiffened locally while other areas are free to flex the result may well be that the flexing areas will finally fracture from fatigue. The reinforcing members should be free to move with the surrounding area, so that the whole structure flexes as a unit and not just in parts.

This is very important in a fibreglass hull, where the bulkheads which are used to stiffen the whole structure must also be free to move a little under impact from waves.

GRP structures are not adequate to fix things like cleats, winches, even portholes to, without local strengthening under the laminate into which the fastening is driven. Suitable materials for this are wood or steel. Wooden pads should be treated with a rot inhibitor, and should not be glassed in completely. The reason for this is that wood will swell if it should get wet and might then crack the laminate. It is easier to leave some wood exposed to allow it to swell locally rather than go through the palaver of gelcoating in one restricted area. This will delay the job for no very good reason. The best woods for making such pads are oak or mahogany. Softwoods, which react readily to changes in the atmosphere, should be avoided.

A relatively recent development in GRP technique is to use carbon fibre mat instead of glass fibre. I suppose this should be referred to as CRP (for Carbon Reinforced Plastic) and not GRP (for Glass Reinforced Plastic). Carbon fibres are much stronger size for size than glass and thus give greater strength without increasing weight or requiring a thicker laminate. It is still rarely used by home workmen.

Now a few words about moulds. Without one it is not possible to shape GRP, which is an impossible material to handle when saturated with wet resin. The simplest mould might be a square box made from plywood. The resin would be laid up inside it on top of the release agent and the result would be a box giving outside dimensions the same as the inside of the box. The small amount of shrinkage would not be noticeable except that it makes releasing the laminate from the mould easier.

If you want to make our mythical hatch the first step is to make a female mould exactly the dimensions on the inside that you want the outside of the laminate to be. Any imperfections, such as being out of square or having an uneven inside, will be mirrored in the laminate.

Local stiffness can be introduced by fashioning a lip along the top edges of the mould so that the laminate is carried over it. It is usual in these circumstances to lay up so that the mat is carried an inch or so over the edge of the mould so that it can be trimmed off afterwards with a saw, hacksaw, or disc, to leave a clean, fully impregnated edge.

Often the mould can be left as part of the structure, as in the case of engine bearers which can be glassed in to a hull both to support the engine and stiffen the hull itself. Obviously such bearers require individual mountings for each foot to enable the engine to be lined up, and there is always the danger that the timber might warp or 'move' due to the absorption of moisture, which might damage the laminate, while in a

wooden boat with wooden bearers this would be less of a problem.

Sometimes, as in the Mirror dinghy, GRP tape applied directly to seams will seal the hull and make it watertight as well as ensuring that the hull remains rigid and that the individual panels do not 'move'. GRP tape can sometimes be used as a form of adhesive in situations where conventional adhesives or any other forms of fixing cannot be used.

A further development of GRP is to use it in conjunction with other materials, such as rigid foams, in the foam sandwich technique. GRP laminates are applied to both sides of the foam which thus creates a light, immensely strong unit, and one application within the confines of this book might be for the construction of wheel houses or other deck structures.

Here again the manufacturers of foams, like Unitex of Knaresborough, Yorkshire, are only too willing to offer technical advice and literature.

Another relatively new material which might well be mentioned here is Plastic Padding and the other similar 'filler/bonders'. These are sold in packs of two tubes, one containing the hardener and the other the material itself. As a rule equal quantities are squeezed out on to a flat clean surface, mixed together with a knife point, and 'knifed' into a hole or crack which needs filling. There are many applications for these materials in boat restoration and repair, and they should not be overlooked. Full instructions are invariably given on the packet or on a leaflet inside.

Often the restorer or repairer will be faced with the problem of creating a mould when GRP can only be applied *in situ*. The answer here is to use plywood, hardboard, foil, or a similar material as a backing member and laminate up to it. If it will be impossible to remove this backing after the laminating is completed, ingenuity has to be exercised to make sure that its permanent presence does not create problems. Often the best method is to laminate the backing member into the completed structure. It will have to be fixed securely into position before work starts by screwing or nailing and often it is the impossibility of removing the fastenings after laminating which makes it impossible to remove the supporting member. Sometimes a G-cramp can be used to simplify removal.

If the backing can be removed afterwards,

however, there remains the problem of how to prevent the laminate adhering firmly to it.

One possible solution is to lay up on top of a polythene sheet which has been stretched tightly over the backing and drawing-pinned down. A polythene bag is perfect. The resin will not adhere to the polythene and its smooth surface will give a smooth surface to the resin, not unlike gelcoat.

There is a great deal more which could be said about GRP but this should be sufficient to encourage you to think about its use in repairing or restoring your own wooden boat.

Sharp glass

There should be no sharp corners if you are trying to do a GRP job. Because it is very difficult to get such corners right, it is very seldom done in the trade. The reasons are if it is on a mould (A) it will be very hard to release the GRP (B) undamaged: it will get air-pockets (C) on outside corners, and either an air-pocket or a resin-pocket on an inside corner and sharp corners are a weakness.

So how do we get over it? If it is an outside corner it is best to radius it with sandpaper. The radius can be as small as a pencil's thickness. This will help the glass to lie better—and it is as near a sharp corner as you should get.

To make this radius, make up a 'screed' (D) to suit the curve. Use a piece of wood about 4in long, ¾in thick and as wide as the radius you want. For a radius screed of 1¼in my screed will have the measurements shown.

When I run the screed along the corner (E) it

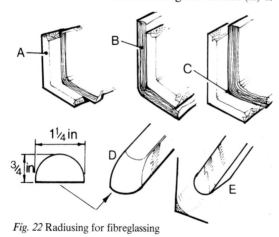

Fig. 22 Radiusing for fibreglassing

will leave a suitable radius of filler behind. The bigger the radius, the stronger the corner will become and consequently the easier it will be to lay up the glass.

Delaminating

Being a traditional boatbuilder by profession, I am really not in favour of carrying out a repair or 'improvement' on wood except by using wood. And by that I mean that sticking copious quantities of glassfibre all over the place does not constitute a repair!

But, on the other hand, I have to live with the fact that those without a certain skill in the use and fitting of wood may have to resort to bodging with GRP if they cannot afford the services of a boat chippy—or cannot find the time required to do a good and proper job with the correct wood.

One of my sorest points is the so-called 'cladding' of a wooden surface with GRP to keep out water.

Most problems here result from the fact that many people do not realise that sooner or later (often sooner, if not immediately) the GRP skin may delaminate from the original surface, and you are left with a flimsy 'skin'. And I have seen such skins torn completely away from a speedboat—and frequently punctured on other craft, so that water gets between the skins and the boat, resulting in excessive weight caused by 'waterlogging'.

Delamination is caused by several things: wood not being thoroughly dry, reactive resins in the wood itself, surface contamination of the wood that rejects the plastic resin, incorrect preparation and keying, incorrect application—and of course the fact that wood 'works' in use, especially in rough seas.

It is also a fact that many boats that have been skinned have had water or damp trapped beneath the skin, and wet-rot has set in. Even if the wood appears to be quite dry, condensation in the boat and/or bilge water can eventually penetrate through the wood and form a damp area between the wood and the GRP. Quite often, an owner pays for a brief period of 'dry' bilges and of keeping the rain at bay a more rapid deterioration in the condition and strength of the basic structure of his craft.

So think before you clad—is it really worth the problems? Perhaps not!

Chapter 3
Painting

Painting a boat is an art

In the UK alone there are something like 500 paint manufacturers, ranging from giants like International Paints Ltd, to small firms employing a few people and specialising in one particular type of paint which is not in sufficient demand to warrant the attention of one of the big boys.

The first rule in painting boats is to decide on one manufacturer and from then on stick with his products. The reason for this is that paint is conceived by the chemists who formulate it and control its production as a *system* for coating

Photo 7 A larger hull beached ready for anti-fouling between tides

surfaces in order to protect them, and the chemistry involved is highly complex. One firm's products are not always compatible with another's especially if you start mixing one chemical type of paint with another.

In the marine business there is a strictly limited number of manufacturers who supply paint to yachtsmen via the chandlers, and most chandlers only stock the products of one because the stock they would have to carry would be enormous if they had all the different types of paint and all the different shades of more than one supplier. There are one or two firms which specialise in varnish and some of these have enviable reputations. As far as the yachtsman is concerned these are one-product companies. Varnish is available today in different formulations—traditional, polyurethane and two-pot, and in finishes which include matt, eggshell, clear, and gloss.

This leaves anti-foulings as another product group, and here again there is often a choice of different products from just one manufacturer, depending on whether you want a hard racing anti-fouling which can be polished, or a cheaper all-purpose material which represents value before anything else. Again, there is a range of colours, as well as primings and undercoats, not to mention stoppers, fillers and all the other bits and pieces.

It makes life easier if you stick with one manufacturer, who must be someone whose distribution is nation-wide if not international. Try to select colours which are not likely to go out of production in a year or two. This is one good argument for painting yachts white, just as Henry Ford said that his customers could buy cars any colour they wanted as long as it was black so the forward-looking boat restorer and fitter out might specify any colour as long as it's white. That sounds like a sensible rule number two.

Rule number three is to study the literature published by the paint manufacturer on whose products you decide to standardise. This should enable you to follow the right sequence of operations with the right products in order to get a good coating. It should prevent you mixing incompatible paints. It should give you a good idea of how much paint to buy because the manufacturer will give an indication of the covering powers of his different paints.

Another golden rule, rule number four, is that proper preparation is the most important part of any paint job. The reason is that a paint coat can be no better than what is underneath it. Why pay good money for good paint and waste it by applying it to poorly prepared surfaces?

One other comment which is relative here is that marine paints are formulated to stand up to the particular conditions of the marine environment, which includes salt in the atmosphere as well as in the water, the flexing of the surface coating which accompanies the 'working' of a wooden boat in a sea, wetting and drying along a water-line alternately every second or so as waves lap, and the need for the paint to dry fairly quickly when applied in an outdoor environment. Paints sold for use on houses, especially indoors, are formulated to meet different conditions, and are most unlikely to stand up to the marine environment as well as marine paint, although their lower cost may at first make their use seem a good idea.

It is not so important to specify marine paint below decks, but if you do use house quality paint below and marine paint outside you are starting to duplicate the systems, with a duplication of primers and undercoats, and the savings you make by buying cheaper house paint may be swallowed up in the quantity wasted in the bottoms of tins simply because you have twice as many tins in use at any one time.

Back to preparation. Before starting any painting the surface must be clean, dry, free of grease, and any loose or flaking old paint must be removed. The tools for doing this include wire brushes, scrapers of different shapes, and a blowlamp—of which probably the most useful are those which work off the small gaz-type cans. They can be bought with different nozzles. Different grades of sand paper and wet and dry paper are essential. Scratches and holes must be filled with the appropriate stopper. Time spent getting back to bare wood with the blowlamp and scraper will often be time well spent.

Boats which have earned their living working may have had some unusual materials applied to them, such as pitch or tar. These bitumastic compounds are almost impossible to get out of the wood, and it may mean that from then on the boat will have to be black. Black paint is sometimes cheaper than white. Sealing coats seldom seem to stop the bitumastic leaking through for very long.

Such boats may have been caulked with oakum or cotton, and it is seldom that working boats will not require close inspection and a certain amount of re-caulking every time they come out of the water. The rule here is that oakum should be used below the waterline and caulking cotton above and in deck seams. The correct tools for the job are essential if the caulking is to be driven in hard, and although the average marina or corner chandler is unlikely to stock oakum, caulking cotton or caulking irons, they can still be obtained from chandlers which supply the owners of working craft, who are usually located in small fishing harbours. If this fails, try the wholesalers who supply chandlers, and the firms which specialise in dealing with fishermen's buying groups.

At a pinch a piece of plywood can provide an edge with which to hammer home caulking, but it is no substitute for the proper tools, especially if you are faced with a complete re-caulking job. (See Chapter 36 on restoration.)

Once you have prepared the surface you can start to make it good by filling in the pin holes with stopper, filler, or by mixing up your own filler. For seams, especially those under water, the traditional shipwright's mixture of putty and red lead powder, is better, and much cheaper, than what the chandler sells. The problem is that finding a supplier of red lead is not always easy—the sort of shop you want is the old-fashioned type of iron-mongers or builders' merchants, and they may have to get it in specially. It is worth it, however, because it takes longer to go hard than ready-made stopping, which is an advantage in seams because it enables them to 'move' without cracking the stopping. It also enables a fairly thick layer to be knifed or trowelled in without having to build up layers with drying time between each, as is the case with ready-made stoppers. You can also paint or anti-foul over red lead/putty immediately, providing you do not slosh it on so hard that the brush pulls it out of the seam!

Red lead is a toxic material, so make sure it does not get into cuts or scratches on your hands, and if you stop work to eat a sandwich or whatever, get it all off your hands before you start to make sure you don't accidentally swallow any.

If you mix up a quantity before you start work you can be reassured that whatever is left over for the next day will not have gone hard and become unworkable overnight.

You may also want to fill in holes where the heads of countersunk screws are below the surface of the wood. The proper way is to make dowels and glue them in, but this is not always possible for various reasons, so you may try to fill them with stopping. This must be allowed to go good and hard before you sand it flat.

If you are painting new work where the join between two pieces of wood is less than perfect it is sometimes better to cover the offending joint with a length of batten and make it look like a structural member than to try and fill the gap. In a corner a length of quadrant can achieve the same objective.

Preparing a surface to be painted provides an opportunity to examine it for the first signs of rot. Any holes you make with your pricker can be filled in as part of the preparation for painting, so if you are at all dubious about the wood it is wise to seize the opportunity to do your own mini-survey.

The first paint coat is the primer on to any bare surfaces, and if you can it is a good idea to give it two coats. Then, following the manufacturer's instructions about drying times carefully, you can build up the undercoats and finally the top coat.

It is the undercoat which does most of the work in a paint system, so more than one undercoat is always a good idea. Work it well into the grain of the wood using strokes up and down before spreading across.

On most boats there will be a line where two different colours meet, as between the boot-topping and the hull colour. This needs careful attention if you are to get a good clean straight division between the two colours without leaving any local areas with insufficient paint.

The way to avoid this is to make sure that the lighter of the two undercoats overlaps the dividing line slightly. Once you have built up the undercoats, the final undercoat should be with the darker of the two colours and this should be taken to the line where the two colours meet. Any slight irregularities can be covered up with the topcoats.

Mark in your line, and paint down to it with whichever paint is higher up on the boat. Build up your topcoats, and when you are ready for the final coat of the colour which is lower, make sure that all the paint is really good and dry, which may mean leaving the job for a few days, and then apply the masking tape to the top of the dividing line between the colours.

You can check that you have got it right by standing back and looking at the whole of the line, and then by standing close up to it and looking along for local minor bumps and dips. Once you have got the masking tape right—and it helps if you stretch it fairly tight and deal with a long length at one time, you can apply the final coat up to the tape and carefully over, just on to it. As soon as you can you should remove the tape, because the adhesive tends to get stronger the longer it is left, and if the tape is removed fairly quickly you reduce the possibility of pulling off paint with it. Also, by painting up to the tape and not down to it you eliminate the possibility of getting a run or a drip over what you had until then intended to be the final topcoat of the other colour.

Where you are touching in a locally blemished but otherwise good paint scheme you have to master the art of 'feathering' the paint to get a good level, even and flat surface. There is only one way to achieve a good result when you do this and that is to practise. It helps if you remember that it isn't what you put on so much as what you take off which counts.

Varnishing is a separate art. There are different schools of thought among the professionals, and these do not always coincide with the suggestions of the manufacturers. Basically, preparation is even more important than with painted surfaces. Stains all show through the varnish, but can be removed by scraping—to a point. Too much scraping will take away so much wood that strength might be impaired. Scratches also show through, so these must be sanded smooth. If the varnish is old but in good condition apart from having lost its shine, a good sanding with a not too coarse paper will be sufficient to give a key.

After this it is better to rub down with wet and

dry paper, keeping it good and wet, and getting rid of all the little 'nibs' and imperfections, before washing it down and allowing it to dry so that the next coat can be applied.

A good varnish brush is essential, and if you have one it pays to look after it. Clean it after use and store it in a mixture of linseed oil and turps, covering the container so that dust cannot get in, and keeping the bristles off the bottom of the jar.

Varnishing is better done by several thin coats rather than one thick one. The initial coat on bare wood should be thinned 50% with turps and the second with 25% turps. It it best to work varnish well into the wood, using a liberal quantity on the brush but spreading it well out, and making the final stroke a long sweeping one, with the grain.

Varnishing, too, is an art, mastered by practice.

Once you have a good build-up it takes several coats and much hard work with the wet-and-dry to get that beautiful deep gloss which is so much admired.

An alternative to varnishing, favoured by many on grounds of practicality and not for aesthetic reasons, is to oil, using linseed oil or one of the proprietary teak or other wood oils. Like varnishing, applying oil requires a dry still day, so that airborne dust does not get onto the wet surface. Enough coats should be applied at any one time to soak the oil well into the wood. The finish is quite pleasing, and certainly the time taken to maintain such a system is much less than the time taken to maintain varnish.

Oiled wood can be varnished in due course if you want to change your mind, but it has to be left a long time—maybe several months after the last oil coat—to ensure that the surface has oxidised properly before the varnish is applied.

We won't say too much here about paint schemes, but it is worth remembering that light colours reflect the sun and make for a cooler boat, while dark colours absorb light and make for a hotter one. Dark colours also make a boat look smaller while light colours make it look larger. The eye tends to follow continuous lines, so that a contrasting stripe along the sheer line or the rubbing strake will make the hull look longer and emphasise the curves of the sheer.

Physchedelic paint schemes look dreadful on most boats and are just plain disgusting on older or traditional boats, which look best painted in traditional colour schemes, with varnished spars, coach roof, hatches and so on. A pleasing touch, absent on modern construction GRP craft, is the white flash along the waterline at the bow, known sometimes as a 'bone-in-her-teeth', and the corresponding white tips to masts and spars.

The origin of these flashes on fishing craft and other working boats was to enable the crew as well as the crew of other vessels to see the ends of the spars and the bow wave of another boat in the dark.

Iron work requires its own separate treatment, especially if the demon rust has been at work. Unless it is all removed it will spread under the paint, and probably the only 100% effective method is sand-blasting. This is not always possible, especially on fittings which may be difficult to remove and could not be treated *in situ*.

Wire brushing and chipping should get rid of most rust, and there are any number of branded products on the market which are claimed to kill rust and prevent it from re-forming. If any of them are absolutely effective we shall be pleased to hear of their names!

The best way to deal with rust is to prevent it from starting by making quite sure that the metal is properly treated from new and the paint film retained intact so that it never can start to "go". But on older boats this will be impossible, so either the fittings have to be dealt with or replaced with new, galvanised ones, or even stainless steel.

A little metal makes an awful lot of rust, so it should not be assumed that there is no steel left just because a load of rust particles and flakes have been removed. The kind of fittings which were made for older working boats will often outlast the boat because they were made of a beefiness unknown in todays' craft. Usually a hard attack with chipping hammer and a wire brush on a power tool will get rid of most of it.

A lot of hard work with the wire brush on the power tool can sometimes result in a burnished surface with lots of rust left in the crevices, which will require attacking with the hand brush and a scraper.

Once you have eliminated the rust the surface must be well primed with an etch primer, and this should be done immediately you have finished preparation because rust starts with oxidisation from the air immediately, even when there is no rain or obvious moisture.

As with wood it pays to give a couple of coats of primer, and work up a good thickness of paint with undercoats and a cosmetic top coat.

Paint does not adhere well to galvanised surfaces, and the cold galvanising systems sold retail are not all that good. The paint is soft and comes off very easily. Epoxy paints are probably a better bet, especially the two-pot systems.

What often makes an older boat really look something is an attractively shaped and well painted set of bow and stern badges with the name of the boat and her port of registration clearly set out. Curlicues and scroll-work all enhance an older boat, and if the name badges can be affixed so that they are a little proud of the hull they look even better. A gilt line along the sheer strake or rubbing band looks most attractive, and often on older fishing boats the original scroll and other decorative work which embellished them in their earlier days can be seen throughout later coats of paint when the light is right.

A special kind of anti-fouling boot-topping paint is manufactured by some firms at what seems to be an incredible price. A little does go a very long way, however, and it is probably better to spend the extra money for a small tin which will give several coats over a period of years, rather than apply a hard gloss boot-topping which will have to be scrubbed frequently.

To conclude this section, here are a few more thoughts on varnishing and painting.

No scratch

When finishing off or revarnishing, you usually start with visions of mirror finishes. But all too often these are sacrificed for the sake of a speedy job—aren't they?

What do you use when you are going to scrape up a handrail, deck covering-board, or a mast? I bet you reach for a Skarsten scraper, slip in a new blade and then groove all hell out of the timber! Well, I use a cabinet scraper—though I must confess I do use a Skarsten scraper on masts and other round surfaces occasionally. But even then I keep swopping over to my trusty cabinet scraper!

So what is a cabinet scraper you may ask. Well, it is a flat piece of metal about 6in long by 3½in wide, and the thickness of a panel saw.

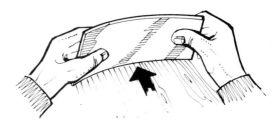

Fig. 23 Cabinet scraper

Why do I think they are better? I find they are easier to control and that I can do any curve, concave or convex—not to mention the fact that once you have bought a cabinet scraper, that's it. You don't have to keep buying blades. If you can bear the initial getting used to it, the way of holding it and sharpening it, then I am sure you will come to agree with me in the end.

A Skarsten scraper is quite a good tool, but you must be very careful how you use it, as it has a tendency to dig in on the ends of the blades. When using a cabinet scraper, however, you have to bend it to scrape with so there is less chance of digging in on the ends.

To use a cabinet scraper, you hold it in your hand as if you are going to hand over a pound note—something you must be all too familiar with! Then take it in your other hand the same way as though you couldn't bear to part with it after all (—as in the drawing). Now pull in with your fingers and push out with your thumbs; this will put a slight curve into the scraper. Now push the scraper away from you along the timber. This will cut or scrape the timber surface. Always work with the grain, never across it.

Moving from the scraping stage to the sanding, there are several different methods to consider:

1 Using a disc sander.
2 Using an orbital sander.
3 The old method of a sanding block with sand-paper wrapped around it.
4 Pass the job on to someone else!

Using a disc sander is very quick—but be very careful that it does not dig in on a soft patch of timber. It should never be used if the job is to be varnished, as the disc leaves a circular mark in the timber which will not come out unless it is planed or sanded out with a block.

The orbital sander is a much gentler machine, but it still can dig into the timber if leaned on too

37

heavily. It also is not recommended to be used on timber which is to be varnished, unless you cabinet-scrape it afterwards and then sandpaper over it again with a sanding block. Why? The orbital leaves circular marks in the timber which show up like rain drops on wet paint.

If you are going to sand for varnishing, the only way to make a good job is to sandpaper with a sandpaper block, and only sand with or along the grain.

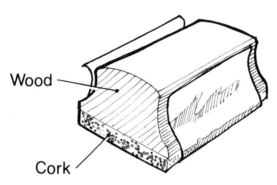

Fig. 24 Sanding block

To varnish new or bare wood you should first use 'half-and-half'. This is half varnish and half white spirit mixed well together. Then lightly sand over (with the grain) with a fine paper of 100 or 150 grit. Make sure you brush all the sanded dust off and then apply a coat of 75% varnish and 25% white spirit. When dry, lightly sand as before and apply a full coat of varnish. Do not put it on too thickly, but work it over so that it does not run. Allow it to dry and then give it one last sand and a final coat of varnish. This should give you the finish you are looking for, and will be a pleasure to look at.

Wet work

While working in a particular yard (which shall be nameless), I saw two painters working on a boat's hull. They were just ready to put on the first undercoat. The weather was very damp and the day was drawing to a close, but they still painted one side of the hull. The next day they were on the other side painting. When they came back to the first side nearly two days had gone by. The paint seemed dry on the surface—until they began to rub it back. They could not rub it back without the paint lifting. So all in all they wasted at least half a gallon of paint and all that labour. Why? Because the surface they painted on to was damp—and paint forms a skin against water, so that it will not stick to the wood, or dry properly. In the end they had to prepare and paint that side all over again!

Chapter 4
Fastenings and adhesives

It is quite incredible how many ways there are of fastening two bits of a boat together. Let's run through some of them, starting with screws.

Select a screw by material (brass, stainless, sheradised or galvanised or somethingised steel), length, gauge (thickness), type of head, (oval, countersunk, round). Don't use screws which are too long and penetrate right through the materials being fastened, or too thick so that they split it. Always drill a pilot hole and make sure it is under-size.

The type of head depends on the type of fastening, but countersunk are usually best for woodwork. Round-heads often need a washer to prevent them being pulled into the wood and damaging it.

I dislike Phillips screws on boats because water can easily collect in the slots.

The type of material depends on the application, but a golden rule is not to mix metals, because this leads to electrolytic action, which destroys fastenings. Especially, avoid all brass fastenings and watch out for cheap screws which are brassed over. Also avoid using steel in oak—acid in the oak and electrolysis both tend to eat away the metal of the fastening so as to make them loose.

All joints should be glued as well as screwed. Good glues are Cascamite, or Aerolite, for general joinery, and Araldite for exterior use, especially to steel, because it provides an incredibly strong bond as well as being unaffected by water. It has valuable anti-rust properties too.

Resorcinol glues are also recommended for exterior work. They come in two pots, must be mixed accurately, set quickly and are not affected

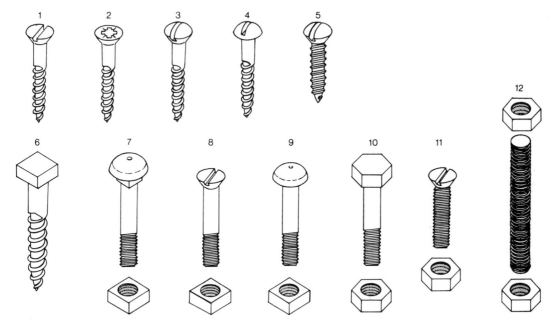

Fig. 25 **1** Countersunk, **2** Phillips countersunk, **3** Raised head, **4** Round head, **5** Raised self-tapping, **6** Coach screw, **7** Coach bolt, **8** Countersunk bolt, **9** Round head bolt, **10** Hexagon-head bolt, **11** Countersunk machine screw, **12** Threaded studding

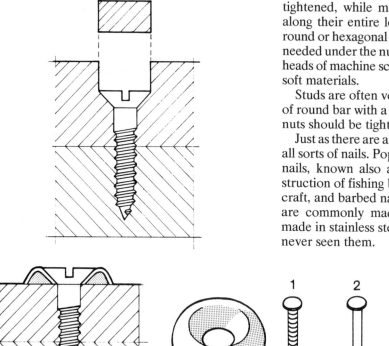

tightened, while machine screws are threaded along their entire length and are supplied with round or hexagonal heads. Washers are normally needed under the nuts on any bolt, and under the heads of machine screws, especially when joining soft materials.

Studs are often very useful. These are lengths of round bar with a thread at each end and both nuts should be tightened simultaneously.

Just as there are all sorts of screws, so there are all sorts of nails. Popular ones are chisel pointed nails, known also as dumps, used in the construction of fishing boats and other heavily built craft, and barbed nails, like Gripfast. Such nails are commonly made of bronze, but are also made in stainless steel, I am told, though I have never seen them.

Fig. 26 Plugged or dowelled screw *(top)* and pressed screw cup

Fig. 27 **1** Gripfast nail, **2** Flat head, **3** Oval head, **4** Panel pin, **5** Rose head nail

by cold. Excess glue must be removed before it can set, otherwise you can never get it off. It may not be easy to buy because it has a limited shelf life, and in the face of all these bogeys I always use Araldite.

Joints must be clamped, pinned or screwed together, until the glue has set rock hard.

Other adhesives in common use on boats are the special ones for bonding Treadmaster or Trakmark to the deck, and Unibond for bonding a cement screed in the bilge to an old one when you are cementing in ballast.

However, internal ballast is often best left loose, or at least removable, so that the hull can be inspected and painted at a future date.

Major structural members are usually fastened with bolts. Coachbolts have a square shank just under the head, to grip the sides of the hole and prevent the head turning when the nut is

Have a care with stainless steel fastenings, because this material can behave in funny ways in a marine environment, unless given good access to oxygen and unless it is of marine quality.

Briefly, the chief problem with stainless steel is that the normal specification stainless items are made to a specification number 18/88. This is fine for conditions where corrosion is minimal, but, as we all know, a marine environment is heavily corrosive and a heavier specification metal (EN58J) is more suitable.

So, if you have a choice when buying fastenings, look at the box or packet, and ask the chandler if you are getting the correct material.

Galvanised nails have their uses, but on small craft copper nails are far superior.

Pop rivets have a place in boatbuilding, and like all fastenings, they are available in a variety of guises. Impartial advice is necessary, if you are unfamiliar with pop rivetting, to make sure you buy the right tool and the most suitable rivets.

A major undertaking will require fastenings to the tune of hundreds of pounds. Scheme things out in advance and buy in bulk. This way you may well save quite a lot of cash.

Before leaving this topic, it is worth quoting from 'Rules and Regulations for the construction and classification of yachts', published by Lloyds Register of Shipping.

'The materials used for fastenings are to be a suitable composition of the following materials: Copper, Gunmetal, Galvanised Steel, Silicon Bronze, Aluminium Bronze, Stainless Steel and Monel . . . Steel and iron . . . . to be hot-dipped galvanised, small screw fastenings . . . electroplated zinc to an approved specification, like BS 1706: 1960 Grade Zn10.
Stainless steel to be of a suitable grade of 18/8 fully austentic type containing molybdenum additions.'

It continues

'Gunmetal may be used but where increased strength and corrosion resistance is desired . . . . silicon bronze should be used . . . . . Brass screws are not to be used.'

Photo 8 Laminated beam in jig while the glue cures. Three different cramps are in use!

'All hull and deck through fastenings are to be of similar composition to any metal members they secure . . . . suitable insulation is to be fitted to prevent contact between dissimilar metals.'

There is also good advice about fastening practice.

'Short dump or nail fastenings are to be the same sectional area as required by the tablets for bolts . . . Cotton or suitable grommets are to be fitted under the heads where bolts pass through outside planking . . . . screw fastenings— the thread must enter a frame or beam a distance equal to the thickness of the planking . . . . . Barbed nails may be used in lieu of screws. Use the same size nail as screw . . . . difficulties may arise should it be necessary to withdraw them.'

Amen to all that.

Broadly, when thinking about a fixing remember that vibration, corrosion and electrolytic action are the biggest enemies when considering the materials for fastenings. The fastening must be beefy enough to bear the loads it will receive in extreme conditions, like rolling 45° each way. It must transmit its load to a member strong enough to bear it, and it must be anchored so as not to pull out, pull through, or snap.

The right tools are essential to enable fastenings to be used to maximum effect.

Glueing

Here are some hints on making the best use of adhesives.

I am certainly not so dogmatic as to say that you can't teach an old dog new tricks, but when it comes to glues for marine woodwork, I would still rather use the well-known, tried and tested methods and materials than some of the new-fangled 'instant-sticks' and suchlike that seem to abound these days.

So, let's have a look at some of the materials I frequently use in the trade. For that job of the split door frame (if it is painted or varnished) I would use Cascomite. This is a powdered resin with hardener, which is mixed with water. It is acidic and gap-filling, it withstands semi-exposure (not totally exposed to all the weather), it is a good joinery glue, and economical in use.

If you are glueing timber which is to be totally exposed, the Cascophin RS216M is the thing to use. It is a resin glue—a liquid with a powder hardener. It is approved by the Admiralty and Lloyds. It is classed as a gap-filling glue, but I would suggest not more than 15 thou. thick for a strong job. It is slow drying, needing about four to five days to cure. It glues wood only, and the moisture content of the timber should be not more than 17%.

Cascophin RS240M has the same glueing properties as RS216M—also Admiralty and Lloyds approved—and is slightly cheaper.

Araldite epoxy, which is best mixed in small amounts, is gap-filling, and glues metal and plastic.

When glueing timber, always make sure that: it is free from dirt or dust; the moisture content is low; you have sufficient cramps or fastenings; you use clean mixing tins and brushes; that you never scrimp (better too much than too little); that you wipe surface glue off before drying; and that there is no salt on the timber, as this draws water and will affect the resin—and you should use barrier cream, as these resins can cause dermatitis with sensitive skin.

Chapter 5
Repairing planks and frames

When they join the ranks of the boating frater-
nity, people generally begin by buying a rowing
dinghy, often an old one in need of repair. Before
the repairs get under way you might consider the
possibilities of adapting it at the same time to
sailing, or even fitting an inboard engine.

We will take as our example a clinker dinghy,
as I feel it is one of the most complicated to
repair. Obviously the first thing to do is repair the
hull and bring the boat up to a seaworthy
condition, which was presumably your intention
when buying the boat. A clinker repair is by no

means impossible for the amateur but I do
strongly suggest that you take plenty of time in
doing the job. Patience and care will be
rewarded!

First consider the materials from which the
dinghy is built. Old dinghies are generally built of
mahogany, wych elm or spruce, but it is not
necessarily vital to use the same timber for the
repair, although you must bear in mind that the
'taking up' rate will be different. I believe that
plywood is still underrated, and can frequently
provide a perfectly acceptable substitute for the

Photo 9 Inside view of a typical clinker dinghy

original, provided of course that you are not planning to get an exact match for varnishing (although even this is possible with care of selection). If you do use plywood I would recommend glueing it as ply does not swell as much as normal timber and, as you know, clinker construction relies on the timber swelling to become watertight.

Now to the job itself. First you must decide on how much of the planking you are going to replace, keeping a good eye open for splits, which are very easy to miss. Having decided where to cut, use a small tenon saw and carefully cut through the plank, making sure you do not run into the next plank. Then go inside the boat and cut off all the rivet heads from the planks which are to come out.

To do this, gently prise a small screwdriver under one end of the rove and twist a little. This should lift the rove enough for you to get a pair of nail cutters under the rove to cut it. If the rove is too tight to do this file off the very top of the riveted nail, slip the screwdriver under it and repeat the first stage. When the rove is cut off, tap the nail out of the plank with a fine nail punch. Have someone on the other side of the plank holding on with a dolly (an iron weight with a steel pin on the end) next to the nail, which helps to prevent the plank splitting.

When all the nails have been taken out, gently remove the planks and before you throw the

damaged planks away re-mark them onto your new timber (i.e. use them as templates to avoid the need for completely re-spiling). If you are putting in a short plank, or the timber is not long enough for it to be put in all in one length, then make the joint a straight scarph, or splay and glue and rivet it. The glue should be a waterproof glue, such as Cascomite or a resorcinol glue. Then when you have marked out your new planks you can then throw away the old ones.

Having removed the damaged planks one invariably finds that the ribs or timbers have also been damaged and as these are essential to the elasticity of the boat they should be replaced if possible, or 'doubled up' alongside. This should be done before the planks are replaced. If the planks are being replaced on the turn of the bilge, which is the most common damage area, the timbers generally suffer, and with the shape of the boat at this point the timbers will have to be steamed. (We deal with this in Chapter 6).

There are two methods of fixing timbers and planks: one is to turn the nail and the other is to rivet. To turn a nail you cut the nail after it has been hammered home at an angle of about 45°, ¼in or so from the timber. Tap the tip of the nail away from the cut part so that it curls away from the angle of the cut. Keep tapping the nail until it becomes flush with the timber, remembering that a dolly must be held against the head of the nail the whole time to prevent it vibrating out. (See the section on riveting in this chapter.) Riveting is a little bit more difficult but is a more satisfactory method as the strain on the nail is spread over a larger area.

When you have cut out your new planks and cleaned them up there are the 'lands' to bevel. The land is the overlap of the planks, where one lands on the other, and needs to be bevelled to make a perfect watertight joint. Look at the old plank, and on the edge measure the thickness of the plank (A). Do this about every 18in and mark the measurements down on your new plank at the same places.

This will give you the running bevel. Plane down to the marks and then the plank will lie nicely against the next one. You only plane a bevel on the top outside land of any plank, so as to enable the plank above to curve to the shape of the hull, and this also ensures that a flat surface then becomes watertight.

The timbers have been replaced, the new

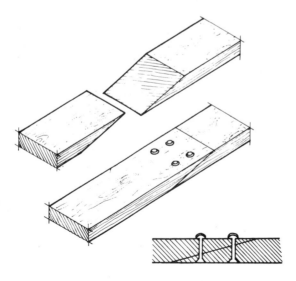

Fig. 28 Scarph glued and riveted

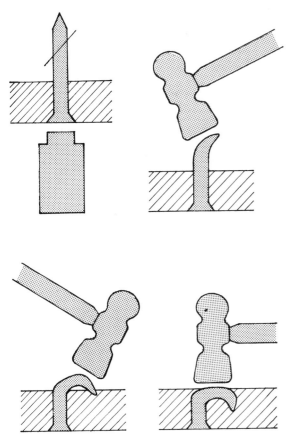

Fig. 29 Turning or clenching a nail

Fig. 30 Bevel or 'Land' on clinker plank

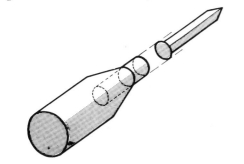

Fig. 31 A riveting dolly

planks have been bevelled and are ready to go in, so now all you have to do is make sure that your planks do fit; it is a good idea to have a dry run, or what is commonly known in boatbuilding as 'offering up' the plank. When you are happy with the result, take the plank out and glue the scarph joints, put the plank in, cramp and nail up. It is best to do one plank at a time as far as nailing and riveting goes, so that you do not have problems with the planks moving before they are fixed, creating a possible leak or strain.

Copper nail riveting looks very easy; so it is, if it is done correctly. First you drill a hole for the copper nail, which acts as a guide for the nail to follow. The hole should be just a bit smaller than the nail so that the nail needs to be tapped home to ensure a tight fit. The knack is to get the hole small enough for the nail to pull together the planks as it is driven home, but not so small as to bend the nail.

When the nail is driven home hold a dolly on the head of the nail—and the steel pin on the end of the dolly should be the same size as the head of the nail (see fig. 31). A word of warning here—never have a dolly too heavy for the nail's gauge or length; the dolly should have a slight bounce to it when the nail is being riveted.

With the dolly held against the nail head you punch on the rove (see 1 in fig. 32). This looks like a slightly cone-shaped washer, and its full name is a yacht rove. The rove is punched on, strangely enough, with a rove punch (2), which is a steel bar about 5in along the width or diameter of the rove with a hole drilled down the centre just larger than the nail (3). The hole in the punch is countersunk to take the shape of the rove (4).

Once the rove is punched home the nail is cut off (5). Now to a most important point: never cut off too much or leave too much on! The best way to estimate how much to cut off is to leave on an amount equivalent to the thickness of the nail. The next stage involves 'dolly hanging', which is simply holding a dolly hard against the nail head while the nail is riveted to prevent the nail bouncing out and the rove falling off. Using a light ball pein hammer hit the cut-off nail, shaping the edges of the copper over the rove (6).

The art of riveting is not to hit too hard; if you do you will get a 'sick nail' (7) which will work loose, and you will have trouble later. Also, if

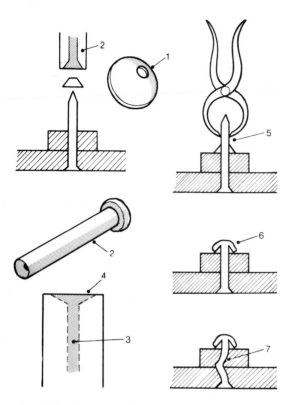

Fig. 32 Riveting copper nails

you hammer too much the nail will get too hard, because the more you hit copper the harder and more brittle it gets; so short sharp hits are the answer, and work around the edges of the nail before working from the centre outwards, which should draw the nail in and tighten up the rove onto the planking. To finish off, get your rove punch and tap it over the riveted nail, which should get rid of any sharp edges left on the copper.

Chapter 6
Steaming

How to make a steam pot

When involved in dinghy repairs you invariably need to bend something, be it a gunwale or a rib, and the only really satisfactory way to do this without producing large quantities of firewood is to steam the timber.

To make a simple steam pot you will need a length of iron drainpipe about six to eight feet long. Make a wooden plug which is a nice tight fit and drive it in at one end, being very careful not to split the pipe in the process. Set the pipe up at an angle of about 30° on some housebricks or breeze blocks. The plugged end should be sitting on the ground—and make sure the pipe is not in danger of rolling off the bricks.

Fill the drainpipe with water to about a third its length and place the timbers to be steamed into the drainpipe and lightly plug the end with a rag. Light a small bonfire as low down the pipe as you can get without setting fire to the wooden bung, and let the water boil. As water expands when it gets hot, and the timber inside the steampot has displaced some water anyway, water might start to bubble out of the top of the steampot when it boils.

Do not try to prevent this by jamming the rag in tight or you will find you have an extremely dangerous steam cannon on your hands. Make sure that you do let some steam escape, in fact, to prevent steam pressure building up. I am not the only boat builder to have narrowly missed a scalding through not being cautious enough in my earlier days.

Fig. 33 Steam pot

Steaming timbers

The timbers in a dinghy are usually oak, though in some classier dinghies they are of ash. Let us assume that the timbers which are to be repaired are two in number, one midships and one at the forward end. It's not really worth making a steam pot for just two timbers, so there is another way, although it is a bit more risky in terms of breaking the timbers. So, if you try this method, make sure that your timber does not have any short grain or knots in it.

What you need are some old rags and plenty of boiling water. Wrap the rags around the timber where the bend is to be and pour the boiling water over the rags. Let the hot water penetrate the timber, and slowly bend the rib over your knee to feel the stiffness or resistance of the wood. One tip to bear in mind is to soak the timber in water for a day or two beforehand; this will help the hot water and steam to penetrate.

Fig. 34 Steaming

Always start on the difficult ribs first so that if you break one you can try the broken one in another place—usually up forward. When you try to put the hot rib in, start at the hog and work towards the bilge, gently forcing the rib onto the planks. Never try to bend it too fast or it will crack, but you must also not be too slow or the steaming effect will wear off.

When you have got the timber in position, drill through the rib and planks with your nail bit and let your dollyhanger hammer home the nails while you dollyhang on the inside, holding the rib in position with your hammer just below the

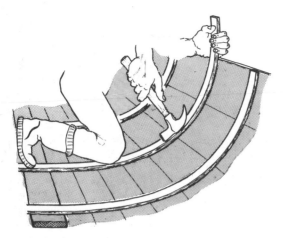

Fig. 36 Wrapping a timber in

Fig. 37 Twisting a timber

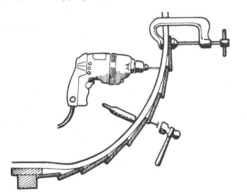

Fig. 35 Nailing a timber or rib

nail hole. This prevents the rib moving and the nail missing the drilled hole in the rib and

possibly splitting the rib on its way through.

Now on to the next rib at the forward end. These ribs do not have the problem of having to be bent almost double, so they look as though it would be a waste of time steaming them. What they need, however, is twisting into the planks, and steaming makes this job much easier. So, fasten the steamed rib at the garboard first, then start to 'set' the rib to the hull.

The ribs in a boat are the same as frames in a larger craft; they should be square off the keel or hog midships and running parallel fore and aft of this. So you will find to keep them parallel the ribs needs to be twisted, clockwise going forward on the port side and anticlockwise going forward on the starboard side.

Chapter 7
Knees and seats

Knees and seats

Now that the hull has been fixed, let us look inside to see what else needs replacing or repairing. It is usually the thwart and quarter knees which sustain most damage, and sometimes the breasthook goes as well.

Fig. 38 Thwart, quarter knee and breasthook

You may get the impression, with their attractive curved shapes, that these are purely decorative, but they have an important function and this is to prevent the boat spreading and moving too much. The breasthook spreads the load evenly over the gunwales when the boat takes a knock on the stem. It also ties the gunwales and stem in together, making them strong and fairly rigid.

The same applies to the quarter knees on the transom which help to tie in the gunwales and transom. The thwart knees serve to hold the shape of the hull through the thwarts—the thwarts being seats running across the boat. The knees are not, as many people think, there to hold up the thwarts, though they do help sometimes.

The thwart knees generally take the biggest poundings, and tend to snap or split. If they are left too long without repair the boat can possibly spread and alter shape, usually ending up beamier and prone to nail sickness.

To replace a broken thwart knee, try if you can to remove the old one without damaging it further so you can use it as a pattern. If this is not possible you must make a template of the knee

by scribing around a piece of plywood the shape of the hull and the curve of the knee. To make a template you roughly fit a piece of ply as close as possible to where you want the knee to go.

Next make yourself what we call a 'dumbstick'. This is a piece of ply about 1in by 2in by ¼in thick. Place the dumbstick against the hull and on the template, with your pencil against the dumbstick, and draw the dumbstick and pencil down the plywood template following the shape of the hull and thus reproducing the shape of the hull onto the template. Take the template out of the hull, lay it on your knee-to-be and reproduce the shape, again with your dumbstick and pencil, onto the timber. This should give you the correct shape and size for your new knee.

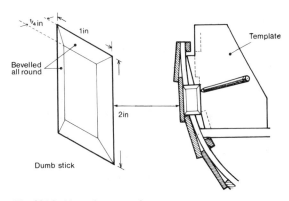

Fig. 39 Marking a knee template

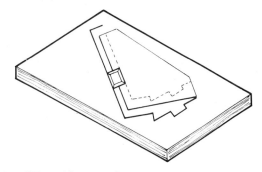

Fig. 40 Remarking a template

49

The traditional method of making a knee is to cut it out of 'grown' timber, which means the grain follows the shape of the curve in the knee. If you care to go out into the forest with your template under one arm and an axe under the other, you too can have a traditional grown knee; however, it is perfectly acceptable to use ordinary straight-grained timber, but you must make sure the grain runs across the knee. If you are using straight-grained wood, cut out the knee after marking on the template and try it in position.

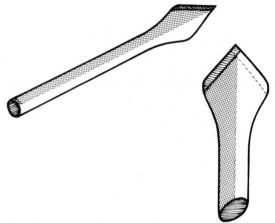

Fig. 43 Spoke bit made out of an old spoke for long nails, e.g. nails into breasthooks

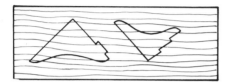

Fig. 41 Grown knees

If you are happy with the fit take it out and cut ¾in off the inside of the curve and cramp the whole thing together. When it is dry, clean it up with a plane and sandpaper and then you can fasten the knee in place in the boat.

Extra thwart

If you decide to make a sailing dinghy out of your boat then you might put in an extra thwart. This could take the end of the centreboard case as well. Leaving that aside for the moment, to put in an extra thwart you must first, of course, decide where. Make sure there is plenty, or as much, leg room as possible.

When you have decided where to position it, you will need two pieces of thin ply about 7in wide and just about two-thirds of the beam at that point. Slip the ply onto the risers (what the thwarts are sitting on) and cramp them together. Prop up the centre of the plywood, otherwise the

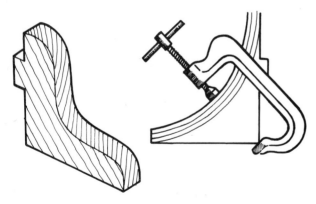

Fig. 42 Half laminated and half grown knees

To refasten, try to follow the old holes. You may have to use the next nail size down (as explained, down in nail sizes means thicker e.g. 13g. down to 10g.) if the original hole is a loose fit. If you are using copper nails, rivet in the way described previously.

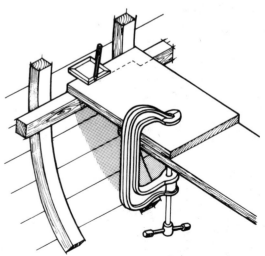

Fig. 44 Making template for extra thwart

thwart will become too long, due to the sag in the middle. Next get your rule or dumbstick and mark the bevels at the ends of the thwarts. Take out the template and re-mark it onto your timber, making sure that you mark port and starboard, as the two sides are hardly ever the same bevel. Cut out the thwart and try it for size. If you are happy then make your new knee templates and fit them—and that's another job well done.

Rowlock cheeks and swells

Having provided an extra thwart, it is handy to make it an extra rowing position and therefore rowlock holes will be needed. These should be positioned about 9in aft of the after edge of the thwart. The gunwale capping may not be wide enough to take a rowlock; if so, it needs to be strengthened.

The first thing to do is measure the 9in, give or take an inch to avoid landing on a rib. Then feel under the gunwale capping to see whether there is any packing already there. If there is not, cut a piece of timber to slip up between the gunwale and planking between the ribs.

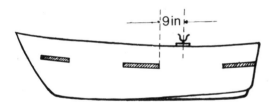

Fig. 45 Positioning of rowlocks

If the gunwale capping is not wide enough to take a rowlock, cut out a pice of hardwood approximately 6in long by 1in wide by the depth of the gunwale and slightly taper or round off the ends. Cramp this piece of wood to the inside of the gunwale and then drill, copper-nail and rivet about an inch in from each end right the way through the gunwale, planking, packing piece and cheek.

Next you drill the hole for the rowlock plate, and screw the rowlock plate down. Drop the

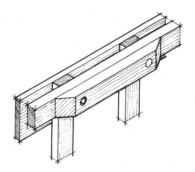

Fig. 46 Fitting rowlock cheeks

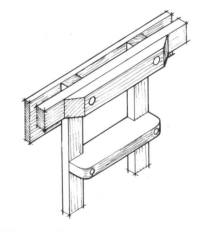

Fig. 47 Fitting swells

rowlock in and mark the bottom of the pin onto the planking. This will give you a guide to prevent you fitting the swells too low.

The swells, too, are made of hardwood and should be about 6in long by 1½in deep and the width of the gunwale plus gunwale cheek. Taper or radius the ends of the swells the same as the rowlock cheeks, and before riveting it to the planking a hole needs to be drilled to take the end of the rowlock pin. Drop the rowlock through the cheek, slide the swell up over the pin into position, and then drill and rivet the swell with the rowlock in to ensure that the position is right. As has presumably become obvious, the function of the swell is to prevent the rowlock rocking about in its hole and making rowing difficult.

Chapter 8
Conversion to sail

Many dinghies can be altered to become a sailing dinghy, but care must be taken not to overstep the safety mark by thinking you can put a large sail area onto a small dinghy. If the boat is going to become a sailer it will probably need a centre board or dagger board. These are not essential, but do help a lot by slowing down the leeway of the boat. I have seen some enterprising sailors, with broomstick rigs and leeboards, hanging over the sides of their dinghies.

Assuming you acquire an old set of dinghy sails the first step in converting the dinghy is to make a scale drawing of the boat in profile and

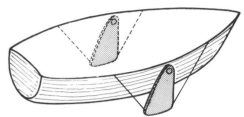

Fig. 48 Lee boards

draw in your mast and sails. The mast should be positioned roughly a third the length of the boat back from the stem, or if there is a jib use that to position the mast. The next step is to find the centre of effort of the sails. This is done by dividing the angles of the two bottom corners of each sail and the centre of effort is where the bisected angles meet. If there is a jib then a line must be drawn between the two centres of effort joining them up.

Photo 10 A simple loose-fitted gunter-rigged pram

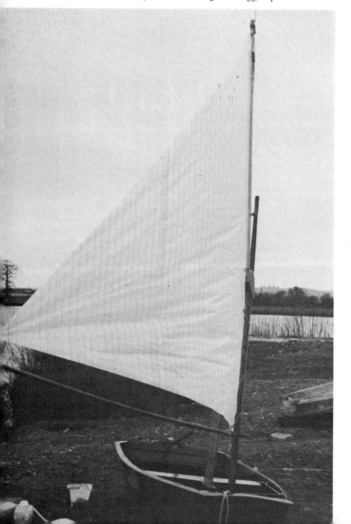

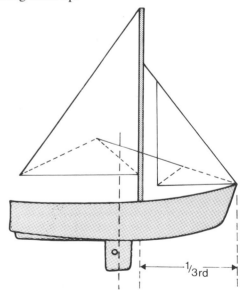

Fig. 49 Making a dinghy into a sailing boat

Let us assume the jib is one fifth the area of the main sail, in which case you need to divide the line between the two centres of effort into five equal parts. The combined centre of effort would then be found one fifth along the line from the mainsail's centre of effort. A line is lightly drawn down from this combined centre of effort through the boat.

The leading edge of the centreboard should be just aft of the centre of effort and this will give you a reasonable balance to start off with, and later on you can move the mast slightly forward or aft to tune it more finely.

Centreboard and case

Now that you have positioned the mast and centreboard in your drawing you can go ahead and make the centreboard and case. The blade or dagger board can be made out of ¾in thick plywood. If you go any thinner, the centreboard is likely to bend under strain.

So, the first step is to make up the case sides which can be cut out of ¼in ply. Put a batten or straight edge across the thwarts and measure down to the hog for the height of the case's sides. If you keep the case's height the same as the height of the thwart it will tie in and look and feel better. Don't make the centreboard too wide—about 14in is ample, and its depth below the keel can be about 2ft. The centreboard case should then be 14in wide plus ½in for clearance of the centreboard plus an extra 2in for batten thickness (16½in total). So, two pieces of ply ¼in thick by 16½in by the height from keel to top of thwart can be cut out. Some 1in × 1in and 2in × 1in battening is needed; the 1in × 1in is glued and screwed down the two ends of the plywood and then the 2in × 1in is glued and screwed on the outside of the casing along the top and bottom.

Before joining the two case sides together, varnish all the inside except where you will glue the second side to the 1in × 1in. It is easier to varnish the inside now to avoid poking about with a ¾in brush on a stick later on. The bottom of the case now needs to be fitted to the hog. If the dinghy is clinker you will have to pack out between the ribs and cut off the centre of the rib which would interfere with the centreboard. When you fit down the packing and the centreboard case, bed them down with plenty of mastic sealant and screw well down. But of course before you do that you had better cut out the hole in the hog and keel to take the centreboard.

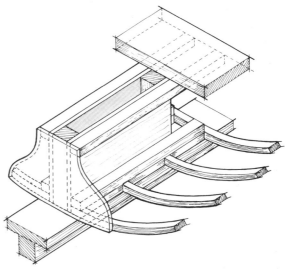

Fig. 50 Centreboard box

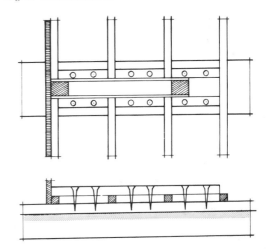

Fig. 51 Packing in between timbers

Mark the hole on the hog and then get a long drill bit or Scotch auger the size of the hole's width and drill the two ends first, making sure that your drill is plumb. Drill as many holes as close together as possible, and then chop out the bits in between with a chisel (fig. 52). When the hole is cleaned out and ready for the case to be fixed over it, a good idea is to fit a flat piece of ⅛in thick rubber, over the whole hole and where the case is to be, with a slit down the centre and Vee'd out at the ends (see fig. 53). This stops a lot of the water sloshing up inside when the centreboard is not in and also prevents the centreboard 'chattering' when sailing.

53

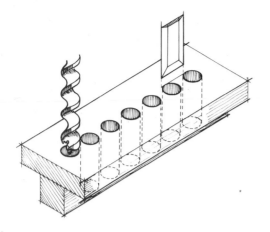

Fig. 52 Slot in keel for centreboard

If the centreboard case is only fixed to one thwart then fit a plywood gusset to the other end. This is easily done by scribing a piece of ply to the hull shape and fixing it to a rib and screwing it to the centreboard case (see fig. 50). This will prevent the case moving and possibly leaking at a later date.

The centreboard, as I said earlier, can be made out of ¾in thick ply, and the leading edge should have a blunt 'round' (see fig. 54) with a

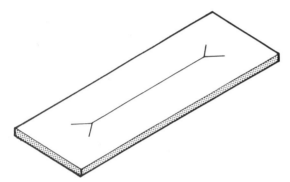

Fig. 53 Rubber to stop 'chattering'

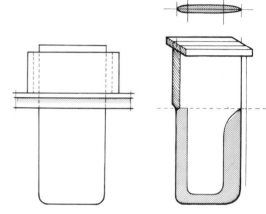

Fig. 54 Tapering centreboard

Photo 11 Plywood racing dinghy showing details of centreboard case ready for thwart to be fitted. This will stiffen it up satisfactory

small radius of about 3in at the bottom of the leading edge. The trailing edge needs to be faired out to about $3/16$in over 6in. Glue and screw some 2in × 1in on the top of the centreboard to act as a stop and handle. Sandpaper the whole centreboard and varnish all over. It looks particularly effective if you choose a nice mahogany ply and the handle grip or stop is a nice white wood.

Rudder and tiller

The rudder for the dinghy can also be made out of ply. It is a good idea to study other sailing dinghies and try to compare yours to others which are similar in terms of sail area and size—so you can use their rudder size and shape for your dinghy. This can save a lot of trial and error.

Draw out your rudder on a piece of ply full size and make a pattern of each piece that goes into it. You must be very careful to get the pivot point correct on the blade and cheeks by making sure that your pattern of the rudder blade pivots well

on your full size drawing without touching what would be the rudder packing pieces. Make up one side as with the centreboard case, with the rudder packing pieces glued and pinned. These packing pieces should be cut out of the same thickness ply as the blade, which can be $1/2$in. When glueing and pinning the packing pieces, make sure that the hole up the centre of the rudder is kept clear of glue for the cord to have a clear run without snagging on anything. Glue and pin the second cheek into position, again double-checking that the cord will be unimpeded.

Next cut out the blade and clean it up. Fair it in similarly to the centreboard, that is by the leading edge of the rudder having a 'blunt round' and the bottom of the rudder tapering to a fine trailing edge as it goes back. Now the hole which holds the pull cord has to be kept inside the rudder cheeks whether the blade is up or down, otherwise the knot in the cord will jam against the cheeks when the rudder pivots.

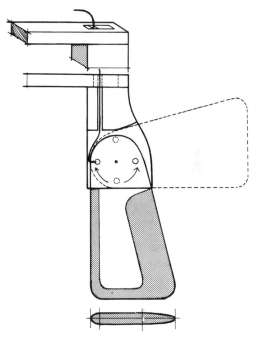

Fig. 56 Rudder assembly

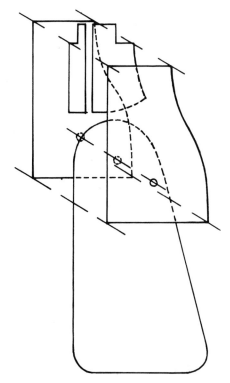

Fig. 55 Templates for rudder

The tiller can be made out of ash or even nice white softwood; and cut a slot in it at the rudder end to fit over the top of the rudder cheeks. This should be glued and bolted together. A simple rudder extension can also be fitted by making it

55

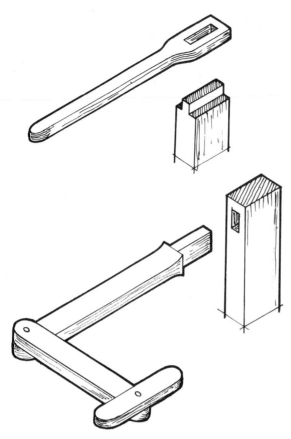

Fig. 57 Two types of tiller

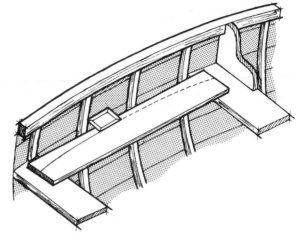

Fig. 58 Scribing for side benches

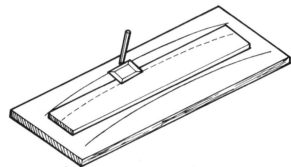

Fig. 59 Marking side bench from template

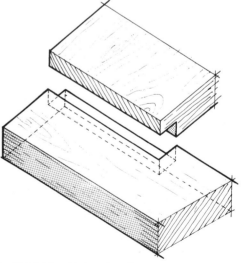

Fig. 60 Joint for side bench to thwarts

out of a piece of softwood or ash 1¼in × ¾in thick with a little cross piece at one end for you to hold onto and a nice brass bolt fastening it to the end of the tiller at the other end.

Side benches

With a sailing dinghy you will need side benches. These run from the transom to the rowing thwart—or the first thwart you come to. Make your faithful template by laying a piece of thin ply down the side of the boat and across the thwart and stern seat. Then scribe the shape of the side of the boat onto the ply. The side bench needs to be about 9in wide and the same thickness as the thwarts. Place your template onto the timber and re-scribe the hull's shape from the template onto the timber; this should give you a slight curve which you then parallel off, to give you the width of the seat.

When you cut out your seats, cut them about

3in too long to allow for fitting. The side bench should sit on the seat riser which is the longitudinal stringer on which the thwarts sit. The side bench is halved onto the thwart and transom seat. Do not try to cut both side benches from the same template trying to save yourself work, as it is unlikely that both sides are identical in shape. It is better to re-scribe your template for the other side.

Screw the side bench to the thwart and stern seat. Glueing is a waste of time with a dinghy as the movement or 'working' of the boat is so great it simply cracks the joints.

Mast and spars

Still staying with our dinghy, if you are unable to get hold of an old dinghy mast and boom to go with your sails then you will have to make them. This may sound a horrifying prospect, but it is not too difficult; in fact, it is easier than some of the work already mentioned.

To make a mast and boom, you first need to know their lengths. Lay out your sail or sails on the floor and measure the luff of the mainsail and along where the boom is to be. Now add to the mast's length the height from the mast step to the sheer plus about another 18in for your head to clear the boom, and about another 12in for the top of the mast. For the length of the boom, add

another 18in or so to play safe, as the extra, if any, can be cut off afterwards once the boom is fitted to the mast on your trial.

The mast can be in one piece, but if you have difficulty in obtaining the length, then you must scarph a piece on. The mast can be about 2¼in in diameter at the bottom, and tapering about one third from the top to about 1⅝in diameter. To do this you first scarph the mast if you have to. This (i.e. the joint) needs to be about ten times in length the thickness of the mast at the point where the scarph needs to be. The scarph needs only to be a straight splice as in the illustration, and glued with a marine glue.

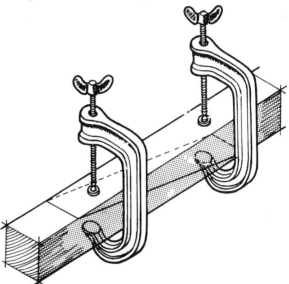

Fig. 62 Scarph for mast

When glued up, mark out the length of the mast and where it will start to taper. Plane the taper out first, by taking equal amounts off each side, keeping it as square as possible. The next step is to make the mast round. To do this it is best to use a spar gauge which is a simple home-made gauge—nothing complicated. What you need is a piece of 2in × 1in wood, about 9in long

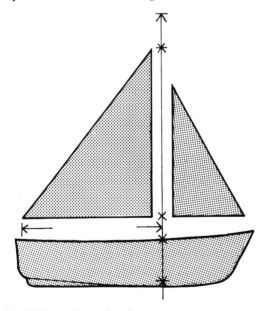

Fig. 61 Mast and boom lengths

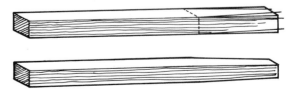

Fig. 63 Mast taper

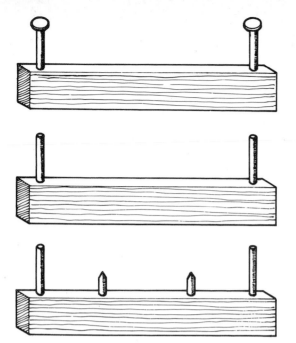

Fig. 64 Spar guage

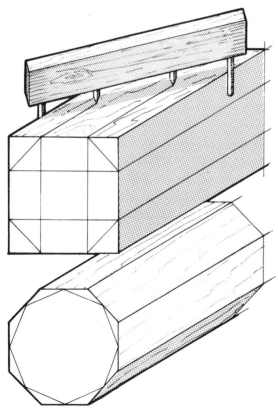

Fig. 65 Rounding a mast

on which you measure in 1in from each end and put a nail. Then cut off the head of the nail and divide the space between the two nails into the proportions of 7/10/7 and put a nail in the two dividing spots. Cut off the heads of these nails about ¼in up from the wood and file a point onto them. You now have a spar gauge which you set onto your square spar, drawing it along the wood. The two sharp points will mark the spar as does a marking gauge. Mark the spar the full length on all four sides and then plane down to these points, giving you an octagonal spar. When that is done, you keep on and on planing off the corners until it becomes round, and then you finish off with sandpaper.

The boom can be left square, or rectangular if you wish, and again it can be tapered for lightness and looks. Starting with a 2½in × 1½in piece of wood you find the middle of the length and taper from there to 1½in square at both ends. The taper is made by planing the bottom of the boom only.

Fig. 66 Simple boom shape

The necessary fittings such as mast track, if needed, and goose-neck fittings can be acquired from the local chandler. The rigging should be kept as simple as possible, just two shrouds and one forestay and the boom can have a block off the boom (pulley) running through another block off the hog.

Here's how to make a mast step

Don't forget that sometimes the inside of the mortise on a mast step is very hard to paint or even to paint at all, and rot sets in.

If you are replacing an old one, make sure that you know where to put the new one, by marking fore and aft on the hog with two nails (see fig. 68) tapped into the hog. Then measure the length of the step and where the mortise was in relation to the step. If the mast step is in a very bad way, take a look at the mast's tenon (see fig. 69) — this may be in a bad way too, and it would be a waste of time not attending to that as well. What I did in such a case was to measure up the mast 6in

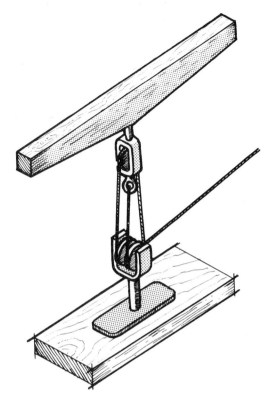

Fig. 67 Simple boom main sheet

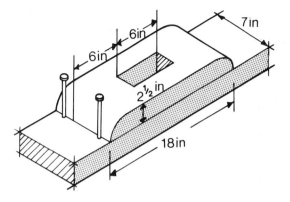

Fig. 68 Mast step

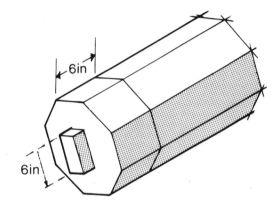

Fig. 69 Tenon at foot of mast

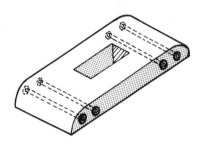

Fig. 70 Mortise for mast step

and scribe a line around the mast as in the fig. 69. Then I cut off the bad timber and re-cut the tenon, leaving the scribed line on. I did not cut back that far.

When this was done, I measured back from the scribed line to the tenon. It measured 5in, so I had lost 1in in the mast height and therefore I had to add 1in to the mast step's thickness. This saved an extra shortening of rigging.

Back now to the mast step. Cut out a block of hardwood 18in × 7in × 2½in thick. Re-mark the mortise and cut it out; put a radius round the ends and give it a few through fastenings to help prevent the timber splitting. I use some ¼in copper rod with washers riveted over (see fig. 70), and the mast step is screwed on to the hog.

How you rig and work a boat is entirely up to you; there is not a right or wrong way of rigging a boat. If the boat sails the way you rig it, and you are happy with it, then fine; but do keep an open mind to other people's suggestions, as they may always think of something that has not occurred to you.

Chapter 9
Making oars and paddles

Oars are an expensive item, especially when you can lose one in thirty seconds. So why not make your own oars—and even three in one go, anticipating the day when you might lose one?

What length should your oars be? As a rough guide, measure the beam of your boat and add a couple of feet. If in doubt, make the oar longer—you can always cut a bit off if it is unwieldy. Get spruce timber if you can, or second best is a good quality clear pine without any knots or pith in it. You will need two lengths about 6ft 6in by 1¾in square, and four lengths of 2ft long by 1¾in.

Glue two of the 2ft lengths one each side of a 6ft 6in length for the blade (fig. 71). The next step is to mark out the shape of the blades. To do this, draw in a centre line on the blade and every 3in from the blade's end square a line across. Then with a thin batten draw in your oar's shape on one side of the blade. (fig. 72). Measure at each 3in line from the centre line to the new blade's shape and put this measurement onto the other side. This will give you identical shapes on the blade. Cut off the waste wood and clean up the curve.

The next step is to thin down the blade, so you again put a centre line, but this time down the edge of the blade. Measure ¼in each side of the centre line at the tip of the blade and with a thin batten mark from there to the top of the blade where it fairs into the shaft. Do this both sides and then put the timber in a vice and plane down to the pencil lines, trying to leave a raised centre line on the flat part of the blade, and tapering to nothing at the tip. This forms a sort of backbone down the blade and gives it additional strength.

Finally, round up the shaft using your spar gauge as a starter and scallop out the handgrips. Paint or varnish, depending how proud you are of them, but do put something on to seal the grain, otherwise the oars will become water-logged and heavy.

Paddles are made in the same way, except that you glue two 6in pieces of spruce onto the top of the shaft and these can be shaped and scalloped as a handgrip (fig. 75).

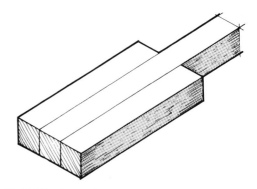

Fig. 71 Glued-up timber

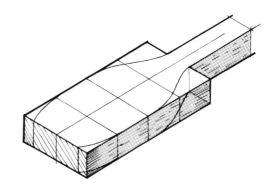

Fig. 72 Marked ready for cutting

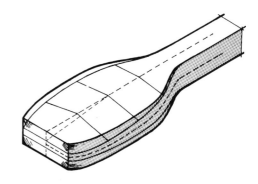

Fig. 73 Remarked for extra shaping

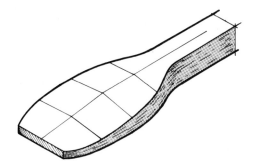

Fig. 74 Ready for final shaping

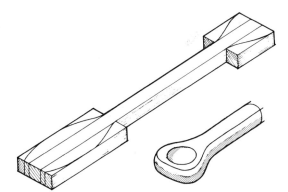

Fig. 75 Glueing up a dinghy paddle

Chapter 10
Installing a small inboard engine

Having put your dinghy into a seaworthy condition, you might not want to go sailing but prefer motoring instead and want to acquire a small inboard engine. I am afraid it means back to the drawing board.

Sketch out the profile of the boat and use the midships, or just aft, as a starting point for positioning your engine. You need the height of the engine's feet to the bottom of the sump—or lowest part of the engine—to make sure that your engine beds will be high enough to clear the hull. You will also need a measurement from the underside of the engine feet to the centre lines of the gearbox (see fig. 76).

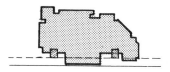

Fig. 76 Engine feet to sump height

Back to your drawing board and put these new measurements where you think the end of the engine will be and draw your shaft line through the boat, bearing in mind that the lower the angle of the shaft, the better the performance of the prop (see fig. 77). Where the shaft line runs below the hull, measure for the prop size by sliding down the shaft line until you get the clearance you require, which should be about 1in from the hull to the tip of the blade.

If the prop has not gone beyond the stern you will not need to alter your shaft line to a steeper

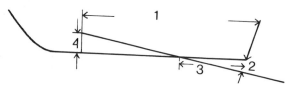

Fig. 77 **1** Distance from transom to end of beds, **2** Propeller clearance, **3** Exit of shaft to transom, **4** Height off hog to top of beds

angle. Try to hit a happy compromise with the shaft line; don't let too much shaft hang outside the hull otherwise it will need an 'A' bracket or a 'P' bracket to support the shaft to cut down whip.

When you are happy with your drawing extend your shaft line on the drawing until it passes the stern so that you can get a measurement down from the stern to the shaft line.

Drill a small pilot hole where the shaft will be through the hull and pass a thin piano wire through. Run the line from the stern outboard side through the hole and secure on the inboard side, either on a bulkhead or batten fixed thwartships at the correct height and forward of the engine's position. The shaft line represents the centre line of the shaft and is also the centre line of the engine. Check constantly what you are doing against your engine drawing to make sure the height of the shaft line relative to the engine feet is correct, as the engine feet become the top of the engine beds.

Next mark the line of the beds on the bottom of the hull, making sure they are the correct width apart for your engine feet to sit on. Then make a template of the bed, using hardboard or ply and draw out the shape and height from the inboard side of each engine bed. This will then allow you a bit extra for bevelling the bottom of the beds to the hull's shape.

Engine beds can become an integral part of the boat's strength if you so wish, so try to run them as far aft and forward as possible. They can also form your floor bearers and sometimes, on larger boats, your rudder strongback.

The thickness of your engine beds will be determined by the size of the engine feet and the bolts being used, but a safe size to work on is 1in to 1½in, and where the engine feet are positioned you can double up with an extra 1in strip which would run from your forward feet to the after feet, giving you that little bit more bearing for the engine feet to sit on. There is no need to use oak or other such hardwoods in a small dinghy; ply is

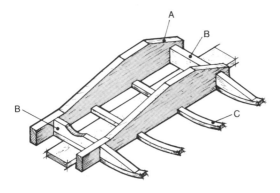

Fig. 78 Engine beds: A. Beds, B. Intercostals, C. Ribs

of the bolt. If your frames are too thin, do as in fig. 78, and if you have no frames at all then sit the beds on the timbers and slide a packing piece between the timbers where you want to put a bolt, and bolt through the hull.

Your engine bed intercostals come next. These help the beds stay upright and spread the torque of the motor—also the load. Depending on the size of the engine, the minimum you would need is one by the gearbox and one directly under the end of the engine. If your beds run through the boat, evenly space more intercostals which can, if you are using the beds as a floor bearer, also become floor bearers themselves.

When the shaft hole is bored, it might be a good idea to deepen the keel to help protect the prop and act as a mounting for the stern tube bearing.

Stern tubes for small boats are usually a length of bronze tube which is threaded at both ends and takes a bearing which threads onto the tube. This gives you several inches of length to play with. The inboard bearing is packed with grease to prevent water entering the boat and the

sufficient provided it has intercostals spaced evenly across the beds as in fig. 78.

If your frames or ribs are thick enough to take a through-bolt through the hull, don't forget to put a cotton grommet around the outboard end

Photo 12 Small engine beds for a Stuart Turner inboard installation. This is about the smallest engine which is suitable for such a size boat

outboard bearing is lubricated by the water itself.

Now back to the keel. What you do is make a plywood template by offering up a piece of plywood along the keel and marking the shaft line on it. The ply must fit along the keel before the shaft line is drawn. If you already have the stern tube, measure its length and decide how much is going to stick outside the boat and mark this on your template. If you have not yet got your stern tube then use your prop size as a guide. The end of the false keel should be cut square to the shaft line, and inside the boat fit a bearer between the engine beds to take the inboard end of the stern tube.

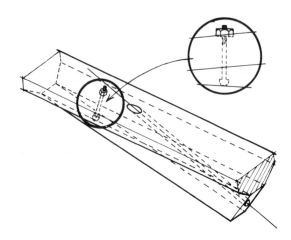

Fig. 80 & 81 Bolting on skeg, and detail

Fig. 79 Checking angle of skeg to shaft line

When you are marking out your template put a pitch mark where the end of the false keel finishes on the hull so that you can reposition the new keel correctly when offered up. When the new keel fits the hull you square around the shaft line on the end of the keel and centre-line it up. Put the wood in the vice and drill the shaft hole out with a Scotch auger a little larger than the outside diameter of the stern tube. This will give you a bit of play when you finally line up the tube on the boat.

Fixing the new keel is done by screwing from the inside of the boat into the keel (see fig. 80 & 81). When you finally fix the false keel, bed it in thoroughly with bedding and a run of caulking cotton. When it is bolted or screwed as the case may be, re-run your piano wire through your stern tube, slide the stern tube into the hole in the keel and connect the wire on the inboard side to the bulkhead or batten which held it before. Tighten up the stern tube fittings just hand-tight and with a pair of calipers centre the inboard and outboard diameter of the tube on the piano wire. This is actually making the stern tube sides run parallel to the shaft line, giving

you a true line-up, and there should be no wearing on the bearings.

All that is left engine-wise is the skin fittings: water inlet and exhaust outlet. The water inlet should be fitted with a pad on the inside of the boat; this pad should be fitted to the hull shape and then screwed and bedded down. The pad should be about 1in larger all around than the fitting. The exhaust outlet again should be fitted with a pad on the inside, and kept above the waterline so that there is no back-pressure on the engine.

Steering

The boat can be steered by wheel or tiller. The tiller method is the simplest, especially if the boat had a tiller before as there could be the old pintles still on the transom.

If you are starting from scratch with your rudder it need not be as big as a sailing rudder. The blade of the rudder needs to be just above the bottom of the lowest point of the prop and about 8in-10in wide. If the rudder is made too wide then it becomes a constant battle keeping the helm where you want it. The tiller arm can be slotted into the rudder stock, or mortised over the top. Both methods are fine, provided that the piece with the hole in it (rudder stock or tiller arm) had through-fastenings to prevent splitting.

If you decide to put in a wheel then your tiller arm can be cut down in length. The simplest method is a cable steering on pulleys, with tension springs. The cable should be flexible steel cable, not too thick—$\frac{3}{16}$in diameter is ample.

Engine box

The final touch to your motor dinghy could be a nice engine hatch or box. This adds protection to the engine from the weather and is also a sound-proofing for your own comfort.

A nice simple box again can be made out of ply, so measure the overall measurements of the engine and allow at least 3in for clearance and soundproofing all round. Use $\frac{1}{4}$in ply and 1in × 1in battens, which can be of softwood. The battens are glued and screwed on all the edges of the ply.

If you cut out the ends of the box first, and the top, you can slope the sides out a bit to take the boxy shape out of it, and if you don't overlap the ply at the corners you can glue some white wood down the joints. This, done properly, looks very smart when varnished against the red plywood.

To fix the engine box over the engine, fit two bearers each side of the engine beds, with notches in them to take the ends of the box.

To conclude this chapter here are a couple of tips on how to overcome (partly, at least) less than perfect carpentry in certain situations.

Fill-in?

When you have made a joint say, for a piece of joinery that you are making, and when you come to glue it together find that it just does not go together as well as it did before you applied the glue—don't despair. It happens to me as well. What I do, if it is not going to be a nice joint, is to mix some of the sawdust of the wood which I am glueing with a very small drop of glue. I rub this into the seam of the joint. When it is dry, I can clean it off level with the joint, and it looks like a good joint. Also, if you have any nail holes you want to hide you can do the same. Mix that particular sawdust with a drop of glue, and this will become better than plastic wood, as it will be the correct wood colour.

Colour-in?

Another way of disguising your screw and nail holes is to mix a quantity of colouring into your filler. Red or yellow ochre mixed together will give you a wide range of shades—or another colouring is burnt umber, which can be added to the other two colours. A boat painter with whom I once worked was something of an artist—so if he was confronted with a filled crack or seam that was conspicuously wrong in colour, he carefully drew-in grain with an artist's brush dipped in black gloss, then spread this while still wet with a stain varnish on a brush, and the result looked very true to life indeed.

Chapter 11
Buoyancy materials

Ideally, small boats will not sink when swamped but will float and support their crews as well, even while they are still full of water. Most will float partly submerged, but it is unlikely that they will support people at the same time.

The easiest solution is to lash buoyancy bags under the seats, blown up and maintained in that condition, and tied with lashing made of web strapping so that they will not burst free and float away when you have a capsize. Buoyancy bags come in different shapes and sizes and do not cost a great deal. They are easily blown up with the mouth, and unless you get one with a slow puncture or a defective valve, will stay inflated for a long time.

Usually they are made of bright yellow PVC, which means that they can be seen from a long distance, which is exactly as it should be to enable rescuers to pick you up from afar.

Better, in many ways, are built-in buoyancy compartments, which are filled with a very light and water-resistant material. These compartments cannot deflate, can be located so that they also provide structural strength to the boat, and by filling with the right kind of material will not become waterlogged and thus useless.

The best places for such compartments are under side benches and in the bow and stern, but if you have one without the other you will find that when the boat is swamped one end will float high and the other low, maybe even to the point where the boat floats vertically rather than horizontally.

A simple way to make these compartments is to build a bulkhead across the boat tight to the sides and to the ribs, or whatever you fasten it to. If a seat can provide the lid so much the better, as this saves having to make a top. Then fill the whole space with either expanded polystyrene or with a two-pot polyurethane foam.

The expanded polystyrene can be obtained from a hardware store and the foam—which I favour—from a manufacturer of glassfibre materials. The reason I prefer the foam is that if

you do the mixing and pouring properly every cubic inch of space will be filled so that water cannot begin to enter, let alone occupy spaces where there is a void.

If you use expanded polystyrene you have to cut the material from a block or from sheets, which is easy enough to do, but it is not so easy to get an exact fit. If you are making the compartment under a bow knee, for example, you cannot fasten the horizontal restraining bulkhead until after the polystyrene foam is in position, whereas with the two-part foam you can drill a one inch hole in the bulkhead and pour the mixture in before it has started to expand. This calls for the sort of quickness of hand which might deceive the eye, especially on a hot day, but is still much better than trying to wedge in chunks of polystyrene.

Mixing is best done in a polythene bucket using an electric drill with a paint-stirring attachment. It takes about half a minute as a rule to thoroughly mix the two liquids, and if you are not going to use all the liquid measure quantities carefully with a polythene cup e.g. an empty yoghurt container. Once the two liquids start to react you have about two minutes in which the stuff expands, and then an indeterminate time before it goes really hard.

If you pour in early rather than late the mixed-up liquid will penetrate into every cranny before it starts to rise. The volume increases by about 25-30 times the original volume. If it oozes out anywhere it is no problem to clean it off after it has set with a knife, and then sandpaper.

The buoyancy of two-part polyurethane foam is roughly that one kilo of polyurethane yielding about 0.03 cubic metres—or about one cubic foot—which will support 27 kilos (60lb) of weight in water. If you select the right foam for the job it will not become waterlogged, because it is a closed cell type. The supplier will tell you if this is the case.

In addition there will be something of a bond between the foam and the skin of the boat, which will prevent it floating away even if the bulkhead, seat or whatever else is holding it in position breaks away.

When it is expanding it is rather uncanny to watch the inexorable advance of this bread-like substance, but it is easily diverted, and there is no danger of it cracking a plank. Some heat is generated, but again this is not sufficient to create problems.

If a plank should be cracked behind the foam below the waterline—through a collison, for example—the foam will not ooze out and will not permit water to permeate its structure.

Polyurethene foam is used as a core in some forms of sandwich construction, and is strong enough to give a little extra strength to the area which it occupies. It does not react with the resins used in GRP systems, unlike polystyrene foam, which means that if you have GRP in the area where you are using the foam make doubly certain that you get the right one.

The same material can be used to stiffen hollow spars, or produce prototypes to mould GRP.

It has certain accoustic and insulating properties, and can be used in many other applications besides making buoyancy compartments.

The material can be cut easily with a saw once it has hardened, so it is a versatile material with many more uses than it is usually put to.

If the ambient temperature is too low, or you do not mix it properly, or stir after bubbles start to appear, or apply it into too restricted a space, or vary the proportions from what is recommended—usually 50/50—you will not get the yield previously suggested.

Another good place to bear in mind when deciding to add buoyancy is under a thwart. It is quite surprising the volume enclosed by a partition on each side of a rowing seat, and with a compartment in bow and stern you should have the extra buoyancy you need.

Chapter 12
Finding it—and finding out if it's any good

A large number of small craft up to about 20ft come on the second-hand market—ex-ship's lifeboats, small work-boats of various types, small inshore fishing boats which are no longer able to provide a living for their owners, large dinghies which were built as one-offs for no particular purpose and a motley array of small sailing or powered craft which are offered second-hand, usually in a pretty bedraggled condition. They may be lacking in paint, their fenders may consist of old car tyres, their warps may be so frayed that only the seaweed holds them together, but among their tattered ranks bargains are to be found, especially for the man who is prepared to have a go and is not put off by a boat which is long on galvanised fittings and short on stainless steel or chrome.

With a certain amount of hard work much can be done with these craft, providing they are still reasonably sound. If they have been working hard for their living, the chances are that they will be in reasonable order, because nothing seems to preserve a wooden boat so much as being used.

The old ship's lifeboat is a particularly likely customer, because they are well maintained during their working life, yet many are replaced at regular intervals, whether or not they are still in good condition, to conform with the law.

So before you go shopping for a new hull to turn it into the boat of your dreams, it is worth examining what is available on the second-hand market. There are a number of ways of tackling this. The normal yacht broker, who can be a valuable ally when it comes to buying a larger boat or an expensive small yacht, is of little use here, simply because you are looking for a bargain at a price which would not justify the broker wasting his time on, in view of a negligible brokerage commission on a very small sum of money.

The best ways to find this sort of boat are to study the small ads in the less up-market yachting magazines, or to go hunting in fishing villages and up the creeks, where small yards are located. A few words with the locals may well unearth the fact that a boat is for sale, and the chances are that it will never be advertised but either sold locally, for a song, or just allowed to rot away.

There are firms which specialise in selling gear from broken-up merchant ships, and not only are they a good source of second-hand gear—although it will tend to be on the massive side—but they also sell the old lifeboats. A proportion of ship's lifeboats are fitted with engines, and others have propellers and shafts but no engines, the power being provided by the crew pulling on levers. If it is your intention to suit your needs with a powered boat, either type will put you well on the way because the shaft, tube, glands and rudder fittings are already there.

Another fruitful source of such craft is the firms which deal in the small craft which have become surplus to requirements by navies and the waterborne sides of the military and flying branches. Some surprising craft come on the market from these people from time to time. Often the boats are sold by auction or by sealed tender, the highest getting the boat.

How much should you pay for such a craft? It all depends on the condition of the boat itself, to which you add the estimated cost of making whatever repairs are needed to make the boat seaworthy, plus the cost of conversion to suit your own individual purpose. Clearly, there is nothing to be gained except a load of hard work in buying a boat which has effectively reached the end of her useful life—and in addition you can easily throw away a lot of money before cold hard reality dawns.

So what you need is a survey, which can be an expensive business. Before calling in a professional surveyor—and no-one else's opinion is worth having—it is worth making your own assessment to be sure that the boat justifies a surveyor's time and cost.

The essential tools of the surveyor are a pricker for testing wood for softness, a hammer

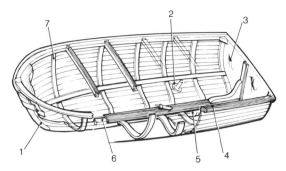

Fig. 82 Check list for bad spots: **1** Forefoot, **2** Skin fittings, **3** Transom, **4** Sheer plank, **5** Keel, **6** Hog, **7** Timbers.

for testing for 'ring', his eyes for testing for hogging, sagging, twisting and general loss of shape, and his nose to sniff out the characteristic odour of rotting wood, mildew and fungus.

Test every piece of wood you can get at with the pricker, having first warned the owner and obtained his agreement to your creating hundreds of little holes everywhere. If the point penetrates easily the wood is almost certainly either rotten or water-logged. In the latter case it may dry out and harden up satisfactorily again. The hammer indicates by its ring whether a plank is still securely fastened to the frame or any other part.

If circumstances allow, a little practice first on another boat might help to educate your ear.

Don't let the shiny paint or varnish or surface fool you. Get on an old pair of overalls and go to town on the boat. Have all the traps, and even the floorboards up—and go through the bilges. If there is ballast in her, try to move it—but if you cannot do this, try to make an assessment of what is underneath from the rest of the hull near it. Also, look behind the linings to see if there are any water stains—which can lead you to possible leaks. Check every possible deck-beam, especially where the carlings are. Coach roof coamings are also bad spots. One tends just to look and not feel. Engine beds and bolts are another spot one tends not to look at—'All that dirty grease—yuk!'

Look at the water and fuel tanks if possible, to see that they are sound and not rusting away—check for pin-holes. Check all pipework as well.

If it is a wooden sail-boat, have a look along the sheer line around where the chain plates are and see if the sheer line has lifted. This will indicate that the boat has been worked very hard at some time, and the hull fastenings could have been strained in that area. Check rigging, spars and masts too.

Work from stem to stern; above, then below, then beneath. And my motto which I recommend to you is: Never fall in love with a boat until you have thoroughly looked at it—for love is blind, they say.

The visual inspection should tell you whether the boat has indeed changed shape, which can indicate, at best, fastenings which must be replaced—a labour of love which costs the earth. Sighting along the boat is the way to do this. Sick fastenings often indicate their presence by rust streaks down the hull, and rust streaks anywhere indicate that corrosion has set in.

Worn pintles and gudgeons can be spotted by eye fairly easily, and so can skin fittings which are corroded. Inside the boat the steering gear can usually be inspected without too much difficulty, for wear and corrosion or seized-up pulleys and so on, and certainly a rusty engine can be seen easily enough. Worn stern tube bearings are reasonably obvious and in most small boats worn or damaged couplings can be spotted equally easily.

With the engine out of gear it should be possible to turn the shaft by hand. Removal of the inspection plates itself should enable you to see whether it is in good enough order to stand a reasonable amount of re-building, if you cannot actually run the engine.

It should not be too difficult to see if the wiring is in good order, if the battery has a little more life in it, if the switches are corroded internally, and so on.

If your inspection discloses a lot of rot, cracked planks, knees which are coming away from the frames and beams, caulking which is falling out, an engine which looks as if it has breathed its last, wiring hanging in loose festoons, and a high tide mark half way up one of the bulkheads, you can take it that calling in a surveyor would be an unjustified expense.

Assuming, however, that you find nothing seriously wrong and the surveyor in his turn confirms this, before you make your offer don't forget that in addition to paying the surveyor, and covering the cost of all the work you intend to do yourself, you still have to transport the boat somewhere and possibly pay for a mooring while you work on it. And if you cost in your own labour, as well, you may find that your cheap buy has changed in character somewhat.

This is not an attempt to deter you; it is a plea to be realistic and not be unduly influenced by wishful thinking. You can be sure that, thanks to inflation and under-estimating, everything will cost about double what any reasonable person would expect.

Check list:

( ) How sound is it?

( ) Has the boat an engine?

( ) Will it be suitable? (Most ex-fishing boats have very powerful motors to work capstans and winches. This power is unnecessary in a private yacht and such an engine will be ruinously expensive to run.)

( ) Are there any electronics? Are they suitable for your purpose? (There is no point in buying unnecessary electronic gadgetry which adds to the price but does nothing for you, and this is what you may find in an ex-fishing boat.)

( ) How much useful gear like fenders, warps, anchors, chain and so on goes with the boat?

( ) If you want a boat to sail, can the hull you are contemplating be modified for sailing, even if it was not designed for this, by the addition of a false keel, or bilge keels and so on?

( ) Are you clear in your own mind before you start what purpose the boat will be used for?

( ) Is your mooring suitable?

( ) Is trailing a possibility, especially for delivery?

( ) Are you contemplating a project within your financial and other limitations?

( ) What size crew have you in mind? Is the boat suitable for that number? (Too big or too small?)

( ) Will you need a galley, toilet, washing facilities, etc?

( ) What will your fuel, water, sleeping requirements be?

( ) Are you after power/performance or comfort/safety?

( ) How much spare time have you? Skill? Tools? Suitable space for working?

( ) Can you afford to hire professional help if necessary?

Chapter 13
Quart into pint pot; planning

Every skipper's mate wants the comfort of a 40-footer in a hull which may be only 20ft long. If space is used to best advantage and thought is given to the materials used, a great deal more comfort can be provided and an illusion of space created beyond one's initial expectations.

Plan it all out on paper first. Mount a sheet of graph paper on a piece of board and try to use 1in:1ft as a scale. Draw the outline of the hull, the outline of the cabin sole and add all the immovable things like the engine, centreboard case and the mast. Underneath this draw in the side elevation of the hull and below that cross sections of the boat for every 2ft along her length.

Ink over your lines with a black felt pen and then fix tracing paper to the top of the board with sticky tape, so that you can sketch in layouts, improve on them, or discard them, until you have found the near ideal plan. You won't have the bother of constantly re-drawing the hull each time, if you do it this way.

If you have the ability to make a decent job of it, try making a scale model of the final layout in paper, card or balsa wood and fit into it scale

representations of cookers, toilets, tables and so on to make sure that the scheme will succeed.

Make sure that fixed objects like the centreboard or engine casing will not prevent doors opening, and that you will have proper access to the bilges and to the engine.

Photo 13 Interior of a well thought out and nicely completed entrance in which the door folds against the engine box to save space and avoid obstruction

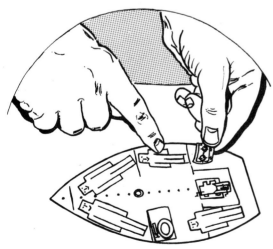

Fig. 83 Layout plans

As far as possible, every item in the layout should perform more than one function. The centreboard case can support a table, a stanchion which forms a stiffener for a bulkhead can support the tabernacle, or an engine casing may double as a flight of steps.

Occasionally this leads to ingenious masterpieces, like a toilet located under the removable cooker, or the locker door which can only be opened by dismantling the engine cover. The finned gremlin has struck again!

The cockpit

Probably the first thing to decide on is the location of the wheelhouse or cockpit, because this dictates so much of what follows.

In many boats there is really only one place for this, right in the stern, with the engine either underneath it or projecting a little into the accommodation, with the steps built into the casing. Don't forget to make sure that the steps hinge upwards, so that no one can step down on to nothing when the casing is removed.

The engine is probably the heaviest lump of matter in the boat. where it is positioned will dictate stability and trim to a large extent, which may be a good reason for mounting it in the middle of the boat, with hydraulic drive to the shaft.

The stern cockpit should not be just accepted without some thought. For many, many years fishing boats had their wheelhouses aft, largely because in the days of sail this is where the helmsman stood to grip the tiller. It took a long time for the habit to die; now many small fishing boats have the wheelhouse right forward, giving better vision to the helmsman, who can still watch the crew through the aft facing windows, while the crew have some protection from the wheelhouse and a large uncluttered space in which to work.

There is no reason why yachts should not have the wheelhouse right forward either, except on aesthetic grounds.

A central cockpit, or wheelhouse, has the advantage of splitting the accommodation into two, bringing a measure of privacy into the boat. Even a small boat can have a stern cabin capable of being slept in by extending the feet of the bunks into the area under the cockpit and on each side of the engine, although noise, smell

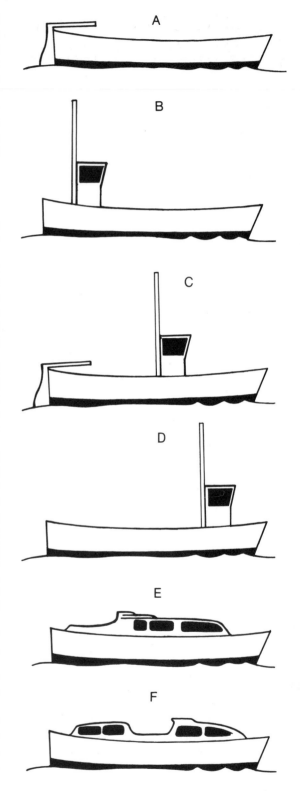

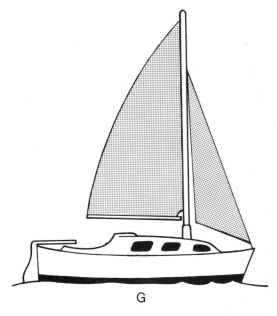

G

Fig. 84 **A, B, C, D**—workboats. **E, F**—cruisers, **G**—Sailing yacht

Fig. 85 Centre wheelhouse cruiser

and vibration may make these less than popular places when the engine is running.

Such segregation may not suit everyone, partly because it means a certain amount of walking from the galley or the toilet to the aft cabin, not always an easy matter in bad weather.

In very small boats the forward part of the boat is usually an area for sleeping, with a single bunk on each side. Sometimes a removable cushion is provided, so that it can be turned into a double berth. For comfort, bunks should be 6ft 6in long and 2ft 3in wide, and doubles 4ft wide at least.

Having located the bunks, the galley has to be fitted in, including sink, stowage for pans, crockery and cutlery, hanging cupboards, toilet compartment, shower (if possible), chart table, booze locker, table, and whatever else you need.

It is current practice to provide even quite

small boats with a dinette, which converts into a double bunk by lowering the table to seat level and using the cushions as a mattress.

The best place for the galley is immediately below the main companion, and this is one part of the boat where headroom, light and ventilation are important. Stoves with gimbals occupy more space than those with fiddles, which are just as effective in many people's opinion, and less prone to make the cook seasick.

If there is no space for a cooker with an oven, the separate oven which sits on burners is a good scheme, if you want to be able to roast, or even bake bread.

If there is no space for a fridge, you might be able to build one *in situ* yourself. Otherwise an ice box is useful. Space for milk and butter has to be found, so it may as well be insulated. Fridges create heat, so this must be ventilated properly.

Fresh water and fuel tanks have to be fitted in somewhere, usually under the cabin sole, again not forgetting that a gallon of water or fuel weighs around 10lb and stability and trim must be considered.

Twin tanks provide a safeguard in case of pollution. PVC or rubber bags can be good tanks, because they take up the shape of the space they occupy.

The cockpit is the best place to provide lockers for items like warps, fenders, general chandlery and for safety gear, like your flares and lifejackets.

Oilskin stowage should be easily accessible from the cockpit or wheelhouse.

The immediate vicinity of the engine must be left uncluttered. Access for maintenance may be required at any time, and loose gear like ropes could get fouled up in the prop shaft or gearbox linkage, with disastrous results.

The engine itself requires to breathe and some form of trunking may be required if the compartment is well-sealed.

In larger boats, it is wise to attempt to build a workbench with a vice into the engine compartment.

Nothing should be stowed too near the exhaust (in case of fire), least of all petrol tanks.

Two bunks can be fitted in the bow of very small boats if one is built at a higher level than the other, with the ends overlapping right in the vee of the bows.

Stowage space

Stowage space above or below all bunks is vital to enable people to have somewhere to stow their clothes and the contents of their pockets when they undress.

Not only is it important to make sure that all doors and drawers can be opened, but it is sometimes possible to arrange one door to hang in two frames at once, thus performing the function to two, by perhaps closing the entrance to the heads in one position and the entrance to the forecastle in the other.

Often sliding doors are preferable. Doors should always open so that it is easy to get through them in an emergency, but in general you want as few doors as possible.

Open plan is better, using light materials to create the illusion of space. Fabrics with stripes will tend to lead the eye along them, so that vertically striped curtains will make a cabin look taller and horizontal stripes will make it seem longer.

Bulkheads and partitions make a boat claustrophobic, and should be kept to a minimum. Boating people soon lose their inhibitions when living on board for even a short time.

Wooden trim and natural materials, like cork and hessian, are more comfortable and 'boaty' than plastics and laminates, although these are useful for working surfaces and can be relieved with wooden fiddles.

In large power boats, the deck saloon usually doubles as a wheelhouse and perhaps eating space, and sleeping space as well. The danger is that it may become so cluttered that it ceases to be able to perform its original function efficiently.

Sailing boats must feature a dry space for sail stowage, and this must be located so that the crew has easy access to them at any time.

When planning a layout, you have the opportunity to tailor-make it exactly to your own requirements, but remember that too unorthodox a scheme may make it hard to sell the boat unless you drop the price to cover the cost of a certain amount of re-building.

Photo 14 Hanging cupboard under side deck before the doors are fitted. The fiddle still has to be fitted to the shelves

Photo 15 right The interior of this Westerly Conway shows how the careful use of suitable materials can give a pleasing spacious appearance

Chapter 14
Which rig?

An analysis of the boats offered to the public would show that of today's new construction the vast majority are bermudian rigged. There are several reasons for this, including the fact that bermudian is the most efficient when close to the wind, and this is where races, it is often believed, are won. Bermudian rig is simpler than any sail plan which includes sails with four sides, because fewer halyards are required and no vangs or running backstays, which in turn tends to make it a safer rig; there is no spar threshing about overhead to frighten people in case a halyard should part and let it crash to the deck and brain someone.

Even yachts with more than one mast are almost always bermudian, including schooners. Cutters, which are becoming more and more rare, usually have bermudian mainsails, although one would imagine that it would be logical to balance the extra sail area forward of the mast with the extra area abaft the mast which a gaff rig would bring.

The fact that so many yachts are bermudian rigged tends to make one overlook the other rigs and their merits. Dinghies are a rich field in which to experiment, because the cost of setting up a rig is not great, especially if second-hand sails are used. It is not difficult to cut a sail with four sides out of a bermudian sail which is too large, and in doing so you have the opportunity to put your own theories about roach and bagginess—or lack of it—to the test.

Equally, the cost of a mast is not enormous, especially if you are able to make one yourself either from timber, which is aesthetically to be preferred, or from a kit.

Balance is essentially having the right amount of sail behind the mast in its fixed position to balance the amount of sail in front of it, in such a way that when the tiller is left unattended the yacht will come into the wind of its own accord. This is called having weather helm. Too much and you have a boat which is hard to steer and which may luff of her own accord, despite the helm being hard over. If you have too little you won't be able to tack.

The opposite to weather helm is lee helm, which means that the balance is such that the boat tends to bear away all the time, and may be quite impossible to tack, so that you have to wear

Fig. 86 **A** Gaff, **B** Ketch, **C** Bermuda

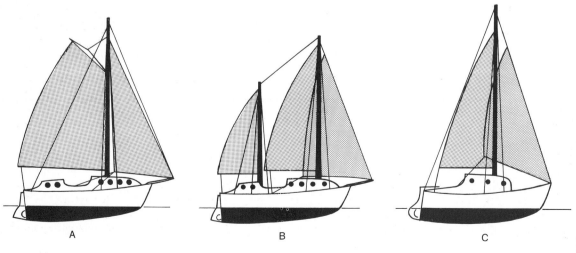

A   B   C

round whenever you want to go on to the other tack, which is plainly dangerous.

To work out balance you find the centre of effort of the sails, join them to find the centre of effort of the whole sail plan, and relate this to the centre of lateral resistance of the hull. This is the point at which the boat would move bodily sideways if pulled by a line attached at that point. If the line is attached too far forward the boat will weathercock, rotating around the point where the line is attached, because there is insufficient resistance from the hull forward of the line to balance the resistance from the hull which is abaft the line. But if you get it just right the resistance from forward and aft will be the same, and this then is the centre of lateral resistance.

The centre of lateral resistance changes when the trim of the boat alters, and as this happens all the time when she is sailing, just as the centre of effort of the sails moves too as the trim alters or as sheets are hardened or eased, it is no easy matter to get the lead between the two centres just right.

What is wanted is the centre of effort a little aft of the centre of lateral resistance, so that the rudder is required to overcome the tendency of the boat to swing round the centre of lateral resistance and come into the wind. The extreme case is a yawl with only the mizzen set. The wind will swing the stern round so much that it may be impossible to overcome it. This is the extreme case of weather helm.

A dinghy will have a quite different centre of lateral resistance when the centreboard is up compared to when it is down, which makes it a matter of skill to know just how much plate to show in given circumstances.

Having said all this, what is the choice of rigs facing the person building, re-building, restoring, renovating or even starting from scratch to equip himself with the boat of his dreams?

The obvious alternative is the lug rig. There are two basic versions, the balanced lug and the dipping lug, and they are both very simple to rig. Either way, the halyard acts as a stay and holds the mast up. In turn, the square shape of the sail enables an adequate number of square feet (or metres) to be set on a mast appreciably shorter than a bermudian sail of the same footage (or metre-age). This means that it will be stronger because it is shorter than the bermudian mast.

The halyard can run through a simple sheave in the top of the mast, pulling a traveller with a hook on it upon which a strop on the yard is laid. A sheet and a line at the tack are the only other ropes required. What could be simpler!

Because the sail is boomless there is no complication like the gooseneck at the mast: all that is required is a rope at the tack to make fast round a cleat on the mast.

The only problem with the dipping lug is the necessity to lower the sail and hoist it on the other tack when going about. This is no problem in a dinghy, and on short tacks it very often not necessary.

Apart from its simplicity, which is its main advantage, allied to the lower cost of rigging a boat in this way, the lugsail is also a powerful one, especially with the wind aft. When running, the sail can be set forward of the mast, thus largely eliminating the chances of a gybe.

Another advantage of the lug is that the centre of effort relative to the centre of lateral resistance can be altered by changing the position of the strop on the yard as well as by changing the position of the cleat to which the tack is made fast. The old Scottish luggers, the Zulus, Fifies and Scaffies, made provision for this on fishing boats which were 70ft and more in length by using cleats and horns in different positions between the stemhead and the mast.

The lug is a great rig, a direct link with the square sails of the earliest known sailing vessels, and capable of easy modification and adaption in the light of experience.

The second rig to consider is the gaff, which is really the lug with everything abaft the mast. It requires a gaff with jaws to straddle the mast, and a throat and peak halyard to hoist it, as well as a boom with a gooseneck at the mast and a topping lift at the sheet end of the spar. That makes two halyards, and the topping lift, plus the halyard for the jib which will be required to balance it, unless the mast is right forward, like the American Catboat or the Norfolk wherry.

The gaff prevents there being standing backstays, so that there is the further complication of running backstays which have to be set up afresh every time you tack. In addition, the gaff often works better with vangs to prevent it charging about, so that the presence of these ropes as well as the kicking strap gives you a lot of ropes to think about. Not only does this complicate sailing, especially in close quarter tacking, but it means that there is more to maintain and occasionally replace. This cost can increase quite dramatically on large boats which use pulleys rather than winches. Every time a rope is reeved through another block it increases its length dramatically. Few gaff-rigged boats look right if they use winches rather than blocks for setting up halyards and sheets.

Setting a gaff involves hauling it up the mast horizontally, with an unequal amount of rope to take in on the throat halyard and the peak halyard, which means either two people working together, or occasionally making one rope fast while you get the other into equilibrium with it. Once the throat is almost taut you can set up the peak, making sure you get out any wrinkles, and then give the final swigging up treatment to the throat to get the luff tight, which will probably mean another go at the peak to get out the new wrinkles.

This labour has been discussed in detail to indicate the difference between hoisting a bermudian mainsail and a gaff mainsail. Problems arise with the gaff if it jams, which means that anything made at home must be the result of careful measuring so that it is neither too tight a fit or so slack that it jumps off the mast. The purchase for the gaff should be as close to the point where the jaws meet as possible, to ensure a straight vertical pull, and the jaws themselves must be protected with soft leather, or maybe PVC, to prevent chafe, lubricated with tallow or vaseline. Parrell balls are essential, laced on a wire running round the forward side of the mast to prevent the jaws jumping off.

As a rule a sail is laced to a gaff, and either hoops or a lacing area used to keep the luff tight to the mast. A tongue which pivots is often fitted between the jaws of the gaff so that there is always a long bearing surface on the mast.

Larger vessels often have the jaws made of galvanised iron rather than steel, which is heavier but stronger than wooden jaws. The do-it-yourself king should have no difficulty in making jaws from a suitable hardwood, or laminating them from marine ply, glued and screwed.

The gooseneck fitting where the boom meets the mast is the same on bermudian and gaff-rigged yachts, and the fittings can be bought from most chandlers. There is little point in attempting to make them yourself.

It should not be forgotten, when evaluating gaff rig against bermudian, that although the latter does not have the weight of the gaff overhead, which is extra windage as well as extra weight, it does have a taller mast for the same sail area, which can create problems, especially on small craft, where the weight of the mast and the leverage high up can be sufficient to capsize the boat in a breeze when she is sitting on moorings plate up, sails down, and unballasted. The lower height of the gaff-rigged yacht's mast and the resulting lower centre of gravity can make a significant difference.

Supporters of gaff also point out that the height of the mast above the hounds, essential to give a decent lead to the peak halyards, also enables a topsail to be set and increase the sail area.

Topsails can be set in all sorts of ways, and in my own experience do not add sufficient extra pull to justify the complications they bring with them. However, in going to windward a topsail adds so much length to the luff that much of the greater efficiency of the high aspect bermudian sail to windward is equalled. The bermudian will always point better, however.

It can be argued that it is much easier to hand a topsail than to put in a reef, which is true. It is also true that with a following wind the gaff rigged yacht does sail better than the bermudian one.

It should also be remembered that when a sail is reefed it tends to bring the centre of effort further forward because reefing reduces the length of sail along the boom. The difference is less with a gaff than with a bermudian sail because of the shape of the sail, which means less interference with the balance between sail and hull.

Bermudian sails need battens to set properly, and battens break. They also jam under spreaders on occasion, a problem not present with gaff sails so frequently.

There is another possibility which might seem at first glance to be the perfect compromise, and that is the Gunter rig. This amounts to setting a bermudian sail on a mast which is only tall enough for a gaff by making the gaff stand up vertically, and indeed this is a very effective compromise on small boats. The Mirror dinghy and the Royal Navy's Admiralty Sailing Craft

(ASCs) are just two very successful small boats rigged this way.

Large yachts do not seem able to carry a Gunter rig successfully, perhaps because the weight and size of the spar makes it difficult to set well.

Few small boats have anything forward of the mast except one sail set on the forestay: that is, they are sloop-rigged. But on larger boats, especially if a bowsprit is rigged, no matter how short, the double headsail rig—the cutter—is common. Splitting the foresail into two areas enables two smaller and more manageable sails to be set, rather than one big sail which will have a mind of its own at all the wrong times. It also enables sail area to be reduced to balance a reefed mainsail by handing one sail.

As a rule, with two head sails the mast is stepped further aft, unless there is a bowsprit, which is really a means of getting a longer boat—as far as the sail plan is concerned—at low cost. By stepping the mast further aft the weight is kept aft so that there is less tendency for the yacht to plunge bows under.

Boats of the size we are discussing here are so small that there is little point in considering yawls and ketches or schooners.

Stepping the mast in a small boat is easily done by making a square base to the mast to fit into a step in the bottom of the boat, making sure that there is sufficient strength to stand up to wringing strains as well as not being driven through the bottom of the boat when the shrouds are set up tight. If the mast passes through a hole in a seat in a dinghy this will also strengthen the mast. It reduces the unstayed length to that above the seat, providing the hole is a fairly tight fit with the mast.

In many ways blocks at the hounds which prevent soft eyes from slipping down the mast are better than spider bands. For a start you save a splice on every shroud except the forestay. With a spider band you have only the given number of eyes—four at the most, whereas with cheeks you can dangle as many blocks as you want by making soft eyes which slip snuggly over the truck and rest on the blocks. The soft eyes should be interlaced so that they tighten on each other and grip the mast when the shrouds are tightened.

For simplicity, cheapness and efficiency to windward the bermudian rig wins. For running and for having fun the gaff rig wins. If you are likely to be taking children sailing in even a small boat there is much to be said for the gaff or the Gunter simply because each mini crewman can be given a rope to handle and to be responsible for, and surely there is more fun for a child sailing when it has responsibility and something definite to do.

One possibility which should not be overlooked is the junk rig. This has been discussed in the yachting press on occasion, and the Kingfisher is available rigged this way as an alternative to the standard bermudian. If the junk rig recommends itself to you I suggest you find someone with experience of it and discuss it with them. The advantages seem clear: simplicity; strength; low unstayed mast; easily handled sail which can be easily reefed. The problem is one's inherent conservative attitudes.

Chapter 15
Repairing transoms, rubbers and tingles

We have discussed in earlier chapters how to replace planks and ribs in dinghies, techniques which can be used to repair the slightly larger craft with which we are now dealing.

Transoms

One area which is likely to cause problems is the transom, so we will start with repairs to a transom on a hard chine cruiser, built of mahogany (fig. 87).

The first repair was below the waterline on the chine (1).

The damage was wet rot, covering an area of about 6in high by 14in wide. I cut a patch out of 9in × 18in to make sure that I had all the wet rot.

Where the nails were poking through the plank ends, I drove them back from the inside and removed them. Then I fitted butt blocks (2) on the inside of my hole.

Next I offered up my new piece of wood, and scribed around the opening onto my new piece of timber. I then cut the new piece out, and made sure that I put the correct bevels on the sides of my new piece where the planks would be fastened. To get the bevels you need a bevel (3). This is placed up the transom face, and also along the plank face.

This was done again on the other corner of the new block or patch.

When the bevel was planed off the new patch, I offered it up to see how it fitted. I was satisfied, so out came my paintbrush and primer and I primed the whole thing. I mixed up some nice thin bedding, and spread it round the four corners of the hole, and on the butt blocks. In went the patch and I screwed it home.

Lastly I fastened the plank ends to the new piece of transom, hardened up the caulking around the area, and turned my attention to the other side of the transom.

This little repair was to a corner (fig. 88) of the transom on the waterline, where it had taken a knock, and wet rot was beginning to creep in. It

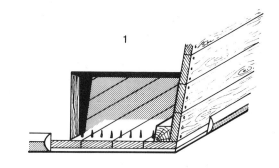

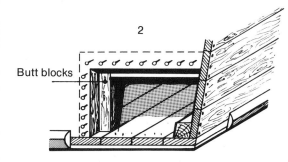

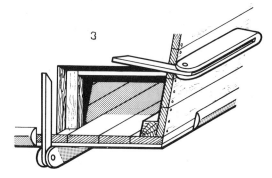

Fig. 87 **1** Cut out rot, **2** Fit butt blocks, **3** Take bevels for new piece

was rather a small area, approximately 6in × 6in. I cut out a patch 7in × 7in, and found that I could not get butt blocks behind as there was steering gear in the way.

To get out of this little problem I rebated the transom hole, and my patch was rebated to suit.

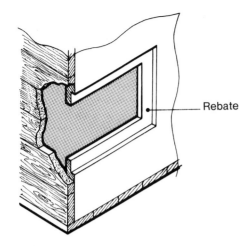

Fig. 88 Cut out rot

This type of repair is a little harder to do, as it must be more accurately fitted but, in cases such as this, there is not an easy alternative (fig. 89). To ensure that you do get a good fit, it is advisable to make yourself a template. This I did by using a piece of ¼in ply, and fitting it to the outside of the transom. Then I re-marked it on to my piece of wood, and cut that out (1)—remembering of course my bevel for the plank end, which was only on one side this time.

When I came to fit this one, I glued it, instead of using bedding or a sealant. Not being able to have a good butt-strap behind, my screws would not be strong enough, as they would only be screwing into half the thickness of the transom (2).

The transom is not the only place where rot

is likely to be found at some time. here's how to deal with small patches where the structural strength of the boat is not yet jeopardised, but where swift action can prevent it spreading and create the need for drastic surgery.

The answer could well be a 'graving piece' (fig. 90). This is a small piece of wood let into the damaged area once it has been cleared of the soft or contaminated wood.

First you roughly measure the damaged spot. Then carefully select an equivalent size piece of wood, which will have a good grain and colour match. This is very important if it is to be varnished.

Having selected the wood, draw out on the area to be repaired your area to be replaced, and cut your new timber to that size. That will be the replacement (or graving) piece (1). One tip to remember is to try to make your graving piece a 'gaining' fit (2) of about ⅛in taper towards the bottom at each edge. This means that as the wood is tapped further in, it gets bigger in its size.

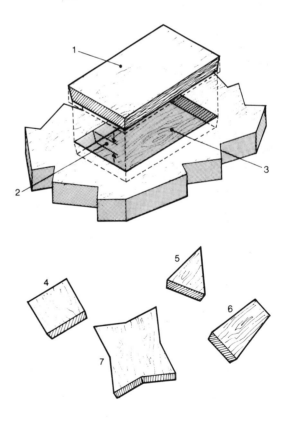

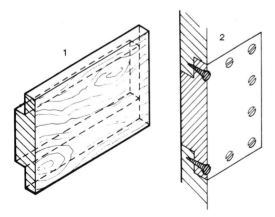

Fig. 89 Fixing new piece to transom

When the graving piece is cut out and cleaned up, it is placed on the damaged spot which is to be replaced. Scribe around the bottom of it with a sharp point or knife—or mark it with a pencil.

Chop out the unwanted wood (3), being very careful not to cut right through—just enough to get out the damaged wood.

Now, spread some glue such as Cascamite around the edges of the hole, and tap the graving piece into the hole. Let the glue dry thoroughly, and then clean off the surface with a sharp plane. If you find that the graving piece stands slightly proud of the remainder of the surface, this will true up with the plane.

If you have quite a few graving pieces to put in, I suggest you try making different shapes—such as (4) diamond, (5) triangle, (6) wedges, and (7) star.

Now, here is how to provide extra protection to vulnerable areas like the corners of a transom where they are likely to suffer impact damage from locks or jetties, or where a cruiser has chafed the corners off her transom, and this has caused the ends of her gunwale rubbers to start working loose. It does not take long with these things for the whole area to start deteriorating.

What I did was to fit a piece of wood (1, fig. 91) on the inside of the transom like a quarter knee. This I then glassed over inside. Then I did a little bit of building up of glass on the outside where it had worn away. I then screwed back the rubbers (2) into the quarter knee, and this tied it all in nicely. It was then sanded over to get rid of rough edges, and painted.

Finally, to stop this happening again, I screwed a piece of galvanised iron rubbing strip (3) around the corner.

Another way to achieve the same result is by fitting doubling pieces on the corners. Such doubling pieces also add strength to an area where a section of new wood has had to be graved-in (as shown here), and protects the area from further damage.

A short while ago the owner of a double diagonal planked cruiser called me to make good some damage to a corner which was ripped on a jetty when the craft was being manoeuvred around and a heavy gust of wind swung his stern in. The first thing to do is inspect the damage on the corner (1, fig. 92).

On this particular job, the boat was still afloat, so it would have been rather difficult to see any

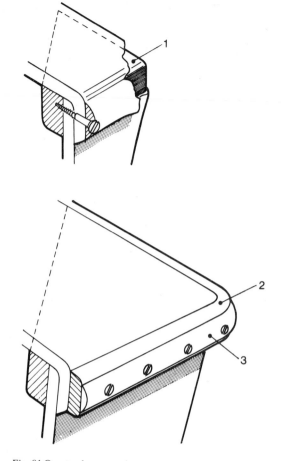

Fig. 91 Quarter knee repair

damage under the water—but one can always put weights on one side of the boat to make it list and enable you to see below the waterline.

In this case, the damage was just above the waterline. It was approximately two planks wide and two or three inches long. This, then, would not be a difficult repair.

Now, get into a dinghy to carry out the job, having armed youself with the necessary tools, a mallet, a good claw hammer, a screwdriver, one sharp chisel—and one chisel you don't mind knocking about a bit. Begin cutting the broken pieces out, trying to make a neat butt end for the new piece of planking.

When chopping out old planking, be careful not to damage the calico (2) in between the skins of timber. If the calico looks dry, before you fit the new piece of wood brush it with a little linseed oil to revitalise it.

Measure the hole for the new piece of

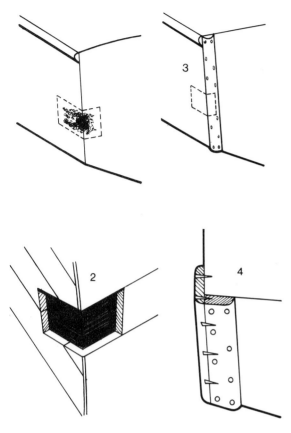

Fig. 92 **1** Damaged area, **2** Cut out damage, **3** Repaired, **4** Chafing pieces fitted

planking, cut your timber and try it for size. If it looks a good fit take it out, paint the underwood (the hidden timber), replace the piece and rescrew.

If it was a longish plank which has been repaired, you would have to nail it as well, along the seams of the plank. Before you do nail it, check that you can get at the nails on the inside of the hull to rivet them. If you cannot rivet them, you could screw along the seams instead, keeping the same spacings.

The damaged planking replaced, you can now put 'doubling pieces' over the corner of the transom and hull to help protect it in future. On this boat I suggested that hardwood be used; one length of timber shaped to the flare or curve of the transom and screwed down the edge of the corner (**3**).

Another piece of wood is then needed of 4in × 1in, which is fitted to the side of the hull overlapping both transom and transom doubling piece (**4**). This piece is screwed to the transom doubling piece and to the hull. This should then form an L-shape around the corner of the transom.

Make sure all the timber is well protected with paint, and that the corners of the doubling pieces are chamfered or rounded to make a nice, neatly-finished job.

Rubbers

It is quite probable that at some time you will have to replace timbers which have pronounced curves, such as gunwale rubbers. One way to avoid steaming the timber is to use coffin cuts.

These are little saw cuts in the back, or underwood of the rubber. They run across the grain and are about ⅜in deep, and spaced out every ½in.

Get the size of the rubber by using a piece just cut off, as a template to the moulding. Mould (or plane) the new piece of wood to suit, and then do the coffin cutting.

Spread putty into the coffin cuts, offer it to the job and proceed to screw it to the planking. As you work around the curve of the sheer, the coffin cuts close up and the putty is forced out. When the new rubber has been screwed home, go round and wipe off all the surplus putty. The reason for the putty is to prevent water getting between the rubber and the planking and so causing wet rot.

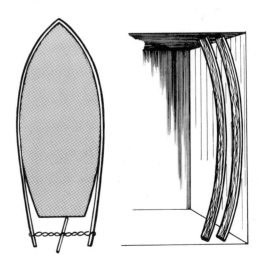

Fig. 93 Fitting rubbers

Sometimes the curve is sharp at one end, as at the bow of a rubber, and reducing in tightness as it gets towards the stern. It has always been accepted by boatbuilders that when a piece of wood has to be bent to the shape of a boat, the tighter curve is made first. Maybe that is not so obvious after all. I was reminded of this by watching an owner fitting a new gunwale rubbing strip. He had got the easy curve from the transom towards the middle of the boat in place and fixed, but he was struggling to push the strip in towards the stem while trying to drive screws at the same time.

If you start with the tighter curve, which is towards the stem in this case, and fix there, you have plenty of length to provide leverage as you pull back. If you are dealing with the two sides, work them in step, then you can draw them in by lashing their aft ends.

Tingles

Another form of repairs you often see and which can be invaluable—even if only a temporary expedient—is the application of a tingle, but only on a small scale.

A copper tingle is a strip or piece of sheet copper, which has been cut about 1in bigger all round than the area you want to cover.

Let us say we intend to put a tingle over a small split which is 3in long. Our piece of copper will then be 5in long by 2in wide. Now we spread plenty of bedding compound over the split and then put the tingle on top.

Use a centre pop to punch a small hole in one corner of the copper, about ¼in in each way. Do this in each corner, then nail home a copper tack.

When you are satisfied that the tingle is where you want it to be, proceed to centre pop all around the edges of the copper at about ½in centres.

Tap home the edges of the copper into the timber as you nail in the tacks.

Chapter 16
Keels and how to add them

Make your own bilge keels

Boats benefit from the fitting of bilge keels, in several different respects. They are probably most beneficial on a boat that is on a tidal mooring, where it must take the ground between tides. The bilge keel spreads the load when the boat comes down on the hard, whereas without the bilge keels it would lean over, placing very heavy loading on just one point of the hull. Also, of course, it assures the boat will stand more or less level when taking the ground, and there is less likelihood of it heeling so far over that on an incoming tide it might get swamped before it becomes buoyant enough to lift!

Photo 16 If a boat is to take the ground very often—as with this converted fishing boat—bilge keels are essential to spread the load.

Bilge keels are also claimed to reduce the rolling action in a lively sea, and also to provide improved directional stability at slower speeds. The general stiffening of hulls is regarded by some as a good enough reason for fitting bilge keels, particularly on older craft—though one must bear in mind that this may result in the transfer of extra and undesirable stress to other parts of the hull which, in some cases, could result in more overall harm than good. So study that point carefully.

First let us look at a round-bilge boat. You set your boat up so that your gunwales are level with each other as in the top illustration in fig. 94. They must measure the same both sides amidships, which will make your boat level.

But if your boat is flat-bottomed or hard-

chined, all you have to do is measure from the underside of the hull to the floor (which will be the distances to the underside of the keel), as in the bottom illustration in fig. 94. This measurement will be the depth of your bilge keels.

However, if your boat is round-bilge, what you must do first is to lay it over gently, and see where it touches the ground amidships. Mark the spot on the hull and then centre up the boat again as in the first sketch. Your mark indicates where the bilge keel should go.

Your bilge keels should run parallel to your keel. Thus amidshps should be the deepest point of your bilge keels. The depth of the bilge keels should not be too great, or they will have a tendency to twist off.

Now we know where they go and their depth—so the next thing is to fix them on. If the boat is GRP, all you have to do is to lay a bilge stringer along the inside of the hull and bolt through it. The stringer should be at least twice as wide as the thickness of the bilge keel, and the stringer's thickness should be enough to take the size of bolts being used.

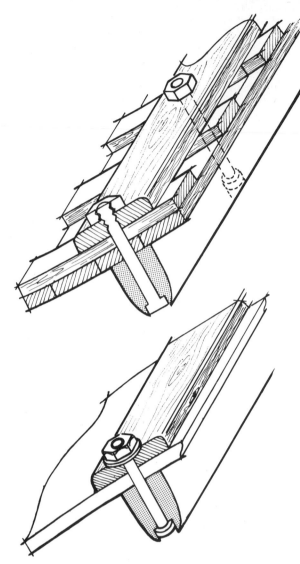

Fig. 95 Fitting bilge keels

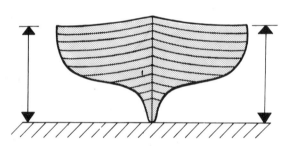

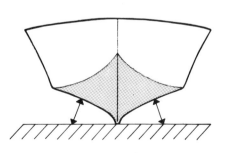

Fig. 94 Levelling up a boat

If the boat is timber, run your stringer over the top of the timbers or ribs. Try to bolt through a timber as well. If you cannot do this, you must put a block or pad under the stringer where the bolts go.

If the boat has frames, then just bolt through the frames. Remember, though, that the idea is to try to spread the load over the boat.

Extra iron keel

If you feel that your boat is a little too tender, you can always add on a little outside ballast in the form of an extra keel.

One method you can adopt is to get a length of steel channel or girder, offer it up under the keel and wedge it there. Then, from the inside, drill down through the keel until you hit the steel. Do this about every 2ft. You can then remove the girder and drill through the steel with a high-speed drill where the bolt holes were marked from drilling through the boat.

The keel bolts can be galvanised coach bolts, which are driven down from the inside, with a cotton grommet around the head. Before bolting the keel up fit a layer of tarred felt between the old and new keels; this will take up most of the uneven surface between the keels.

When it is bolted up mix some cement and fill in the channel of the iron keel. This will add a bit more weight to the keel.

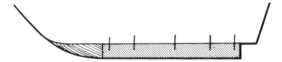

Fig. 96 Bolting a keel

Where the keel starts and finishes make some fairing in blocks and bolt them to the wooden keel (fig. 97); these should stop anything snagging onto the keel.

Whichever type of keel you decide to fit, remember that is is best to do the work before you start any more work on the inside of the hull. You have to have good access internally to make the fastenings, and once you start to re-build the interior or install engines you will almost certainly lose this accessibility.

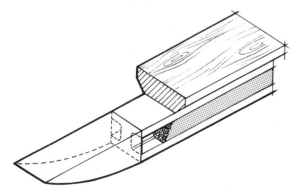

Fig. 97 Fairing a piece for keel

Chapter 17
More about installing engines

There are many reasons why it is best to deal with the engine installation as early as possible. As we have seen, it is often wise to plan the whole of the boat around it, but another factor is that an engine is a large inanimate lump of metal which may be virtually impossible to get into position once the accommodation has been started on.

With the deck laid and bulkheads in position, there may literally be no way in which it can be taken below, let alone positioned on its beds, because the apertures through which it would have to pass are too small. This is a point to be borne in mind if you are working on a boat which has an engine which may have to be taken out for replacing or reconditioning—often there is no way it can be got out without first taking up the deck. The reason is that the deck was laid after the engine was in position.

And it is also hard to guarantee that your scheme for a lay-out really does provide adequate access to the motor for maintenance and repair until the engine is on its beds. On the other hand, you may have wasted space by being too generous with accessibility.

What is true for the engine is also true for fuel tanks and possibly stern gear and steering gear. All these items are best located in their final resting place before the laying of decks and the fitting of bulkheads make it impossible—and this might easily apply to other large awkward things like cookers, water-tanks and even large sheets of ply.

Here we discuss how to make engine beds for a larger boat.

The general principles are the same, but you must remember that we are now dealing with larger boats and therefore with more powerful engines which are heavier and more sophisticated than the lightweight units we dealt with earlier.

First you set up your shaft line, using a piano wire or good quality chalk line. Run the line from the stern outboard side, through the shaft log or shaft hold, and secure on the inboard side, either on a bulkhead or batten fixed thwartships at the correct height and forward of the engine's position. The shaft line represents the centre line of the shaft, and is also the centre line of the engine.

If there is a reduction box on the engine, this must be taken into account, as the shaft line will step up here a few inches. Check what you have done against the engine drawings, to make sure the height of the shaft line relative to the engine feet is correct, because the engine feet become the top of the engine beds.

If you have not got a drawing, put a straight edge along the engine's feet and measure down to the centre of the reduction boxes' coupling, which couples the shaft. This measurement is then added parallel on top of the shaft line, which will give you the height of the engine beds. You then have a height to which the beds can be made, and also the angle of the beds.

Next, mark the line of the beds on the bottom of the hull, making sure that they are the correct width apart for your engine feet to sit on. Then make a template of the bed, using hardboard or ply, and draw out the shape and height from the inboard side of each engine bed. This will then allow you a bit extra for bevelling the bottom of the beds to the hull's shape.

Engine beds can become an integral part of the boat's strength, if you so wish. So try to make them run as far aft and forward as possible. They can then form your floor bearers, and sometimes your rudder strongback.

Now—the materials. If the beds are to be glassed over, douglas fir or pine will do. The thickness will be governed by the size of the engine feet and the bolts being used, but a safe size to work on is 1¾in to 2in—which will take at least a 100hp engine.

If the weight factor is important, use douglas fir or pine with a marine ply covering, which is glued and screwed or nailed. Use marine glue such as Cascophin or Airoduct.

The size again will take up to about 140hp.

Photo 17 A popular small marine diesel engine is the Perkins single cylinder 1.18(M) which gives 5hp at 2500 rpm

Photo 18 A heavily built SABB diesel engine which can be hand-started and was originally designed for small inshore fishing craft where its reliability is essential

The ply should be around ½in and timber 1½in thick. If you are not worried about weight, then use a hardwood such as iroko or afromosia. Oak is nice but, as I warned you before, if you use oak don't use any galvanised fastening or bolts, as the acid in the oak will attack the galvanising.

If your frames are thick enough to take a ½in or ⅝in bolt you can bolt right through the hull. If you do, don't forget to put a caulking-cotton grommet around the outboard end of the bolt under the washer. If you haven't any frames at all, sit the beds on the timbers and slide a packing-piece between the timber where you want to put a bolt, and bolt through the hull.

Engine bed intercostals come next. They help the beds stay upright and spread the torque of the motor—and also spread the load. These need only be about half the thickness of the beds.

Bolts for the beds, through the hull, can be about ⅝in diameter. If into cleats, ½in or ⁷⁄₁₆in diameter is fine. The bolts which hold the cleats to the frames can be ⅜in to ⁷⁄₁₆in diameter.

If they bolt the outside intercostals to the cleats, then use ⁷⁄₁₆in to ½in. The intercostals can be 3in diameter bolts where bolted to the beds, or screwed with 14 gauge screws. If ply is used on the beds, then screw with 10g. screws, or use 10g. or 8g. nails—Gripfast or copper. If copper, then nail right through and turn on the inside.

Final reminder—the most important thing is to line it all up perfectly before you start.

Chapter 18
Navigation lights

Recently introduced regulations by IMCO (the Inter-governmental Maritime Consultative Organisation) have changed the rules regarding the provision of navigation lights. The principles remain the same, however, although there are now precise specifications for colour, range and arcs of visibility. In general there are tough requirements as far as the range is concerned, and a tri-coloured light is permitted at the masthead of a boat which is sailing, although not when under power.

An example of the requirements of the new rules is that boats over 40ft in length must have 25 watt bulbs in all navigation lights with the exception of the stern light, which can be 10 watts. This is because the stern light is white and a white light gives the same candela for 10 watts as a coloured one does for 25 watts. Boats under 40ft must have their lights visible for one nautical mile, and a properly designed navigation lantern will achieve this with a 10 watt bulb even in a coloured lamp.

It is also permitted to fit a combined red and green 'sidelight' unit at the pulpit, to be used in conjuction with a white stern light and white steaming light when under power.

My feeling is that all multi-coloured lights are hazardous in the extreme, because a red and green combination light closing with you head-on will appear to be some distance away, whereas in actual fact the boat is right on top of you. If two yachts are manoeuvring in a harbour at night the skipper of each can well be fooled into thinking that the other yacht is some distance off and there is no risk of collision, when in reality the two yachts are only feet apart. If the helmsman has lost his night vision because of the general battery of lights all round the harbour, or has been partially blinded and confused by them, the situation just described could occur more easily than you would readily believe in the comfort of an armchair in the middle of the off-season. (See Appendix for the relevant extracts from the International Regulations for Preventing Collisions at Sea.)

For this reason we are here discussing installing stern lights, masthead light, and separate sidelights mounted in proper old-fashioned sidelight boxes.

As far as the electrical part of the job is concerned, make sure that the lights you install are well designed, so that bulbs can be changed by stripping the unit down by hand, so that the arcs of visibility of the lights are correct, so that they are watertight (it is not unknown for side or stern lights to be completely immersed on occasions), and ensure that the battery is man enough to cope with the drain when all the lights are on for several hours. The wiring must be thick enough to make sure that there is not so much resistance in the circuit as to cause voltage drop.

There is also a school of thought which advocates paraffin (kerosene) navigation lanterns on the grounds that anything electrical is bound to fail eventually through corrosion, battery failure or short circuiting (probably through damp). A good short circuit can be responsible for a spectacular and expensive fire. Hard worked boats are certainly liable to any of these eventualities. On the other hand, small craft used by professional seamen are fitted invariably with electrical navigational lights, and if the whole system is installed properly, battery kept maintained and charged, and the wiring run so that it can't get wet and corroded with the result that it shorts, these lighting systems are as reliable as any other.

Paraffin lamps are not always easy to light, they suffer from a tendency to blow out in strong winds (especially sudden gusts), will run out of oil if not filled up before lighting, cannot be re-filled if the oil reservoir on board runs dry, and in general can create just as many problems as electrical navigational lights.

Here again, the solution is to buy good quality

lamps. These seldom blow out and if you get the heavily galvanised type, rather than copper or steel ones, they will last for ever.

There is a debate about the best type of lenses for navigation lights. Many have reeded glass, which concentrates the beam so that it can be seen further away. Others have dioptric lenses which also concentrate the beam, but if a small boat is heeled the dioptric type send the beam skywards like a searchlight, so that the light cannot be seen by an observer whose eye is near sea level. For this reason many experienced yachtsmen do not favour dioptric lenses.

Navigation light boxes

These can be made out of ply or timber and the simplest way to make one is to sit the navigation light on the bench and measure its height and width. Mark the base out first—and it is best to make the box a little longer than you need in case you get it wrong. It is easier to cut it down than to make it longer!

So for a navigation light say 5in high and 3in wide make the base 4in by 12in long. The sides run down past the base, so add the thickness of the material on to the sides, i.e. 5in plus ½in minimum for the base.

The sides should be glued and screwed and rounded over at the ends, as in the drawing.

If the boxes are going to be fixed on the roof then they will have to sit on levelling blocks. Put the navigation box into position and slip little wedges under each corner until the box is level, then measure the gaps where the blocks will go. The blocks can be screwed to the roof and the boxes to the blocks.

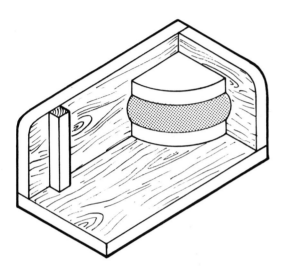

Fig. 98 Navigation light box

Chapter 19
Making bulkheads, and other matters

So many people look at a complicated bulkhead fitting, for example, and ask how on earth I fitted it in—or "How many attempts did you have on that one?"

Well, it all boils down to scribing it, if you want it to fit accurately the first time. Scribing is to draw out the exact shape required on the piece to be cut.

For instance, if I have a bulkhead to fit into a boat I will first make a template, as you see in fig. 99. This is made up of strips of thin wood or ply offcuts. They are all tacked together into as near the shape as possible. Then I scribe the template, as in fig. 100.

To scribe it, I first decide on one or two measurements which will span the gaps between my template and the hull. I then make up a 'dumbstick' (fig. 100). This will be a piece of ply the size of the measurement I have decided on. A pencil is held in a groove in the dumbstick, and I then draw all around my template, following the shape of the hull and other obstructions.

When this is complete I take the template and place it on to the sheet of ply which is to form the bulkhead, and nail it lightly on to stop it moving about.

At this point it is a simple matter to re-scribe back on to the bulkhead, once again, using the dumbstick. The edge of the dumstick is held level with the mark on the template, and a pencil mark made on the plywood. The dumbstick is then moved along the line on the template very slightly, and another pencil mark made on the plywood. This is repeated every inch or so around the whole thing. When completed, and the template taken away, you have a series of dotted marks all the way around. These are joined up, and that is the shape your bulkhead needs to be. Takes time, of course—but you only need to do the job once!

Making a fore-hatch

No matter how small the boat, if it has a cabin it

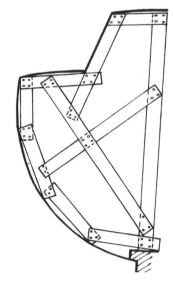

Fig. 99 Making a template

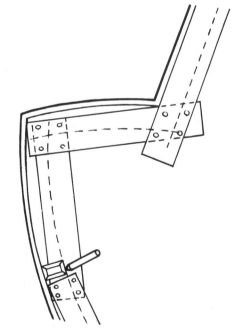

Fig. 100 Scribing a template

Photo 19 The template has been made and is being used to set up the timber of the bulkhead framing ready for glueing and screwing

Fig. 101 New hatch opening

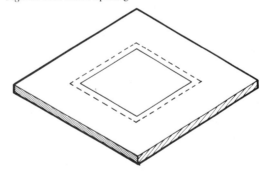

should have a fore-hatch. And why? Because otherwise it becomes a fire-trap—and under certain circumstances it could also be your avenue of escape if the craft were to sink by the stern. Additionally, it just happens to be compulsory in numbers of waterway authority areas.

So if you have a cabin boat without a fore-hatch, here is how to make one. Bearing in mind that the average hatch opening is about 22in wide, mark out your hatch on the deck and try to get between the deck beams—if you have to cut through one it must be strengthened up by fitting short carlings between the beams.

When the hatch opening has been cut out, fit a piece of ply over the hole and draw around the opening from underneath. Then add on 1in all around the opening which will become the inside measurement to the hatch (see fig. 101). Make the hatch about 4in to 6in high.

Now there are two ways of doing the joints at the corner, the better of which is to dovetail

them, though you can do a shoulder joint with a slight dovetail effect (see fig. 102), but in either case use glue and screws on the joints.

The top can be of ply, and this is glued and screwed to the frame—let it overlap and plane it back when it is dry. If the deck is a laid deck and you want the hatch to be the same, just lay your decking over the ply and fit a beading around the edges to cover the end grain of the plywood (see fig. 103).

93

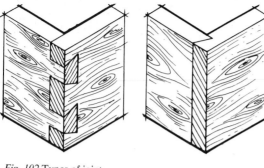

Fig. 102 Types of joint

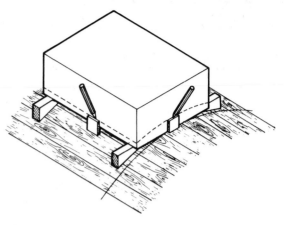

Fig. 104 Scribing down a hatch

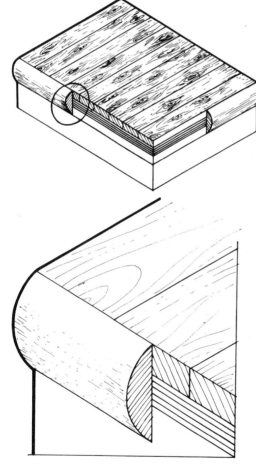

Fig. 103 Hatch top

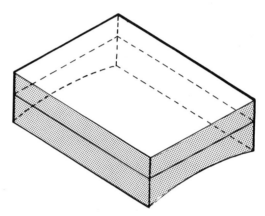

Fig. 105 Cutting a hatch to open

fit perfectly without any strain or twist being put into the hatch.

When it fits the deck, measure down from the top of the hatch about 2in and scribe all around at that measurement (fig. 105), then cut the hatch in two all around that line. It's a good idea to mark on the top and bottom of the hatch which is the fore end before you cut the hatch in two. Sit the bottom part of the hatch onto the deck and cramp it into position, then drill off your screw holes. If the hatch sits on a carling or beam then screw down into them, but if the hatch just sits on the deck and misses the carlings then screw up into the hatch. When all the screw holes are drilled, lift up the hatch and put plenty of bedding on it and sit it back into position and screw down.

Where the deck comes through to the hatch opening, fit a hatch coaming, which is well bedded and screwed in to the carlings (see fig.

To fit the hatch all you need to do is to sit it in position and slip in small wedges to prevent it rocking, and then scribe all around the hatch (see fig. 104). Take off as little as possible, but make sure the scribe goes all around. Plane off the unwanted timber and try the fit again. It must

94

106). Let the coaming stick up above the deck by about 1in. If you drill four drain holes, one in each corner of the hatch, any water that gets through the hinged part will drain out (see fig. 107).

Sliding hatches are usually fitted onto coach roofs, and their construction is quite simple (see fig. 108). One of the important things to remember is to make sure that there are no water traps between the slide and the hatch coamings. Usually, if the sliding hatch is leading from the cockpit into the boat, there are drop boards or hinged double doors—sometimes even both. Make sure that the doors open outwards; if they don't it is very difficult—sometimes impossible—to make them watertight.

Keep it rigid

One of the problems you may encounter when working on the hull of a boat is that the sides may move. They won't exactly flap about in the breeze, but they may flex a noticeable amount,

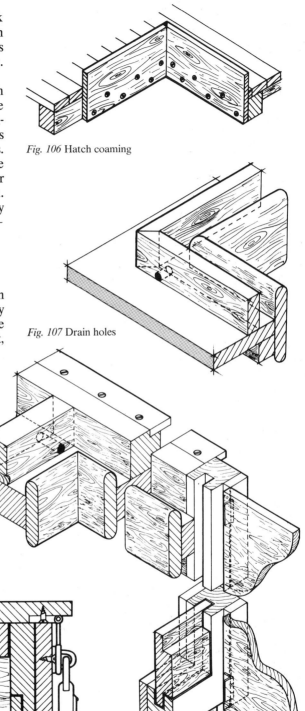

Fig. 106 Hatch coaming

Fig. 107 Drain holes

Fig. 108 Sliding track *(top left)* and sectional drawings of sliding hatch and drop boards with hinged doors

especially if you take out seats, knees, deck beams and so on. One function of deck beams, in addition to providing a support for the deck planking and being something to fasten them to, is to stop the sides of the hull falling apart outwards.

In turn, the knees help to unite the structure in the other plane.

Hence, you have to make sure that the sides of the hull are locked absolutely rigid when you are working on such things as making a deck where there wasn't one before, or replacing thwarts, or making new gunwales or bulwarks.

To do this may mean making temporary deck beams to tie the sides of the hull together, using almost any spare piece of timber which is long enough for the job. If you possibly can, use clamps to fasten it to the hull to avoid making screw holes, or if you have no alternative other than screws try to ensure that the same holes can be used for permanent screws later. If you can't manage either, don't forget to plug the holes once the screws have been withdrawn to prevent water getting in and creating rot.

To steam or not to steam, that is the question . . . .

To steam or to laminate? That is the decision you will have to make on many occasions when you have a repair job to do on some timber section of a boat. So it is a matter of analysing a list of pertinent factors.

For example, let us consider that I am going to carry out a repair on a gunwale rubber—my list would look something like this. To steam, I would need:

1 Steam box or steam pipe.
2 Good working area for wrapping hot timber around boat.

3 Cramps for holding timber in place.
4 Electric power for drilling, shaping, finishing, etc.

I must also consider these points:
1 Is the finish to be paint or varnish?
2 Is the hull wood or GRP?
3 What is the shape of the gunwale rubber—pear-shaped, half-round, or square?
4 How much flare is there in the hull or the sheer?

Then I must consider that if the craft is afloat I would not have a steam-pipe, whereas in a yard I would be able to manage. I want to know whether I could actually use cramps on the job.

Then there is the business of getting at the job easily. If a craft is ashore, I would have room for staging (something rigid to stand on), from which I can push and pull as required. Doing the job afloat presents problems.

Whether the rubber is painted or varnished is important. If I laminate the section and it is then varnished, the glue lines may be rather conspicuous. But this may not matter so much if the remainder of the rubber and/or the one on the other side is a laminated piece. However, it is not important if the finished job is hidden under paint.

So to shape. If you have a pear-shape, and you laminate, you will have to be careful where your fastenings go, as there will be a lot of cleaning and shaping to do. If the section is steamed, you can shape it before you steam it and so get it to fit the flare.

If you laminate, and there is a lot of flare, you will have to spile your laminates first.

So you can see that it is not an altogether straightforward decision whether to steam or laminate. You must weigh up all the pros and cons of the particular job.

Chapter 20
Making good use of space

Later in the book we deal with accommodation, related to slightly larger boats. Much of this is relevant to the smaller boats we are dealing with here, except that there just is not the space in 20-footers and so on to build the more complicated units discussed later.

So what we concentrate on now is space saving dodges, starting with fo'c's'les.

If you are thinking of fitting out the fo'c's'le with a couple of bunks, and it looks as if one of the sleepers is going to end up with his knees under his chin, here is a way of providing sleeping accommodation— unless you practise Yoga!

The general layout one sees in small fo'c's'les is a bunk each side, meeting at the centre line.

This is all right if the sleepers are children or dwarfs. But if they are full size then one gets all the foot-space and the other has to sleep bent double— or kick!

The alternative is to stagger the bunks' height. This way you will get two full-length bunks and plenty of foot space. If you do it this way, make sure that the under-bunk sleeper has enough space for his feet to stick upwards— and that the top-bunk sleeper does not try to lift the side deck or roof top with his shoulder as he turns over! Fig. 109 shows roughly how it should work.

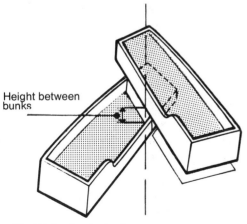

Height between bunks

Fig. 109 Overlapping bunks

Tables can take up a lot of room, especially if they are supported from the floor, perhaps by the centreboard casing (which is quite common), or hinged at one end from a bulk-head. There always remains the problem of what to do with your feet when sitting at it.

One way round this is to make a chock on the mast, if it comes through the deckhead, or on a bulkhead, to support one end of the table, and support the other end by suspending it by rope from the deckhead. A cord can be used to go round the mast to stop the table swinging or coming off the chock. When the table is not required, it can be easily unshipped and stowed away— perhaps as part of a bunk, seat, engine casing, or even as a cover for a sink or cooker.

If the cords are good quality white rope with perhaps a few fancy knots worked in, and the table surface varnished or (better still) oiled with teak oil or Danish oil, the whole effect can look very attractive and not in the least a bodge.

One problem which can arise when you are attempting to squeeze the accommodation of a 40-footer into a 20-footer is that heat from a stove can set fire to a bulkhead or other part of the boat because there is not enough air space between them. It is astonishing how far the flame from a burner fans out when there is a pan on it. If you are ambitious enough to install a cooker with an oven, you will have to protect the adjacent areas from scorching.

On the face of it, putting asbestos around anywhere there is a flame seems a sensible thing to do. But it is no use fixing it directly on to wood, because although asbestos will not burn, it will transmit heat. It can absorb and carry sufficient heat to char the wood with which it is in contact.

Official advice is that there should be a gap of 1in between the asbestos and any wood behind it. In a pocket-size galley this may be felt to reduce space rather a lot. If you reduce that 1in you will still get some protection, but if the asbestos gets really hot, the surface of the wood may suffer.

If you can get at the screws as they go through the gap, you can use tubes as spacers. There will then be no wood in contact with the asbestos. Otherwise you will have to fix battens first and screw to them. If these are positioned away from the parts where greatest heat is anticipated, they should not suffer. However, do not completely box in the space. A free flow of air there is what provides the insulation. Let there be gaps— battens can be in parts and there can be spaces rather than close fits where they meet.

Other ideas for saving space include work surfaces in galleys which fit over the sink unit when a flat area is required for preparing food, but which lifts off and goes in the cockpit when the sink is required for washing up—or even, with a little ingenuity, fits over the cooker to provide a draining board. To do this it must be slotted into bearers so that there is a gradient towards the sink. A plastic surface is essential, or well varnished wood, kept scrubbed clean.

Another problem in a galley is where to fit the rubbish bin. Domestic pedal type buckets are hopeless and many of the products designed for boats are so big that they get in the way.

One possibility is to make a pocket out of plywood off-cuts on the inside of a door, preferably one under the sink; there waste pipes create a space which is difficult to fit out with shelves. A disposable polythene bag of the appropriate size slipped inside will prevent the pocket from being dirty and unhygienic.

A problem in galleys is where to fit the water pump so that its presence does not impede access to shelves or cupboards. One answer is to fit a pump under the floor boards which is operated by foot pressure on a lever. These pumps are made in different configurations, so that there is either a pedal which sticks up through the floor, or a lever pedal to enable the pump to be installed inside a cupboard, under the sink for example, in that space which is so awkward to use.

In designing a galley do not forget that it is

Photo 20 Best use of the space under a bunk is provided by these compartments made by fitting mini bulkheads. Access is from the front on the outside of the bunk and by lifting tailor-made lids from above at the side nearest the side of the hull

very hard not to create blind corners where access to the back of a cupboard or a shelf is difficult because there are other cupboards or shelves on both sides of the right angle. One way round this is to construct wedge shaped units in the corners, which won't beat the problem but go some way to overcoming it. If you have sufficient ingenuity it is not impossible to make the whole wedge shaped unit slide out to give access at the back.

The problem of access at the back of very deep cupboards can also often be solved by making the whole unit slide out on castors. Basically, you make a cupboard within a cupboard, with castors on the base and small wheels running on bearers to enable you to pull out the whole unit. A rubber stop prevents the whole unit coming out too far. You can only do this if there is enough uncluttered floor space in front of the unit to take the front to back dimension of the internal cupboard.

By pulling the internal cupboard out you can get at the backs of the shelves by standing at the sides.

Don't forget that drawers are wasteful of space because the bearers and the gaps between the drawers all take up space in which you can't stow goodies, while shelves have the disadvantage of enabling you to pile in so much stuff that nothing is visible or accessible. Drawers. too, will jam shut if you cram in too much.

Drawers must be made so that they won't shoot open every time the boat rolls. Fig. 110 shows how to make them so that this doesn't happen. An alternative is to fit catches at the tops of the drawers so that they lock but can easily be opened by pressing a button, for example.

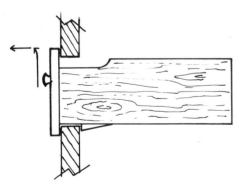

Fig. 110 Bunk drawer wedges

Another thing to remember when making drawers or any other joinery which is a fairly snug fit but which must be free to open or slide easily is that wood will 'move', especially in a wooden boat. Not only will it swell or contract with the temperature to a greater or lesser extent, but the shape of a wooden boat will change a little from time, when it is out of the water, for example, and the weight is all taken on the keel and the supporting struts.

For this reason it is best to avoid very close fitting doors or drawers in a wooden boat, and if you decide to opt for loose drawers with snap catches to keep them from shooting open do not make the fitting of the catches so tight that the catches themselves jam tight when the wood moves!

A fairly common way of saving space in very small boats is to install a bucket type of toilet below a wash basin or shelf, because the toilet can easily be slid out when required; there is no fixed plumbing to stop if being shifted about.

I am not too keen on this idea because if the toilet is free to be slipped out it is also likely to be free to go charging about when the boat rolls or pitches! Restraining chocks and guides are all wasteful of space, so in. the end you tend to defeat the objective of the exercise.

Better to make the toilet immovable—until you want to take it out for emptying, and make whatever you fix above it hinge up out of the way, like a shelf for toilet gear or a folding wash basin.

Needless to say, the ideas some people have of a combined toilet/galley compartment, with food storage and preparation in the same area, is not one to be supported. I mention this because I have come across boats with the food larder above the chemical toilet. . . .

A chemical toilet under a hinged seat is acceptable, but not if the seat is also a bunk. And it is not a good idea to locate the toilet in such a place that everyone has to get out of the interior of the boat when some one wants to use the loo, least of all in the middle of the night.

This subject leads us naturally into mentioning ventilation. This is very important in all small boats, not only for the reasons hinted at already, but to make sure that there is an adequate supply of air right through the boat at all times. Without clean fresh air circulating you get musty clothes and bedding, evil smelling cupboards, food

which goes off rapidly, rotting wood, foul bilges, fungus, almost anything in fact except a sweet smelling, pleasant interior. If petrol vapour or LP gas leaks get into the bilge you also create a nice highly explosive mixture which will one day explode and probably destroy the boat and lives.

So air must be encouraged to circulate. Today there is no shortage of off-the-shelf ventilators which will allow air to circulate easily and which can be closed when it rains or when spray begins to fly. It helps if you construct a wooden box over them with access for air in a different place to the opening for air to be drawn below. A drain hole of generous size in the wooden box to enable what water does penetrate it to escape easily is a must.

The natural flow of air inside a boat is from aft to forwards, so allow for this fact in planning ventilators.

Having got the air below you have to encourage it to flow through cupboards and lockers, and the way to do this is to cut holes—up to 1½in in diameter low down and high up in each compartment—so that cold air can enter at the bottom and hot air is drawn upwards from the top. These holes can be made to look pretty by fancy carving, but as they are functional and normal in small boats there is really no need to be ashamed of them.

All engine compartments require good ventilation, because a constant supply of fresh air is essential for combustion, but also go get rid of fumes, fuel and oil spills, and fumes from batteries, which can also be lethal during charging,

As a rule portholes, especially towards the forward end of a boat, spend most of their time closed, so don't rely on them alone.

There is another point not to be overlooked when sorting out the accommodation in a small boat, and that is the location of skin fittings. One good rule is the fewer the better, because that way there are fewer places for corrosion, blockage, fracture, and general problems. Another good rule is to get good hefty fittings with a seacock and a filter, especially for the outlet of a sea toilet or an engine exhaust, when the size is very important, and a filter is of course pointless.

It is not a bad thing, on the belt and braces principle, to have an alternative seacock and filter in the engine compartment, so that in an emergency, if the engine cooling water intake gets choked, you can rapidly close the cock and transfer the hose to the number two cock.

There are different opinions about what is the best material for seacocks and skin fittings. I favour Delrin or Nylon because they do not corrode and are quite strong enough for the job

Photo 21 above left Stowage for the chemical toilet is provided under the hand basin. Many people think that having two toilets is better than installing a holding tank which may be difficult to have emptied

Photo 22 below left A well designed plastic ventilator manufactured by Electrolux

Photo 23 below Ventilation holes in the lids which make up the bunk top

they have to perform. They do not encourage electrolytic action either. They should be made so that you can close the seacock to get at the filter for cleaning, and all seacocks must be easily accessible.

To install a skin fitting you wait until the boat is out of the water, cut a hole just big enough to accept the fitting, and bolt it in with through bolts, nuts on the inside, with plenty of good quality grease under the flange or plate. But before you do start drilling make sure that there is nothing in the way, inside the boat or out, which could make it a bad place to locate the fitting. This includes things like frames which prevent the valve that closes the opening from closing properly, bilge keels so close to the fitting that you can't get the bolts in, fairings for transducers, and so on. It is easy to place the skin fitting so close to a frame that you physically cannot get the hose or pipe on to it.

We talked earlier in this chapter about tables. Now let's return to chart tables. Many small boats have them—but how often are they used? It may create a salty image, especially in the brochure put out by the manufacturer of production yachts, but unless you are anticipating long passages and intend to make full use of electronic navigational aids to help you plot courses, make fixes and so on, there is really little point in having a chart table in a very small boat because most of your navigation will be of the buoy spotting and identifying variety.

If this is the case all you need is a space to lay out a chart so that it can be read easily and somewhere to sit while you make notes about tides and weather forecasts. So why waste space on a chart table?

Better to make a ply clipboard, large enough to take a chart folded in half, with perhaps a pad for notes. Then you can take the clipboard into the cockpit or wheelhouse with you and use it without leaving the helm, which makes visualising your course much easier.

Such a clipboard should have a sheet of plastic overlaid on the chart both to protect the chart and to enable you to plot on it without eventually covering the chart with pencil marks which are difficult to erase.

With a little ingenuity it is possible to make such a clipboard slot into some sort of fitting on the cockpit side so that it cannot shift, and so that it can be seen easily by the man at the helm without having to move. This is so much a matter of horses for courses that it is pointless to make firm suggestions about achieving it.

Another space saving idea is to use nets for stowage. Netting is not so hard to obtain—from some chandlers (especially those stocking gear for fishermen), or from the shops which cater for anglers. Netting can be slung under deckheads in areas where no one is ever likely to want to put their head, and used for stowage. It is especially useful over bunks for clothing at night or bedding during the day, or in toilet compartments, where there always seems to be overhead space which is completely unusable in any other way.

The fixings will have to be strong because it is surprising how much weight can be jammed into such nets, and what you don't want is for the whole lot to suddenly rip off the deckhead at night while you are asleep and smother you.

Resist the temptation to rig too much net stowage in case you create such a claustrophobic atmosphere that no one can bear to go below.

There are many more ides for making best use of space in a small boat. Regular reading of the more practical yachting magazines is a good way to jog your imagination into dreaming up something which is appropriate for your own needs.

Chapter 21
Making and fitting screens

Many small boats look better and are more comfortable if a windscreen is fitted. Not only does it deflect the spray but it can also provide a space which can be used as a shelf for standing cups of tea, glasses, binoculars, and so on, and even somewhere to mount a compass, although this last is not a good idea if the compass will be located near wiring for instruments or close to anything else which will interfere magnetically.

A screen from a manufacturer can cost a small fortune, besides being unlikely to be the exact size and shape you want, but it need not cost too much to make one yourself.

Softwood can be used for the frame providing you do not intend to varnish it—in that case you really must use a hardwood.

The first step is to measure the cabin top and make up a template on a piece of ply of the exact shape and size of the finished screen. This will enable you to cut it out and offer it up to make sure that the finished job will fit in with the general style of the boat. Nothing looks worse than too tall a windscreen, nothing is more pointless than one which is too low and achieves nothing except diverting the spray or rain into your face.

Having satisfied yourself that what you have cut out on the template is what you want, you can take off the timber lengths. Give each length a number or code—'port side upright' for example—so that you know what each length is for when you start to assemble.

It is always worth marking any length of timber or piece of ply when doing carpentry work, not only by function, but which side is which —'port upright—aft side' and even add 'top' or 'bottom' when the two ends are not interchangeable. This way you won't find that you have used the wrong chunk of wood and maybe created a situation where you run out of timber or have to throw away an otherwise perfectly good length.

Having cut the timber to the right lengths and shape you have to cut the joints, fit them to make sure that they go together properly, and then drill and countersink the holes.

A screen of the type we are discussing will be much stronger and more rigid if it has side pieces, as in the photograph, and these side pieces will also make it easier to fasten the screen down strongly.

The next step is to assemble the framework, and this is best done by applying the glue to the joints, cramping them and then screwing. The size of timbers will be dictated by the overall size of the screen, and this in turn will dictate what size screws you use. Make sure that the whole thing is strong enough for its function, but do not use such heavy timber that the whole thing looks ungainly or clumsy. Examining other boats with screens will help you get it right.

Once the framework has been completed you have to scribe it to fit the cabin top. We have already discussed scribing as applied to bulkheads and the principle is the same here. First offer up the screen, and let it sit so that the centre point of the screen is making contact with the cabin top, and then slip blocks under the side members so that it is level and square. Now use a block of wood or the side of a tape rule case, and draw a line on the bottom of the framework so that it follows the line of the cabin top exactly.

You can now mount the framework upside down on your work bench and cramp it, making sure it doesn't move about while you shape the base of the frame along the scribed pencil line so that it follows the cabin top contour. Don't forget that it will have to be chamfered at the same time because it is unlikely that it will be square to the cabin top.

You may find that a fillet is needed, especially underneath the side screens, although if you make the bottom timber too deep and there is not too much camber on the deck this may not be necessary. If a fillet is needed you must take careful measurements and then cut and chamfer it to ensure that it fits snugly between the bottom of the frame and the cabin top.

Photos 24, 25, 26 Scribing a screen down on to the coach roof.

Once this is right it can be glued, cramped, and screwed to the frame. Remember during this fitting process that the more snug the fit the better the end result will look and the less likely it will be to leak.

Now you can fit the screen. Locate it accurately on the cabin top and draw pencil lines each side of the base members. Remove the screen, and drill holes from above through the cabin top, and then countersink them below—the reason for doing this is so that you can fix from below, which looks neater, is stronger and will probably be more watertight.

Once the holes are drilled you can replace the screen, fix it firmly in position, and then drill from below through the holes in the cabin top into the framework, using the holes as a guide. It

is very important here that the holes go squarely into the framework as any which are out of true will come out, poking through the side of the framework.

Once all the holes are drilled and you are happy that you have got them all right you remove the screen (yes, again!) and fill the space between the pencil lines on the cabin top with a layer of bedding and then locate the screen—for the last time—properly in position and make sure it cannot move. Now fix the screws from below, starting at the centre and moving outwards. The excess sealer will be squeezed out, and it may be necessary to give the screws a second and final turn with the screwdriver, starting again at the centre, once all the excess sealer has escaped.

Scrape away all the surplus sealer and wipe the surfaces of the wood and the cabin top clean with a rag soaked with thinners or petrol.

Plane and sandpaper the framework, fill the screw holes and sandpaper off any excess filler, and finally paint the whole framework—or varnish if you prefer.

Once you are satisfied with the paint and it is good and dry you can fit the glass. The first stage here is to make a brown paper template and get the glass cut to size. Most stockists will cut to shape and size for you if you give them a template, and in my experience this is a much better bet than trying to cut it yourself. The art of the glazier depends on good tools and lots of experience, and unless you have both it is wise to pay a few pennies extra and let the expert do it.

To make the template you may have to fix the paper to a backing piece of ply with sticky tape to stop it slopping about.

The glass should be cut about 1/16in smaller than the hole, to allow the sealer to work.

You can now fasten the rear beading to the framework with brass or copper panel pins (not brassed), using glue between the two faces of wood (the beading and the framework). By rear beading I mean the one which will allow the glass to lean against it *in situ*, while the top beading is fixed later with more panel pins.

But before doing this apply a thin layer of sealer all around the beading so that when the glass is laid into position it can be pressed gently into the sealer until the excess is squeezed out. You may have to apply a little more sealer before

positioning the top beading and fastening it.

The final step is to remove the excess sealer and finish the painting.

The type of glass and the thickness will be dictated by the size and type of boat and the type of use she is put to. A larger cruiser which is going out to sea will require stronger glass than a canal boat, possibly even laminated glass.

The most difficult part of all this is fixing the final panel pins into the top layer of beading. One mis-hit and you have to go back to the glass shop for more. To avoid this use a small light hammer, aim carefully—and keep the templates just in case!

Chapter 22
Deck fittings – comfortable cockpits

This book would not be complete without some mention of deck fittings, and this seems to be the most appropriate place to discuss them. It is also a good place to talk about how to make best use of cockpits and small wheelhouses, with the accent on making them as comfortable and functional as possible.

The main points about deck fittings are that they should be strong and functional, and that they should be fastened down absolutely securely. There are many firms now engaged in manufacturing deck fittings – cleats, bollards, winches, windlasses, fairleads, eyebolts, fillers for water or fuel, tabernacles, pulpits and stanchions, but unfortunately not all the manufacturers know too much about the practical use of their products on boats, especially in adverse conditions.

So the first thing when selecting fittings when undertaking a repair, restoration or renovation is to make sure that what you buy is suitable for the job. If you are buying new fittings (or second-hand, which is often to be recommended) you can make quite sure that they are also big enough and strong enough. The pitfall which the manufacturers of production boats often fall into is in providing deck fittings which are too small and too flimsy. I always tend to go to the

Photo 27 A selection of deck fittings in stainless steel

Photo 28 This tabernacle is bolted through a solid pad and through the deck underneath

other extreme, but then I mistrust 'yachty' fittings anyway, especially those made of stainless steel (is it the right grade?) or described with the jargon of the ad man—'satin-finished in gleaming phosphor bronze' etc.

For the sort of boats we are writing about in these pages it is probably best to go for good, old-fashioned, galvanised fittings of the type specified and used by fishermen and other professional small-boat seamen. These folk know best and to follow their example is good practice.

The other major point is to make sure that deck fittings are properly fastened down. Deck fittings should be fastened through the deck and through a beam underneath with hefty through bolts, never less than four of them. Often they should be mounted on a pad as well. This is particularly important with cleats—to enable there to be more space underneath the arms for

ropes to pass, as quite often cleats have insufficient clearance under the arms. It is vital, too, with winches, where loads must be spread as widely as possible.

Fairleads often benefit from being mounted on pads so that the ropes passing through them will not chafe on anything on their way to the fairlead.

Other deck fittings which must be beyond reproach as far as size, robustness and fastening is concerned are chain plates—they must be big enough to take adequate-sized shackles, and davits, if you run to such exotica. Davits are subject to enormous leverage stresses, and this must be allowed for in their size and fastening down.

Bilge pumps must be well fastened down. The time when you really need them is the time when the boat is being thrown about and they will be

Photo 29 A well shaped and fitted pad takes one leg of a pulpit stanchion. Note the bedding being pressed out as the bolts are tightened, showing it is doing its job properly

used as secondary grabrails and stanchions, and thus subject to much greater strains than being used for their primary function. Bilge pumps, too, should be mounted so that they can easily be stripped and cleaned in acute moments of stress.

Anchors are deck fittings, and they should be provided with chocks on which they can sit and be lashed to without any risk of breaking their lashings in a heavy sea.

And so it goes on.

Navigation lights must be positioned so that they not only perform their prime function of being clearly visible but also so that they can be maintained easily. If a bulb is to be replaced it should not be necessary to take the whole fitting to pieces to do so.

Some boats sport sockets for flagpoles. As sure as fate at some time the flagpole will be called upon to act as a spare bollard or even used

as a towing eye, functions for which it was not designed, and to meet stresses for which the fastenings were not intended. Be warned, and if you have these fittings make sure that they are strong enough and well enough fastened down to perform these additional duties.

Now turning to cockpits—and here again the same rules apply. Fittings must be strong enough and secure enough—imagine the strains on a helmsman's seat, for example, when a heavy man, weight increased by bulky foul-weather clothing, is clinging tight in a seaway.

Grab rails are just as important in a cockpit as on deck, and they must also be strong enough to withstand sudden very heavy strains.

There is plenty of scope in cockpits to exercise ingenuity to make good use of space. The space under lockers is often devoted to fuel or water tanks, but can also be used to stow rope, fenders,

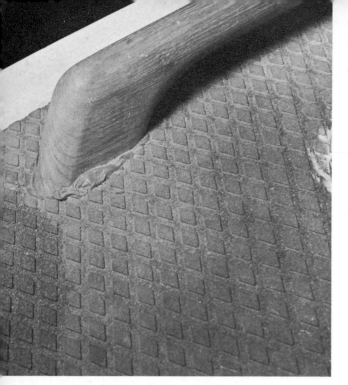

Photo 30 This grab rail has been drawn down onto its bedding by bolts from underneath

bosun's stores, lifejackets, and so on. The difficulty is to decide on whether access should be from the top, which can create problems in making the lids watertight, or from the front.

Much depends on whether there is a canopy or not and on whether there is sufficient space in front to give access from there. It is little use providing a locker if you cannot get things in and out.

Locker tops are often used to make bunks, providing that the cushions are thick enough and the area available big enough.

An important feature of virtually all cockpits is that they should be fitted with self-drainers. Here the important thing is for the holes to be large, the pipes of big diameter, and fitted so that they discharge on the opposite side to the side they fill. This means that if the boat is heeled the water will not syphon back in to the cockpit.

A comfortable cockpit is one with some pretensions to aiding the well-being of the people using it. To encourage this there should be a few shelves if at all possible, with fiddles, so that drinks can be left standing without sliding about or spilling. Gimbals are useful for this, and it has been reported that one delightful feature of the late Humphrey Bogart's yacht was the number of such gimballed holders for glasses in the cockpit!

Also very necessary for comfort and good navigation is a safe stowage place for binoculars. A locker, binocular sized and shaped, padded with foam rubber, and with drain holes at the bottom, should not be difficult to fit into most cockpits. Construction consists of a batten framework well screwed to the bulkhead and clad with plywood. Allow for the space occupied by the battens when you are designing it.

Other lockers can be provided for such items as flags, and pockets can be built for winch handles, horns, and other movable gear. For smokers a place to keep cigarettes and matches dry might be worth making.

A canopy over a cockpit is worth considering, even for a sailing yacht. The boom can be used as a ridge pole and a simple PVC roof stretched over with drawstrings running through long pockets to enable it to be lashed to the guard rail. Such a canopy provides a spare cabin when at anchor or in harbour and need not be costly or difficult to make.

A cockpit locker is often the place where a gas cylinder is stowed; this is fine as long as access is from above with an airtight interior, and a vent over the side to enable leaked gas to discharge itself outboard. The interior of such a locker can be made airtight by cladding it with fibreglass, which will adhere well to the timber sides of the locker.

Gas stowage should ideally be as near to the cooker as possible so that there are no long runs of piping to get damaged or fractured. There are different regulations on this subject in different countries, so find out what applies in your area before starting work.

When buying—or making—cushions for cockpit seating, try to provide at least 3in thick foam and waterproof seamed PVC covers, so that the cushions can be left out in the wet.

Another possibility is to get the type of cushions which float and are sold with rope lifelines along the edges. Not only are these comfortable and decorative, but can also be thrown in the water after someone who has gone over the side, not so much to act as a buoyancy aid or lifebelt but to be a marker to help you find them.

Another idea, not so daft as it sounds, is to bear in mind the possibility of your taking a pet away in the boat with you, and to think about making some provision for an animal's dirt box.

Photo 31 A simple cockpit arrangement in which the helmsman's seat folds away when not in use and the table also stows when the boat is under way

Photo 32 The same cockpit, with the beds in position

Chapter 23
Converting lifeboats

The average conversion around the 30ft mark is usually an ex-ship's lifeboat. Nowadays they are GRP, but you can get them in steel, aluminium and timber. Whatever they are they make a fine conversion and there is plenty of scope for them as motor cruisers or motor sailers.

Designing and building the superstructures calls for the same advance thought and planning as any other boating job. Before you start, ask yourself what the structure is intended to do. How will it affect the rest of the boat?

Perhaps you have in mind some form of shelter for the helmsman on an open dayboat powered by an engine, for which the obvious thing would be to erect a kind of sentry box at the back end somewhere and leave it at that. But is this necessarily the best place?

All deck structures offer additional windage, and a large wheel house in the stern will act as a mizzen sail, which may have advantages, but may pose problems too. It will certainly alter the way the boat lies to anchor, with wind across the tide, for example. A better place may be amidships, or even right forward; as mentioned earlier, there is nothing sacred about the stern for a wheelhouse.

Locating the wheelhouse amidships effectively cuts the boat in two, which leads to thoughts of a large stern cockpit and a cuddy forward, with access from the wheelhouse. The wheelhouse might then be wider than you originally envisaged, and the cuddy may have enough room for bare necessities like two bunks, a toilet and a cooker. But without too much bother you are now converting an open day boat into a weekend cruiser!

The best way to tackle this will depend very much on the size and construction of the basic hull, but one possibility is to bolt new frames on the original ones and raise the sides of the hull. The whole of the foredeck can then be laid over new beams, and the wheelhouse structure can be blended into the raised hull.

Alternatively, if this type of boat is to be used for fishing, it may be better to erect the wheelhouse right forward so that the whole of the after end is free for working the nets, with some shelter from the wheelhouse. This layout may also be suitable for boats which cater for angling parties.

A major modification like this will mean altering the steering gear. A wheel in the deck structure will have to replace the tiller, not a difficult job using cables. It might be better to leave the tiller in place, as an alternative steering position for emergencies if the main steering breaks down.

Engine controls may also have to be moved. With an engine positioned well forward, often the case in boats like this, linkages for throttle gear will probably be simpler than when they are led off to the tiller area.

It is a common practice to locate the wheelhouse over the engine, which is fine for protecting it from spray, but make sure that in the process you don't lose accessibility to it, especially ease of making minor checks or adjustments when under way.

It is absolutely vital that the wheelhouse is securely fastened to the hull. A trip on a boat which had a wheelhouse secured to the deck by angle brackets whose fastenings had worked loose was terrifying, as every roll of the boat was accompanied by a separate and independent lurch of the wheelhouse, feeling as if the whole structure would go over the side at any minute.

Apart from the excess windage created by too large a superstructure, there is the danger of fitting too many windows, too large, or made from too light a weight of glass. Perspex is probably better, although it is prone to scratching, but at least it won't break if someone bangs it with an elbow, nor will it shatter if struck by an invading wave top. But it has been known for big seas to push them in, clean out of the rubber strip surround.

When a wheelhouse also provides access to the accommodation, there is a danger of leaving

Photo 33 This type of superstructure is dangerous on a boat which will go to sea

Photo 34 Careful planning has produced a layout in which the starboard door is well forward and the port door is well aft

a large open hole, down which the unwary can plunge at the risk of breaking a limb. Make the opening for the companion in a place where it cannot be stepped on blindly, and provide some type of banister or grab rail round it.

The exact place where the helmsman stands and the location of the companion opening will influence the position of the doorway into the wheelhouse from on deck, and the side from which the doors are hung. Sliding door have some advantage over conventional hinges.

It is becoming fashionable on some fishing boats for the forward face of the wheelhouse to rake forwards, the idea being that rain and sea spray do not catch on the windows so easily. It also enables the helmsman to peer out better when the windows are open.

As far as sailing boats are concerned, a forward-raking wheelhouse can look different and more businesslike. Most of these points apply equally to sailing boats, but an additional factor to remember when scheming things out is that the new structure must not be so high that the boom will not clear it!

If this should happen, you may have to re-rig

the boat, which may involve cutting canvas from the foot of the sail, unless you re-step the mast on a pedestal to raise it enough for the boom to be able to move freely.

An open day-sailing boat can be converted into a weekender with a simple cuddy forward, from which a doghouse leads naturally. Not only will this provide shelter for the man at the helm, it will also make a place to set up a table.

The alternative to raising the sides of the hull and flushdecking right across is to build a central coach roof with side decks. This usually looks better on a sailing boat, although it does involve more work. Flush decks can look good, but it does require thought to get the lines just right.

It would be nice to be able to get full standing headroom below, although you may have to settle for sitting headroom on smaller craft. Make a side elevation drawing, with the cabin sole drawn in, so that you can measure off just how how much headroom you are providing down below. Don't forget the thickness of the deck supporting beams as well as the decking itself.

The critical part of any superstructure is where it meets the original hull. On a sailing boat this is the very point where it may be partially submerged for periods when the boat is tacking. It is therefore essential that the join is absolutely watertight and the whole affair so rigid that it

113

cannot move under the considerable wringing strains imposed when sailing.

Making a coach roof on a sailing boat will affect the stepping of the mast. In the kind of boat we are discussing this will most likely be stepped on the keel. You will have to decide whether to leave it there, with a hole in the coach roof through which it passes—always a likely source of leaks—or whether to step it in a tabernacle on deck. The tabernacle will have to be reinforced from below, probably with a bulkhead.

The tabernacle idea is better in some respects, and the mast can be stepped more easily without enlisting the help of a crane.

Sailing boat coach roofs are usually lower than on a power boat; port holes or small windows will provide the only source of light and air. Some thought should be given to the provision of ventilators, therefore, at the scheming stage, before some structural member makes their positioning impossible.

There is no reason why an attractive open boat should be less attractive just because a lid has been set up on it. The thing to avoid is square boxy Noah's-ark-like cubes, by drawing it all out first on a piece of paper, to scale.

Lots of curves in all planes are essential. Remember, too, that the eye tends to follow a line, so that some of the 'height' of a super-structure can be lost by using tongued and grooved planking for the side cladding.

If the the original hull has a nice sheer line, this can be picked out along the rubbing band with a

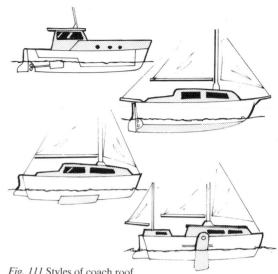

Fig. 111 Styles of coach roof

colour contrasting to the basic hull colour. A reverse sheer on the top of the coach roof, blending easily into a raked doghouse or wheel-house, can then make a boat look very pretty.

The construction of a deck saloon, on a larger yacht, can provide a safe sheltered steering position, with bags of room for crew members, regardless of the weather. Seats can convert into bunks, and a folding table can give it a further function as a dining area.

Too much top hamper, however (which is the danger with this kind of structure on too small a boat), can create tremendous windage, and the weight, including that of the people, can alter the whole stability of the boat. Deck saloons should be well thought out before being tackled.

Photo 35 This narrow boat hull has been given two steering positions—one aft where the tiller is fitted for fine

weather, and the sheltered centre cock-pit for rainy days

Chapter 24
Raising a deck

We have discussed some of the basic problems which have to be solved when designing a superstructure. Now we look at the essential work of building it, and in order to bring out the vital points we are going to describe work on a lifeboat hull conversion as an example.

The amateur builder will probably find it easier to work in wood rather than aluminium, steel, GRP, C-Flex foam sandwich, or any other material, and in this context wood includes marine ply. Wood is easily obtainable, it is easy to work, easy to fasten, easy to replace if some mistake in cutting or shaping should mean scrapping a length, and a well-made and properly varnished wooden superstructure can look more handsome than one in other materials.

It is nearly always better to stick to one material for the basic form of a boat, because a wooden deck on a ferro hull, for example, poses problems when it comes to making the junction rigid, strong, secure and watertight. Hence the amateur should avoid building a GRP wheelhouse on a wooden hull, or an aluminium one on a GRP hull.

We are taking an open wooden boat and raising the whole of the foredeck, making an opening hatch on the forward end, with a low coach roof amidships. We will turn the after end into an open cockpit, with fairly narrow side decks, and an open-backed wheelhouse, which will provide the forward fixing for a canopy to cover the cockpit.

There may be a small tabernacle for a mast to carry a steadying sail.

The work falls into fairly clearly defined stages. First, make a large scale working drawing and study it to see that nothing ridiculous occurs (like bulkheads being located in places where there is no access through them), and also that the structure is going to be aesthetically pleasing.

Using the basic drawing, work out a schedule of quantities of materials required. Include everything—framing, battening, cladding, knees, carlings, deck beams, windows or portholes and doors; paint, varnish, fastenings, adhesives, deck-fittings, bulkheads, shelving, spars and navigation lights; interior fitments like bunks, cookers, toilets and sinks; canopy, shrouds and bottle screws; and make an enormous shopping list, putting like with like.

Decide on what timber you are going to use for the different applications, and take each type of timber in turn to work out a cutting schedule, so that you buy only enough timber and in lengths which will enable you to cut it without wasteful off-cuts. Nothing is more infuriating than finishing a job with 19 off-cuts, each 18in long. Put them all together, and you have a length of 28ft 6in. You could have saved all that if you had specified the exact lengths of timber required when ordering.

This is particularly true when working out the best way to use sheets of plywood. Plywood sheets are normally 8ft × 4ft, but some firms stock sheets 8ft × 2ft, or 4ft × 4ft. Fastenings are also very much cheaper bought in bulk, and it is quite incredible just how many will be required for a major undertaking.

Your shopping list divides itself naturally into two sections: materials required for the basic structure and materials required to fit it out.

Catalogues are also an ideal form of check list, to make sure that you don't overlook some major and expensive item like the anchor winch!

Having worked out the likely cost, you can then make an estimate of the time the job will take to complete. It is as easy to under-estimate the time factor as it is to under-estimate the cost.

The average chap is unlikely to be able to devote more than three hours, three evenings a week, and ten hours on Saturday and ten hours on Sunday, three Sundays out of four. Family commitments, crises at work, annual holidays and many other pressures make it impossible to divert every spare minute to the project.

To do this is also to stifle one's enthusiasm by over-exposure, which will make it seem like all work and no end result, if you go at it too hard.

There will be whole months when a lot of hard work will produce little in the way of tangible results, and it is easy to become discouraged by an apparent lack of progress, especially if you are stretching yourself.

It is much better to pace yourself over a period. Excellent, too, if you are able to get some use out of the boat while the work is in progress. This way, the boat will seem to be a boat which provides pleasure, and not just a shell into which sweat and cash is poured.

The first thing to do is to build some kind of a shelter over the open hull, so that you can work in the dry and warm whatever the weather. As soon as this is completed, run an electric cable to it so that you have light and power.

Some of the battening for the interior can be used to build the basic framework, later to be salvaged for its proper function. An old lorry tarpaulin, which may well have to be patched to make it serviceable, or a heavy gauge polythene sheet, makes a good cover.

Photo 36 A lorry tarpaulin supported by softwood planks which were later used for joinery provide a snug area in which to work during the winter

And now to work. The first thing to tackle is the new frames, which will support the beam shelf and the hull planking, as well as the deck beams, chain plates and rubbing band.

These frames are best made from hardwood, and should be through-bolted to the original frames or timbers, having been notched to fit round the original bulwark capping and stringers. Cut them all a little overlong, so that they can be sawn off to fit the new deck line when they are all in place (see fig. 112).

If the new posts are over 2ft high, then one or two stringers should be put in. These can be about 1½in × 1in hardwood. Let the posts run up higher than needed so that a fairing-in batten for the sheer can be tacked on (see fig. 113). The hardest part to fit on will be the new stem. This will have to continue the shape or rake of the old stem, but this may be scarphed and bolted on (see fig. 114).

When your new sheer line has been drawn in, space down the stem your number of planks. A word of warning here: the narrower the planks (eight as opposed to five), the easier they will be to spile and fit. But don't make them too

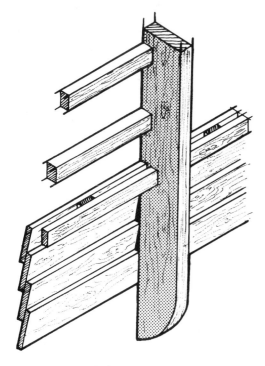

Fig. 112 Setting up the frames

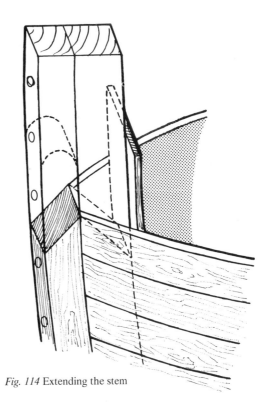

Fig. 114 Extending the stem

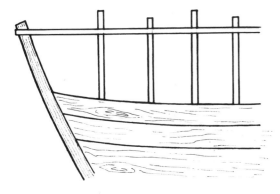

Fig. 113 New sheer line

narrow—remember all those caulking seams!

Now, when you have marked off the stem for the planks, move aft about three frames and, with a pair of dividers, space off the same number of planks. Then again move aft about three or four frames and space off the number of planks on the frame. You will notice that the planks will be getting wider as they go to midships.

When the sheer is scribed in you can run through the new shelf or gunwale. This should be

Fig. 115 New beam shelf and planking

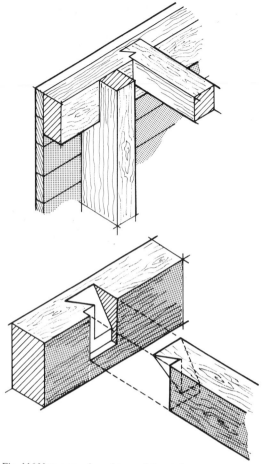

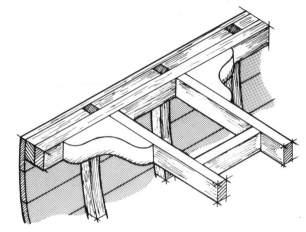

Fig. 117 Lodging knees and gunwale packing

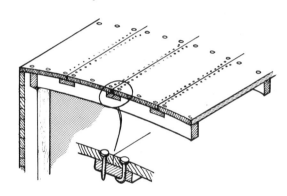

Fig. 116 New gunwale and type of dovetail

Fig. 118 Deck seam battens and fixing

kept the thickness of the beams below the sheer if you are not going to dovetail them in.

If the boat is going to have a sail, then lodging knees should be fitted on each beam next to the mast. These should be bolted and should be the same thickness as the beams (fig. 117).

If the deck is going to be ply then you will need seam battens let into the deck beams. These should lie 4ft from the centre line of the deck. The thickness of the batten can be the same thickness as the deck: e.g. ⅝in batten, ⅝in deck (fig. 118).

The deck can be glued to the beams and seam battens, and bedding compound used along the gunwales and sheer plank. When fastening, nail and clench along the seam battens. Screw into the beams and gunwale.

If you are going to build in any hatches, companion-ways, or superstructures which will

pierce your decking, allow for them by building in carlings. These will give you the outline of the hatches etc., and you can cut away the central part of the beams when you are ready to consolidate the hatchway.

In fact, unless you are prepared to make a really super job of it, it would be better to keep the number of breaks in your deckwork down to a minimum, because they all tend to lengthen your working time.

So work out your deck beams to suit the bulkheads, companion-ways, skylights, hatch-ways and so on, which should also be checked on your plan drawing.

The next step from that is to fit and fix the gunwales. This can be very difficult, as nearly every gunwale has to be either steamed or laminated. For the amateur, I would recommend laminating, as it can be glued and left on the job.

118

When you come to do your laminating, you must decide on the size of gunwale and the thickness of your laminating strips. I would say an average size of gunwale could be 3in by 2in for a 30ft boat and the laminations can be ¼in thick. Thus, there would be eight laminations to each gunwale. The laminations should be glued and nailed together around the inside of the boat along the sheer line.

When you start the laminating, the first two or even three laminations can be screwed from the outboard side of the hull. This pulls the laminations to the shape of the hull. The rest of the laminations can then be nailed and glued from the inside.

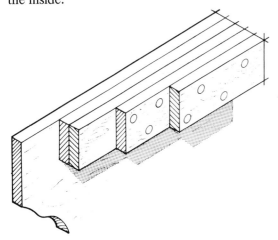

Fig. 119 Laminated gunwale

When the gunwales are glued and dry, they are ready for fairing in. This is done by using what we can call a beam crop, which can either be a template of your beam, or an actual beam.

You place the beam or template across the sheer, resting on the gunwale and measure the gap on the inside of the gunwale, which is then measured down the outside of the gunwale below the sheer.

Do this approximately every two feet, and when you have done this, you should link up all the marks with a nice long fairing-in batten, scribing along the hull. This is then planed down to the marks. In theory this gives you part of the radius of the beam crop.

Next comes the spacing of the beams, which is governed by the main bulkheads, as the bulkheads should be fixed to a beam. So in between your bulkheads, you space out your beams

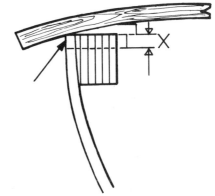

Fig. 120 Sheering down gunwale

evenly. When you are satisfied with all your beam spacings, you should dovetail them into the gunwale, making sure that the beams are let in flush with your fair gunwale.

When all the deck beams are dovetailed and glued, put a strong-back down the centreline of the deck, to support the deck beams. This can be of any rough sawn timber, but must be straight and strong, i.e. about 6in × 3in.

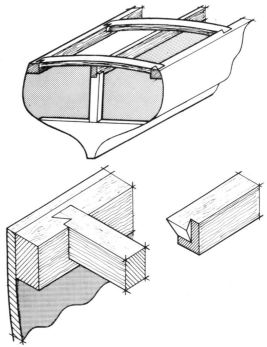

Fig. 121 Beam strong-back and joints

The principle of the strongback is to keep all the beams at the correct height and camber, on the centreline.

119

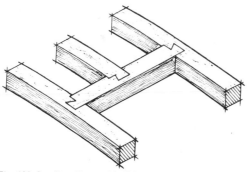

Fig. 122 Small carling and half beam

If there are any skylights or hatches to be fitted, then their carlings should be the next thing to do. These are again dovetailed and glued into the beams and, where they cut a beam in half, the beam (which is now called a half-beam) is itself dovetailed into the carling. The same applies to the skylights and even the companion-ways.

The ends of the beams are glued and jointed so they do not require sealing.

If the deck is to be plywood, which is generally the case nowadays, seam battens have to be let into the deck beams at 4ft centres, working from the centreline of the boat outboard (fig. 123). Seam battens can be the same thickness of plywood as the deck itself, and their function is to join the butts of the plywood together.

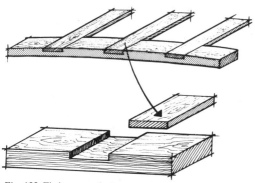

Fig. 123 Fitting seam battens

When the seam battens are fixed, you fair in the whole deck with your jackplane making sure that there are no high or low beams and that all carlings and seam battens are flush with the deck beams.

Now you can put your lid on. It is advisable to start from your main bulkhead, working forward and along the centreline. In other words, lay all

your full sheets of plywood down, before you start cutting shaped pieces. This is done by tacking down a sheet of ply in position and working away from it with your other sheets, fitting them as you go.

When you have laid all the plywood, number the pieces in an order that you will remember and then take all the sheets up again ready for glueing and nailing. I need hardly add that you then glue and nail!

The treatment for the laid deck depends rather on individual preferences, but what you are trying to achieve is to make sure that the deck, particularly where the hatches, skylights and companion-ways grow out of it, is absolutely watertight.

This means that all wood members must be sealed or glued before screwing. The deck itself must be so solid that it cannot flex. It is astonishing just how much an apparently rigid ply structure can flex (and do so imperceptibly, but sufficiently to permit the passage of water) when a heavy object is dropped on to it.

One method of waterproofing a deck is to cover it with light canvas, laid on to a thick coating of sticky paint and stretched as it is tacked. Several more coats of paint will make the canvas watertight and largely rot-proof for a long time.

This top coat may be mixed with silver sand from your local chandler, or it may be top-coated with a non-slip deck paint.

Quarter round beading will anchor the edges of the canvas around hatches and alongside the cabin sides, while a toe rail holds it down the gunwale. This beading also hides the tacks.

Another possibility is to cover the plywood with one of the standard deck coverings. Tread-master is probably the most durable, but some of the others can be damaged, and once so, water may get underneath to start the rot process unless remedied quickly.

Further alternative deck coverings are some deck coatings in brushable form, with cork or other particles, which lay on thickly to protect the underlying deck and still provide a gripping surface.

A better idea still is to lay a wood plank deck on top of the plywood, but it is expensive and very time consuming. The plank seams should be caulked with cotton and pitch, or a flexible sealing material.

Chapter 25
Planning a deck layout

Once again, a plan of the boat to scale, drawn heavily on a piece of graph paper, with a flimsy overlay on which to sketch possible alternatives, is the starting point for deciding on the best deck layout and the most suitable position for fittings.

What you decide to do will depend very much on the location of the main companion-way, on the position of the deck beams, and on whether or not you go for a flush deck, or the more normal coach roof and side deck configuration.

A flush deck may well be better and should be easier for the amateur to build. The location of the masts on a sailing boat will also be a factor.

The size of the main companion and hatch should not be too limited. Large doorways are dangerous, but small ones can restrict movement when you are fully clad in several layers of sweaters and oilskins. About 18 to 20in width is about right.

Too low a doorway or too restricted an entrance is also dangerous because you will be liable to bang your head when using it in bad weather.

It is also a temptation to design your entrance around your personal vital statistics, which may be unwise if you are 6ft 2in, like me, or smaller than average. The result will be either an entrance which is so sloppy that a smaller than average person can be thrown about dangerously, or so tight that anyone of average or larger size will be unable to pass through easily, which might well be dangerous in an emergency. It might also create problems in future years, when you try to sell the boat.

If you are converting a sailing boat, the first thing to do is to make some firm decisions about rig and the position of the cockpit, because these are inter-related.

A centre cockpit is attractive, as it enables you to provide sleeping space in the after end, with a degree of privacy, and this can be achieved in even a small boat by providing quarter berths, which run forward from the foot of a short vertical ladder leading to the cabin.

But bear in mind how this centre cockpit will affect the working of the boat. In many boats, spray seems to come on board just at the point where the centre cockpit is located, which means that there will be discomfort on most points of sailing.

You have to think about access to sheets, halyards, warps, kicking straps, vangs and everything else. You have to think about the lead of the sheets, especially the main sheet on a sloop. This is going to be difficult to control unless you lead it forward through snatch blocks, or fix it to the boom some little distance from the outboard end. The distance is likely to be so great that the sail will not set properly and there will be a considerable loss of efficiency.

One way to overcome this partly is to opt for a ketch rig. This way, the main sheet will probably lead naturally to a point at the after end of the cockpit, which is fine, and the mizzen sheet can be left to itself almost, unless it is a big sail.

With this arrangement, the helmsman can look after the main sheet as well as the helm, and either the crew look after the mizzen sheet, once the headsail sheets are secure, or the helmsman can look after the mizzen too.

On a Thames barge, which is yawl rigged, the mizzen sheet is usually made fast to a cleat on the top of the rudder post, and is seldom touched. Because it is led to the cleat via a block on the top of the rudder blade, the angle it makes alters as the rudder is moved. This might provide food for thought for many aspiring conversionists!

Another problem of the centre cockpit is that, if a large headsail is set, not only may the headsail sheets want to be led to a position too far aft to be workable, but the position of the sheet winches is likely to coincide with the position of back stays. It is very difficult to have a standing backstay with a ketch rig, and not only are running backstays something of a nuisance in this case, they are also downright dangerous, especially if you have an accidental gybe, when you may well knock the mast out of her.

The cost of rigging a two masted boat will be greater than for a sloop, because you have to double up on virtually everything. And just to kill the myth of the centre cockpit ketch, where are you going to stow the dinghy if you do not want to tow it? On most sloops you can lash it, capsized, on the coach roof between the cockpit and the mast, but on a centre cockpit yacht there is unlikely to be enough room.

Sailing conversions are better, safer, cheaper and easier if sloop rigged with a standing single back stay!

Having made this decision you can decide where to locate the mast, horse or track for main sheet—and do not despise ring-bolts with a block on them to provide a one point fixing—sheet winches, chain plates, kicking strap, vangs, and the whole of the sailing gear.

If you want to be able to get at the halyards without having to go walkabout on the foredeck, you might be able to design the main hatch so that it lifts up to enable you to get to the foot of the mast from down below, or by making a hatch just forward of the mast for the same purpose, although this could be a hazard in some circumstances.

Reverting to the best place to fix the main sheet on its boom, many modern yachts have the sheet attached to a claw ring some little distance inboard, while on loose-footed boomsails it is common to make the attachment point for the

sheet some distance inboard of the clew. Either way, the sheet also acts as a kicking strap, to an extent.

On a power-only craft there are none of the problems associated with sailing gear. Here the question usually is how big to make the wheel-house? Excess top hamper is the enemy of the small motor cruiser, and this is a point to be borne in mind. It might be better to design a relatively small wheelhouse with an open back, and rig some sort of tent or canopy to enable the open area to be used for living space overnight. This is common practice on small sailing day-boats, where the boom doubles as the ridge-pole for a tent, which is only rigged when the boat is not moving.

Also common to both power and sail is the necessity to fit cleats, bollards or samson posts. Although individual preference and depth of pockets to dictate what you have, remember that it is better to go for something perhaps a little larger than might be thought necessary at first glance, and that samson posts with a cross member or double cross bollards are probably best from the purely functional point of view. It is often possible to pick up such fittings, galvanised, from old working craft, and these are always a good buy.

A bollard or cleat amidships, on each side, is very useful for docking, locking in and out, and for semi-permanent moorings, where springs

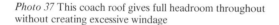

Photo 37 This coach roof gives full headroom throughout without creating excessive windage

and breast ropes can be taken from them. Fairleads are essential to make sure that warps lead true to the bollards.

Apart from sheet winches, most yachts today have a capstan or winch to help get in the anchor. These winches must have gypsies matched to the anchor chain, and if you are converting a large boat do not overlook the possibility of a hydraulic winch operated by a pump running from the main engine.

Fishing boats and commercial craft almost invariably use hydraulics for such gear, and as a result the hydraulic gear available is very efficient and reliable. It is probably a better bet than equivalent electrical equipment.

A fairlead is essential on the stemhead, to carry the chain over the bow, and on larger yachts a small single davit is valuable as an aid in bringing the anchor on board. Hoisting umpteen fathoms of chain, plus a 75lb anchor, can be no joke.

Masts on sailing boats are probably best stepped on deck in tabernacles. This way, if the mast is stout enough and stayed adequately, you have a mast which is man enough for its job, but which can be stepped and lowered by your own efforts from on board, using sheer legs, and removing the dependance on a crane, which is part of having masts stepped through the deck. It avoids leaks, too.

The size, position and shape of pulpit, taffrail and guard rail stanchions is also a matter for consideration. Many small boats, especially mass-produced cabin cruisers, have guard rails which may be only 18in high, and are lethal because they do not stop you going over the side; they tend to trip you up and make sure you go! Anything less than 27in is unwise.

Guard rails and pulpits must be securely fastened down, of course, like everything else we have discussed. It is no use just screwing them to the deck, or even into a pad below the deck. They should be bolted through the deck and, if possible, through a beam as well. So should sheet winches, anchor winches, tabernacles, grab rails and bollards and cleats. Chain plates should be bolted through the beam shelf as well as the side planking.

It is this need to fasten down all fittings really well that led to my comment earlier that the layout will depend on the position of the deck beams.

Whatever deck material you opt for, it must be fixed down well and to good solid hard-wood beams. Although the centres at which these beams are located depends to an extent on their dimensions and the thickness of the deck itself, they should also be positioned so that they can act as a fixing point for all these fittings, as well as for bulkheads and coamings.

To some extent, the distance apart of the frames dictates the location of the deck beams too, so that the whole structure must be considered as a unity.

Even the provision of a toe rail can be useful to help tie frames, deck beams, knees and beam shelf together, in addition to its main function of preventing things dropped on deck from rolling over the side.

What kind of non-slip deck surface you decide on will in turn depend, to an extent, on what material you make your deck from and on how you waterproof it. As good as anything is a sandwich of timber laid on deck beams reinforced with steel knees, with a plywood layer on top and Walker's Treadmaster glued on top of that.

Back to fixing down fittings. Don't forget that windscreens often receive very sudden shock loads, so they must be fastened very strongly too. Even ventilators are liable to a kick, especially if someone slips, so they require secure fastening.

All the fittings which are fastened through the deck must have a good layer of sealer on their bases and round the bolts before the nuts are hardened up.

Other matters to be thought about and located on your plan before you start work are the provision of cockpit drains, equally essential in power craft as in sailing yachts, and the positioning of filler caps for fuel and water. You don't want to find that the only possible place for a water filler cap is the exact spot where the sheet winches have already been fixed.

And navigation lights: where should they be located so that they conform to the new Collision Rules and yet fail to become obstructions? With some thought at the planning stage, this can be achieved.

Thinking it out first is the name of the game.

Chapter 26
Engine choice

A sure way to acquire a few grey hairs is to put a new engine into a boat. There is so much to think about before you even look at the gearbox, transmission, propeller and so on. Selecting an engine is really a matter of narrowing down an enormous field by elimination, in the light of your own specific requirements.

The first question is what kind of fuel? In most cases the answer must surely be diesel oil.

At one time petrol engines were favoured in yachts, because they are light and compact compared to a diesel engine of the same power. They cost less, and run with less vibration and smell.

In order to reduce fuel bills, a number of petrol/paraffin units have been designed. The engine is started on petrol and the paraffin fuel line is pre-heated in a special manifold by the exhaust gases. After the engine has run for some time and has reached its relatively high operating temperature, it can be switched over to run on paraffin, cheaply and efficiently.

Many such engines run well on tractor vapourising oil (TVO), and this is a good system in boats which are worked hard for long hours, like fishing craft harbour launches and other work boats.

Today, however, TVO is hard to come by, especially on the continent, paraffin is not as readily available in marinas and harbours as it was, and few petrol/paraffin engines remain in production, although many of the older engines soldier on, like the Kelvins you find in fishing boats. They were built to last.

If weight is important, as in racing power boats or sailing yachts which are entered for races, petrol engines are better, because they are generally lighter for the power produced.

There is also the matter of safety. The danger of fire or explosion in a boat with a petrol engine is much greater than in a diesel boat, although a properly installed and maintained engine should present no hazard. The operative word here is 'should'.

The second matter for consideration is power required. Most modern yachts are over-powered and many of them laughably so.

The economical speed of a small displacement boat can be calculated by using the formula: speed in knots equals the square root of the waterline length in feet multiplied by 1.4. The exact value of the multiplying factor varies with the shape of the hull, but is unlikely to exceed 1.5 for the sleekest of racers. Even 1.4 is a high factor for most small craft.

The effect of this rule is that once a boat has reached its maximum economical speed, it will only go faster as a result of an enormous increase in power, with a corresponding lavish rise in the amount of fuel consumed.

It is a different story when planing hulls are concerned, of course.

Take a cabin cruiser with a water line length of, say, 25ft. Her maximum economical speed will be five (the square root of 25), multiplied by 1.4. That is seven knots, which should be quite fast enough for most pleasure yachting.

So why try to pack more horse power into the boat than is needed to push her along at that speed? All you achieve is to spend money on an engine which is seldom used at its full power, is needlessly thirsty, is bigger than it need be, and which may never even run at its most economical rpm.

There are no simple hard and fast rules for calculating power required, but the table gives a guide and here we deal only with displacement hulls and inboard engines.

The only benefit, to my mind, of an outboard engine is that you can take it home for maintenance. Otherwise an inboard beats the outboard hands down on performance and efficiency, not to mention noise, lack of pollution and life expectancy, assuming that weight is not a factor.

After fuel and approximate horse power required, you should think about the engine in the boat. Its location will dictate its size, configuration and weight.

Type of craft	BHP	RPM	Fuel	Weight LB.	Speed Knots	Comment
18ft sailing boat	4-6	1,500	petrol	200	5	Folding or feathering propeller
25ft sailing boat	10-12	1,500	petrol	200	" " "	
30ft motor sailer	25-40	2,500	petrol	400	8-9	
34ft sailing cruiser	25	2,500	diesel	450	6	
35ft motor cruiser	35-40	2,000	diesel	650-800	9	
35ft fast fishing boat	110	1,000	diesel	2,600	15	Single screw
	140	2,000	diesel	2,200	22	Twin screw
	250	2,000	diesel	2,750	25	Single screw

At this point the range of possibilities begins to narrow. When you start to think about the problems of fitting the engine into the space available, and the ways in which it can be lowered into position on its beds through the openings in the deck, the range narrows further. There are fewer problems if the engine can go straight into the hull before the deck and bulkheads are in position—but one day it may have to come out again!

Remember, too, that it is one thing to pack an engine into a hull, but you must also have working space around it for maintenance and repairs. Sometimes these activities have to be carried on while you are at sea. Many of us have the scars from exhaust pipe burns to stress the point.

Weight is important, because too much weight in the wrong place creates its own additional problems. Fuel tanks, for example, may have to be located in awkward places to compensate for the concentrated weight of the engine.

The ideal scheme is to have a light engine well aft, with good access all round. This reduces the shaft length, itself a benefit, and stops the engine room intruding into the accommodation.

If you are working on a conversion, like lifeboat hulls for example, you will have to plan the whole layout of the boat around the location of the engine.

It helps if you make a hardboard template of the engine and offer it up to see how it fits. To make one you need the manufacturer's literature. Most firms include scale drawings as well as other vital information, like power curves and details of weights and sizes, in their leaflets.

If your thoughts are turning to a second-hand unit or a home-marinisation project, this kind of information is vital.

By now you will probably have narrowed the possibilities down considerably. At this stage it helps to make a comparative table.

It is surprising how much the units of much the same power output from different manufacturers will differ in size, weight and configuration. If they have a fishing boat pedigree, they will almost certainly be larger, heavier, slower running and more expensive, but probably cheaper in the long run if they are to be hard worked. They will probably stand up better to abuse than marinised vehicle engines.

Make up a table of your requirements. One column should be devoted to method of starting, and, if at all possible, you should specify an engine which can be started by hand as well as electrically, in case the battery or wiring lets you down.

You should also have a column for the type of cooling, because you will have to decide whether you want it to be by air, raw water or by heat exchanger, each with its advantages and disadvantages.

The method of cooling and the best means of fitting the exhaust system must be borne in mind when you consider the physical installation in the boat. The exhaust should not have to be run in such a manner as to bring hot pipes into close proximity to inflammable parts of the boat. There must be access to the seacock and filter, or the skin fitting which brings water into the boat if you have a water-cooled unit, and there must be room for the swan's neck in the exhaust between the silencer and the outlet. This is to prevent sea water syphoning back into the engine when the boat is heeled.

This may lead you to serious thoughts of an air-cooled installation. There is less plumbing for a start, and no danger of choked water inlets. Adequate ducting is required, however, and fans, as well as protection to prevent water getting into the ducts, which can present problems of its own. The ducting tends to conduct noise, too, making for a rowdy and heavily vibrating installation, unless you take steps to stop it.

What else must be borne in mind?

The engine must be securely bolted down to the fabric of the hull and its weight well distributed to the frames. These may require doubling if the hull was not designed to take an engine. You will require access to the mountings to enable the engine to be aligned and later re-aligned, you may have to replace flexible feet, and if you are opting for a straightforward conventional drive, with a shaft running in a tube, there has to be room for the couplings and the bearings. This must be worked out before the engine is installed.

The manufacturer's literature will tell you the maximum angle from the horizontal which is permissible. Although most engines are positioned out of the horizontal, there is a limit to the angle.

Give some thought now to fuel. The more powerful the engine, the more thirsty it will be, so it is important to make some calculations based on the manufacturer's performance figures to estimate just how large your tanks must be to give you an adequate cruising range with a good safety reserve. Calculate the weight of tanks, plus fuel, and then decide where they should be placed, again remembering that tanks require access, have to be provided with fillers and vents, and that the weight will affect stability and seaworthiness. You may decide, at this point, to select a small engine!

Batteries have to be provided, producing the same problems of access and weight, as well as raising the question of the voltage of the whole boat. You normally have the choice of 24, 12 or 6 volt systems of which 24 volt is probably the best.

If you have decided on an engine with a hand-start capability—essential in my view—make sure that the installation will permit you to turn the handle and put some beef behind it! Some engines can be adapted to accept the handle at either end, which might be a point in their favour.

Nowadays, virtually all new boats are built with their engines installed down the centre line, with the propeller in front of the rudder. At one time quarter engines were quite popular, and in conversions of boats which were not designed originally for engines, like pulling lifeboats or Montague whalers, there may not be enough meat in the stern post or enough strength in the hog to accept a tube poked through it. Hence, it may be better to go back to a quarter installation with the shaft off centre and the tube passing through the hull beside the stern post, with considerable local strengthening.

There will also be boats in which it would be better to think in terms of two less powerful engines with props each side of the stern post and probably two rudders, and discard the idea of one central unit.

One possibility we haven't touched on yet is the outboard engine mounted permanently through the hull. To my mind this is achieving the worst of all worlds: an inefficient unit which cannot be removed easily and which is difficult to get at for maintenance.

There may be times where it has its advantages, however.

One way in which a great deal of money can be saved is to buy a second-hand diesel engine from a scrapped vehicle and then to marinise it yourself. To do this you need expert advice. I heard recently of a 1.5 litre BMC diesel engine, one favoured by many for home-marinisation, which was bought for £40 from a van breaker. The van rusted away, but the engine, with all the robustness inherent in a diesel engine, had many hours of life in it, and then would justify an overhaul.

After all, how many hours does the engine in a yacht run, compared with the number of hours in a lorry?

Chapter 27
The right drive

In a majority of small boats the transmission system is still a conventional arrangement in which the engine transmits its power through a mechanical gearbox with an ahead or astern rotation to the propeller which is fastened to the end of a shaft.

The engine itself must be fastened down absolutely securely on heavy bearers fixed immovably to the boat's frames.

There is no future in the sort of installation I heard of recently in which the engine was bolted to lengths of old railway line which just lay on the frames. My informant was a member of the life boat crew which effected the rescue!

Flexible mounts are becoming popular, but they allow the engine to bounce around, so all fuel and water connections as well as electrical leads will bounce around too, resulting in fractures, if precautions are not taken.

The crankshaft drives the propeller shaft via the gearbox, which is usually a mechanical unit operated by a lever or sometimes a small wheel, although hydraulically operated gearboxes are becoming more common.

The type of box and the reduction ratio have to be considered as part of a specification including engine power and speed range, size and length of shaft and its bearings, as well as the pitch and diameter of the prop, and additional factors such as shape of hull and function of the boat.

Thus a 20hp auxiliary in a sailing boat will require a completely different specification to what is required for the same engine in a narrow boat used exclusively in the canals.

Expert advice from engine manufacturer, propeller manufacturer or an experienced and knowledgable engineer is advisable, and give your informant as many facts to work on as possible.

There are many boats afloat which are being used for quite different purposes than those for which they were designed, and they would perform with greater efficiency if their transmissions were modified to suit their new role. Many boats have had quite unsuitable systems right from their launch!

The usual shaft arrangement works like this: A flange is bolted to the flange on the outboard end of the gearbox and the shaft is keyed to this with the propeller on the other end. Usually this is driven up a taper and secured with a key, a locking nut, and a safety split pin.

Often there is an intermediary shaft, and universal joints are sometimes used to connect two shafts instead of couplings.

Universal joints compensate for a certain degree of misalignment but without them the engine and the shafts must be lined up immaculately, otherwise expensive problems like hot and worn bearings, worn bushes, excessive vibration and damaged engine components result.

Engines are aligned by packing shims under the feet with the aid of a jack, until the coupling faces are in perfect alignment. Feeler gauges can be used for this or a pencil held on one face while the other face is rotated. The engine is shimmed up until the pencil indicates that the two faces marry exactly.

The shaft passes through the hull via a tube with some form of bearing at each end. There are different systems, a common one being the Cutless type, which has a rope-packed gland at the inboard end, often having a grease nipple screwed into it. Water fills the tube and lubricates the shaft as it whizzes round.

Engine installations must be done properly: a badly done job will cause trouble, usually miles from anywhere, in bad weather, with everyone on board sea-sick and lacking tools and parts! This is one area where professional help can be justified when making an installation.

An alternative to straight-through drive, especially where lack of space makes it difficult, is hydraulic drive. Here the engine can be mounted anywhere, almost—in the chain locker, sideways under the saloon sole, or even on deck.

The engine drives a pump connected by high pressure lines to a motor on the propeller shaft, eliminating, as a further benefit, the alignment problem. In addition you can go straight from full ahead to full astern, which could be disaster on a conventionally transmitted engine of some power unless revs are cut right back. A rope round the propeller will cause no damage because relief valves in the pipe lines operate so that the engine power does not go to the shaft.

Hydraulic drive creates less vibration, especially vibration due to mis-alignment, and the same system which drives the propeller can drive the anchor winch and the battery dynamo or alternator. Manufacturers claim an efficiency of 80% to 85%, and certainly there are many installations which would have been impossible any other way.

Also growing in popularity is the Z-drive, sometimes known as the outboard drive or outdrive. Here the engine can be mounted tight against the transom with a drive unit looking rather like an outboard engine fitted to it via a mounting collar built into the transom itself.

The engine drive changes direction through 90° to turn a vertical shaft which turns the propshaft after another 90° turn.

The whole of the drive unit lifts up and down to alter the trim of the propeller which can give maximum efficiency under different sets of circumstances, while the whole unit also rotates in the other plane to steer the boat in a similar way to an outboard engine.

The Z-drive is more efficient than an outboard and it enables beefy diesel engines to be used in situations where they could not be considered in any other way.

Unlike the outboard, the Z-drive does not lend itself to easy theft. Installation is easy, because there is no tube to be fitted and virtually no lining up to be done. Also claimed for the Z-drive is great manoeuvrability.

A further method of transmission is the jet. Although this has not been developed to the extent of Z-drives or hydraulics, I have seen a very effective installation on a Thames barge, where the lack of a propeller to set on made it a natural for a type of craft whose ability to dry out almost anywhere became a prime virtue.

Ropes, polythene bags, weeds, each the enemy of propeller propulsion, can be dealt with easily when powered by jet, and other advantages are good manoeuvrability, positive control, easy installation and the small space required. The safety aspect should not be overlooked, a prime benefit because there is no propeller to damage people, making the system a good one for rescue and ski boats.

A further possibility, much neglected, but invaluable in some circumstances, is the arrangement where space limitations make it desirable to turn the engine through 180°, so that it is facing backwards, driving the shaft which is located underneath it, by means of Vee belts.

Dodgy though it may sound, it does work, and modern industrial belts are strong and efficient. Tensioning wheels are easily rigged to compensate for stretch in the belts, and a little cunning in the installation makes it easy to replace a belt with a minimum of dismantling.

The engine will continue to run even if the propeller is fouled, but the belts will burn out or snap, protecting the engine and the propeller.

Photo 38 left A small runabout powered by jet

Chapter 28
Into the interior

We keep saying it is essential to have planned the interior before starting any work, and with this in mind we can assume that the main bulkheads were positioned when the deck was built. What we have to do now, therefore, is to plan the detail of the interior and then build it.

These remarks are equally applicable to sailing boats and motor cruisers, and apply basically to yachts of any length.

We will assume the fairly conventional layout of a sleeping cabin forward, with a compartment immediately aft of that which is split by a passage down the middle into a shower compartment on one side with the toilet and washbasin on the other side.

Photo 39A This production cruiser features a dinette layout which converts into a double bunk

Coming aft, where the beam of the boat is beginning to reach maximum, we have the saloon, which is laid out with a dinette on one side, intended to be easily convertible into a double bunk, with the galley facing. A chart table may well be built into the after end of the saloon with immediate access down the companion-way which leads from the cockpit/wheelhouse.

The engine is located under the companion steps, so that access to it is gained by shifting the steps out of the way. The cockpit/wheelhouse seats double as bunks, only possible with either a wheelhouse roof, or provision for setting up a tent type cover over the cockpit using the boom in its crutch as a ridge-pole if the cockpit is open.

As far as possible, lockers are built into the

seats in cockpit or wheelhouse. At the after end of the cockpit there are more lockers for stowing fenders, warps and so on. The compartment for stowing the calor gas cylinder is in the locker under the cockpit bunk on the same side as the cooker to simplify the pipework, and it is vented outboard. Tanks for fuel and water are in the 'wings' of the engine compartment.

Electrics

It is best to tackle each compartment in turn, starting forward, and bearing in mind that you can install the lights, switches and wires in one part of the boat before you have even decided where the main fuse box and panel is to go.

But it is better to decide, roughly speaking, where all the lights are to be located before you tackle any wiring, to make the runs of cables and the positioning of junction boxes and switches more logical. This way there should be few occasions where cables have to be run under the deckhead and down a bulkhead just because the main cable is on the wrong side.

The same reasoning is true of water pipes and calor gas fuel lines. If you think it out in advance you can make sure that you don't waste time and material running unnecessary cable or pipe.

It is logical to start work in the fo'c's'le. You won't be running the risk of damaging work already done when you cart tools around, or of

Photo 40 Final plumbing must be done before the joinery is completed

knocking chunks out of timber when you bring lengths of copper pipe into the interior. Your work bench can be set up conveniently in the saloon where there will be maximum access round it.

The amount of shaving and off-cuts of wood you create once you start the interior carpentry is uncanny. To avoid being swamped it is good policy to have a good sweep out at least once a week.

Another problem is that the amount of sawdust in the air, in addition to general atmospheric dust, makes it difficult to varnish or paint the interior on the same day as it is completed. It is better to allow the dust to settle for 24 hours after sweeping up, and then have a paint and varnish day.

It is also wise to paint and varnish as soon as you can when any item of joinery is complete, to protect it against accidental damage and spilled grease or paint.

Bunks

In most boats there is a small bulkhead at the forward end of the fo'c's'le to separate the chain locker from the accommodation. This is unlikely to have been fitted as part of the deck structure, so it is the first thing to be built now.

It needs to be considered in conjunction with the bunks in the sleeping area immediately behind it, bearing in mind what floor space you must have for access to the bunks and for dressing and undressing.

The height of the bunks above the floor is critical because there is a temptation to make them too high in order to create large locker space underneath them. If there is not enough headroom between the bunks—plus mattress and bedclothes—and the deckhead, the result will be claustrophobic.

It may be possible to create an area above the actual chain locker in which to store linen or clothes by building-in a hefty shelf above the space the chain will occupy, and leading the chain into it by means of a heavy PVC tube of really big diameter from the hawsepipe.

Access to this cupboard also needs to be considered, which may affect the height and exact shape of the bunks.

It is essential to provide bunk boards in any boat which might go to sea.

The drawing shows how you construct a Vee-shaped pair of bunks in a typical hull. First find the centre line of the floor, so that the cabin is divided into two.

This will help you to make both bunks the same (assuming the design calls for even bunks).

Then up the bulkhead measure the proposed height of the bunk—say about 22in—and using your level draw a line across the bulkhead. Where it strikes the boat's side, measure back along it 3in or 4in for linings, then measure your bunk's width (about 2ft 3in) and using a level plumb a line down. This will become the bunk front.

Next you measure the bunk length—6ft 6in if you can get it—and measure the width of the bunk top at that position (X) to make sure there is enough leg room. (Fig. 124).

If it is alright then you can make the bunk fronts. I would suggest 8mm ply for these, so that you can cut them out in one go. You know the height and the length, so simply cut out two pieces 2ft 3in × 6ft 6in.

What comes next is what you fix the front to. I would suggest 1¼in × 1¼in softwood, and this needs to be screwed and glued where it comes in contact with either the bulkheads or the hull respectively. The joints only need to be halving joints set out roughly as follows. (Fig. 125).

Put plywood partitions under the bunks to add strength and make locker spaces. This is done by cutting out little plywood partitions, like mini bulkheads, which are glued and nailed to the bunk bearers which run athwartships. The shape of the mini bulkheads is determined by making a template with offcuts of ply tacked together and then laid against the hull side, so that a parallel line can be scribed off the hull to give the shape, which is then transferred onto the piece of ply which will be the partition (Fig. 126).

The bunk front can go on next and should be glued.

The bunk top should be made out of 8mm plywood and locker openings for each compartment need to be cut out. Do not fix down the bunk top, but leave it loose so that if at any time work must be done under the bunks it will be easier to get at.

Last of all come the bunk boards (Fig. 127). These should be 1¼in × 9in hardwood and cut out so that the centre of the board is approximately the height of the mattress.

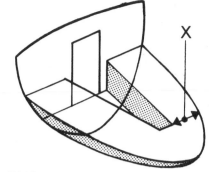

Fig. 124 Measuring up for bunks

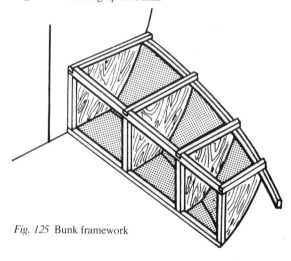

Fig. 125 Bunk framework

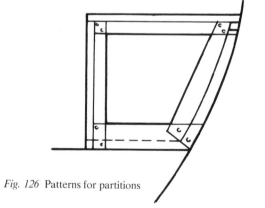

Fig. 126 Patterns for partitions

Fig. 127 Bunk boards

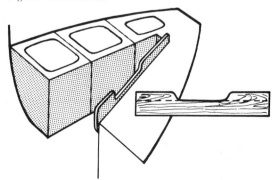

Chapter 29
Designing a toilet compartment

Cramped. Badly-lit. Poorly ventilated. Plain unhygienic. Any or all of these could describe too many toilet compartments—especially on older craft, but too often on newer ones too!

It is just as important to have a comfortable toilet compartment as it is to have a warm, dry bed. On a yacht the amount of pleasure to be had from using the boat is surely related just as much to the comfort, hygiene and general utility of the toilet compartment as it is to the galley, sleeping accommodation or any other part of the boat.

The layout discussed here is that of a sea-toilet mounted on a plinth, so that there is a firm base to anchor it on, and so that ones feet are in what might be descirbed as an ergonomic position when the actual 'thunderbox' is in use. The height of the plinth is also dictated partly by the headroom under the side deck, and by the front to back dimension of the plinth itself.

The only way to get all this right is to mock the thing up with old wooden boxes from the greengrocer's, sit on one, and imagine that the whole structure is pitching and tossing in a seaway. Handholds will be located after experience at sea.

I suggest a Lavac sea-toilet, the advantage being that with two-way valves it is easy to make its one pump also discharge the contents of a shower tray. A second two-way valve enables the same pump to perform yet another function, that of pumping the bilge. The pump itself is a robust diaphragm type, and the skin fittings can be Maranyl.

As a rule the amount of gear to be stowed in a toilet compartment is limited, but there is no reason why this space should not be put to good use for storage of other things.

Rather than opt for either a chemical toilet alone, or a flush toilet with holding tank (which is difficult in a small boat), you can have a conventional sea toilet, and a chemical toilet as well.

When use of the sea toilet is permissible, the chemical one is stowed in the cupboard under the sink; when the boat is on inland waters, the chemical toilet can stand on the grating beside the sink.

This technique seems to me to offer the best of both worlds. It eliminates the cost and problems of the holding tank system, and gives the advantages of the sea-toilet when at sea.

Building a toilet compartment is pretty straightforward. The plinth is ply, screwed and glued, and fastened to the hull.

The whole area of the compartment is bounded by three bulkheads which are part of the fabric of the boat. So, again, fixing is easy.

The bulkheads are made by cladding both sides of a timber battening framework with ply, and filling the spaces between the battens with Rockwool, or glass insulation material to deaden the sound from one compartment to the other. Without this infilling, every time the bulkhead is knocked on the outside there will be a resounding boom inside the compartment.

The timber framing for this bulkhead provides solid fixings for the ends of the battening which supports the plinth.

The most difficult part for the amateur is making the framework for the front of the cupboards. Frames are constructed ashore from an accurately made template, using off-cuts of ply.

There is a point to be borne in mind when making a framework off a boat: it could be too big to squeeze through the opening to the accommodation, leaving no alternative to making it on board, in what will normally be less than ideal conditions.

The last thing to make is the door frame and the door itself. Follow house construction techniques and you won't go far wrong. With a little ingenuity the door can be arranged so that when someone is in the compartment the door shuts it off and ensures privacy, but with it open the same door seals off the fo'c's'le and ensures privacy there instead.

The toilet compartment can also double as the

wet clothing drying-off cupboard if it is big enough, which means locating fairly hefty cup-hooks or coathooks on the appropriate bulkhead so that wet oilskins, sweaters, trousers and other garments can be hung up to dry.

For cladding the bulkheads one very pleasant, functional, and above all 'boaty' material is cork tiles. These can be bought from do-it-yourself shops in a variety of sizes and finishes, but the best are the thin, already varnished and sealed 1ft square tiles, which can be glued down without difficulty. Don't forget to draw a datum line in the appropriate place and work from that outwards.

Another possibility for cladding is Formica or one of the similar materials. Usually, in a boat, nothing is more calculated to give the interior a terrible plastic look, but with careful selection Formica can add to the appearance of a toilet compartment, as well as being easy to clean and easy to fix.

If there is space it is easy to make a toilet compartment double as a shower compartment. Build a GRP shower tray down into the bilge, and provide it with a means of pumping it out. A grating of the kind you see in the cockpits of new yachts and all over the place, especially near the steering position on restored 'Wooden Walls' men-o'-war, can sit on bearers and allows the water to fall through easily.

Gratings are best made from a good hardwood, and can be either varnished or left as God left the tree. They must be easy to lift to enable you clean underneath.

Domestic shower mixer fittings and taps are perfectly suitable here, but some ingenuity may be required to heat the water and feed it through the mixer unit. The easiest answer is a gas water heater, of which there are many types on the market, and a pressure pump, plumbed and wired in so that turning the taps introduces a flow of water through the heater and then into the mixer head.

A word of warning about water heaters. The gas requirement to enable them to deliver piping hot water quickly is quite heavy, and you may find you need a heavy bore pipe to lead the gas from the cylinder if you are to avoid starving the heater of gas and thus providing only lukewarm water. You also need a good vent to get rid of the hot exhaust gases. The fact that the whole of the compartment gets drenched with water every

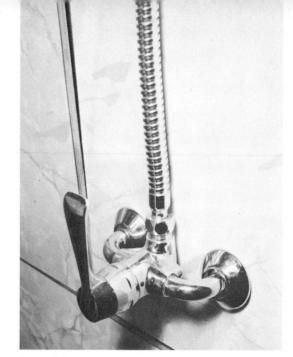

Photo 41 A domestic type fitting is perfectly adequate in this yacht shower

time a shower is taken is really no problem; all you have to do after is mop it all out, which is no great chore in what will inevitably be a small space. But it is easy to arrange shower curtains if this seems a good idea.

It is often possible to arrange for all sorts of little cupboards and shelves in a shower/toilet compartment. All that is required is a little ingenuity and all those old off-cuts you were too mean to chuck away. Don't forget that if you do intend to rig a shower they will have to be made watertight somehow.

An alternative is to use netting slung from the bulkhead like a naval hammock. Then all you have to do when a shower is be be taken is to unhook the net and roll it up complete with contents and take it into the saloon.

Ventilation is very important in toilet compartments, especially when the boat is at anchor or tied up in a marina, when there will be no help from the movement of the boat through the air which induces extra ventilation while under way. Equally, when you are under way, spray may make it difficult to open a porthole, so you need a deckhead fitted ventilator of some size.

Light fittings in the compartment will have to be waterproof if you are going to use it as a shower compartment too. This should present no problem with the aid of your friendly neighbourhood chandler.

Chapter 30
Flooring a cockpit

It seems easy, one might think, to lay a ply cockpit floor—but, one can run into a lot of little snags. Let's see what we can do.

The first job to do is lay the floor bearers. These are usually put in to the boat's level line; some cockpits have a slight fall aft so that the water will drain to the aft end—so we will put a fall in ours.

At the main bulkhead (A, fig. 128) we fix our first bearer, 2½in × 1¾in. This will be screwed and, if the bulkhead is ply, glued as well. Now clamber aft and put in your last bearer against the transom. Aha—first snag now! The boat is floating or not level so how do we get the fall correct? What we do is make ourselves a big 'square' out of scrap wood or ply. Get three lengths of wood about 3in × ½in, and measure off very accurately one 3ft length, one 4ft length and one 5ft length. Fit them together as I have illustrated and they make a nice big square (fig. 129).

Now sit your square on the main bulkhead (A) on the first floor-bearer. With your second pair of hands run a chalk line (B) from the bulkhead bearer to the transom (C). Make sure the chalk line is level (D) with the bottom of the square. When it is, mark the transom.

Do this to port and starboard sides—and even in the middle will help. Then measure down from the marks on the transom ¾in and fix your transom bearer to these marks. This will give your cockpit floor a fall aft of ¾in. Don't make the common mistake of putting too much fall on the cockpit floor, for the feeling it gives will be very uncomfortable.

We have created our floor line, so what we must do next is run two or even three longitudinal floor bearer supports.

We plan to make our floor as watertight as possible, but we will have two traps in it, so that must be remembered when working out the spacing of the floor bearers. What you must do is to decide which way your ply is going to run. If it is going to be laid across the cockpit as in the

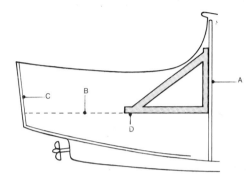

Fig. 128 Setting up floor line

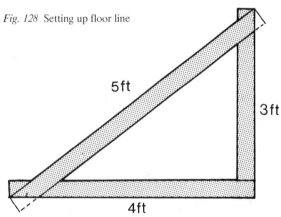

Fig. 129 Make a 'square'

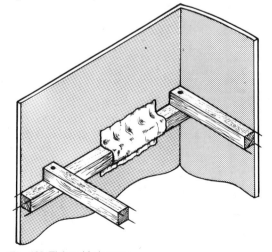

Fig. 130 Fixing side bearers

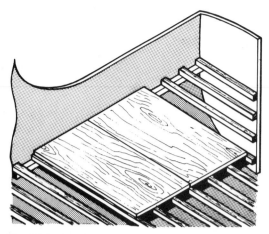

Fig. 131 Laying sheets of ply

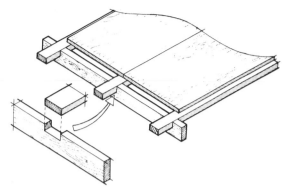

Fig. 132 Seam battens and floor

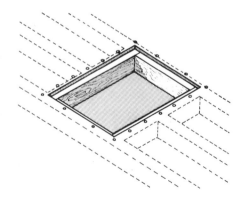

Fig. 133 Deck hatch opening

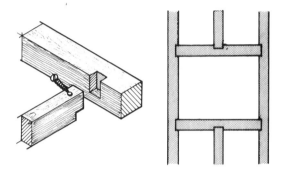

Fig. 134 Hatch surrounds to help water-tightness

drawing (fig. 131) you must make sure that there is a bearer every 4ft.

These will take the butt joint. If the ply is to run lengthwise, then every 8ft there should be a bearer to take the butt joint.

If the cockpit floor is a big one and the ply is laid lengthwise, you must let in seam battens every 4ft.

The seam battens should be the same thickness as the floor and about 4in wide, and these are screwed down to the bearers.

Now that the laying of the ply has been decided and the floor bearers fixed, it is time to mark out the traps. One is to go over the shaft coupling, and the other over the shaft log.

If the floor is high enough for someone to get underneath, then make the trap large enough for someone to get down under. This, then, can mean cutting a bearer in half, in which case do it as follows. Mark out the trap opening on the floor bearers and then take out the bearers you are going to cut—but don't cut it yet. Now you must fit in two trap carlings to support the cut beam, and joint them as in the drawing (fig. 133).

When you come to cut the ply, make sure that the trap sits on half the bearers and carlings, and when you fasten down the floor, make sure that you nail or screw all around the opening.

To try to make the trap watertight, without fixing it down, is pretty well impossible. But try to make the trap as neat a fit as possible and this, with the help of the floor's slope, will only allow a few drips in.

Now you fix down the floor; if it extends right out to the hull, you can fasten it or glass it into the hull. This also will give the hull extra strength.

What about your butt joints? You can either bed them in on resin, glue, or even thick paint and putty.

Now what happens to all the water that gets into the cockpit? Here are three suggestions. First, I suggest a simple hand pump fixed to the

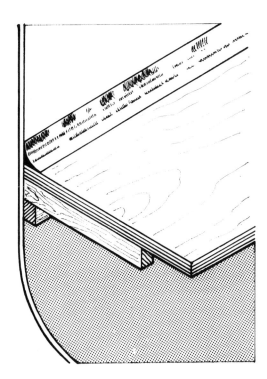

Fig. 135 Sealing deck sides

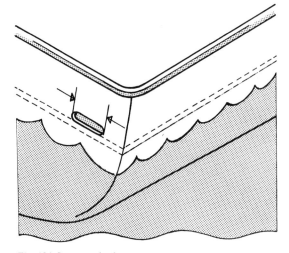

Fig. 136 Scuppers in the transom

transom on one side, this being the lowest end of the floor.

But, if the cockpit floor is above the water line then the other two methods can be used. You can put in scuppers (A), which again should be at the lowest end, the transom — and put one in each corner. They need to be about ¾in high and

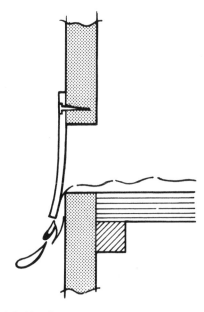

Fig. 137 Rubber flap

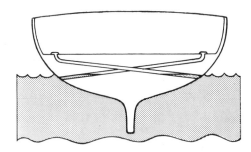

Fig. 138 Cockpit drains

2in long. Make sure that the hull is bonded to the floor. You can even fix a strip of ¼in thick rubber over the hole to act as a flapper, which will help to stop any waves coming in. Just tack it along the top, and let it overlap the scupper by about ¾in.

The third method is to have cockpit drains, which can be of 1in diameter flexible pipe fixed to a skin-fitting. The only thing to remember with this one is to run the port drain to the starboard side, and the starboard drain to the port side (fig. 138).

This is done so that if the boat rolls to port its outlet will clear the water and will thus prevent the cockpit filling up, as the drain hole on the port side will be below the waterline — and of course vice versa.

137

Chapter 31
Cab-sides, carlings, and coach roofs

Normally, the deck is the first thing to deal with after raising the gunwale or sheer line and doing hull repairs. We shall take as an example the putting in of new side decks and cab-sides. This is a nice stage as it grows very quickly and one feels a great satisfaction with its progress.

So, scale off your drawing the width of the side deck at about four places, and transfer these onto the boat. To do this, put cross braces across the boat at the points where you have scaled off, and make sure they are the thickness of the carling below so that the carling can sit on the braces (fig. 139).

If you have put in the main bulkhead and beam after fitting your cockpit floor, then use that as your main starting point. Measure forward to where the cab-side finished and put in the fore main beam if the front screen is to be in two, or even three, pieces. These are just halved and screwed in, and then you measure the width of the side deck at the forward end and the two evenly spaced points in between the bulkheads.

Now fit two plywood gussets where the marks are on the braces. These will help to keep the

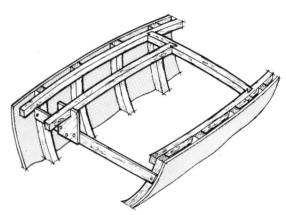

Fig. 139 Ply gussets holds the carling while half-beams are fitted

carling in place while the half beams are fitted. The beams should be dovetailed in, as the carling is trying to straighten itself and halving joints will let the carling move. Space out your half beams to take the joints of the ply deck.

If there is a sharp curve, which can happen in lifeboats, then it might be a good idea to fit in tie bolts every other beam. These are long iron rods which are threaded and run through the gunwale and carling alongside a beam.

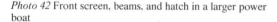

Photo 42 Front screen, beams, and hatch in a larger power boat

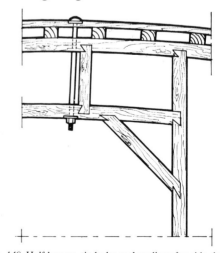

Fig. 140 Half beams, tie bolts and carlings for side decks

When all the half beams are in, fair in the deck beams with the carling and gunwale and then fit the deck. This can be glued down or bedded down along the gunwale and carling.

When all this is done the carling can be bevelled in to take the cab-sides, which is known as the declivity of the cab-side. To find this, do a full size drawing of the cab-side and half deck view. Make a declivity batten and use this with a level to bevel your carlings (fig. 141).

The cabin sides come next and a template should be made for this, as mistakes easily happen. Don't bother about marking your windows yet; fit the cab-side first. Plywood again is probably best, and if a joint is to be made (as the cabin might be longer than 8ft), make the joint a double lip scarph (fig. 142) and glue. If it is possible also, try to get the joint over a bulkhead as this will help the strength and even hide one side of the scarph.

It you cut out both sides first and you make a bad scarph joint on one side, then you might be able to change over sides and hide that bad joint behind the bulkhead post. Cramp both cabin sides in position and make sure their declivity is correct, then put some battens across to hold them.

Next, you can make the templates for the front screens. This part is quite important as it can either give the boat the amateur look or, what you are really aiming at, that pro look. If you have any cabin roof beams made up, then put two or three at the fore end about 1ft apart on top of the cab-sides. Get a piece of ply and fit it as your template to the deck and rake of the cab-side. Then, with a straight edge sitting on top of the beams, mark off the camber onto the template. Because the front screen is raked back and running off square to the centre line, the camber of the roof beam of the screen is completely different from the roof beams. Where the cab-side joins the screen let the screen run past so that the end grain is on the side; this can then be covered by a beading, or you can fit a rebated corner post. This can be done two ways (see fig. 144).

However, this must be decided before the screens are made. The style and construction of the windows must also be decided, and is elaborated later.

Now, to carry on with the front screens. These generally sit on top of the deck and are bedded

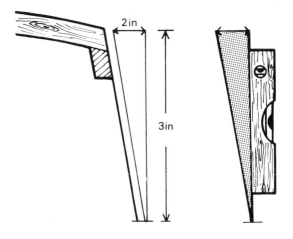

Fig. 141 Making a declivity batten

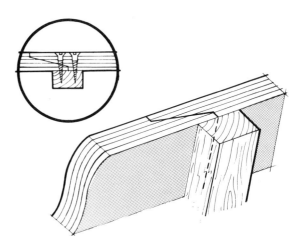

Fig. 142 Scarph in cabin side

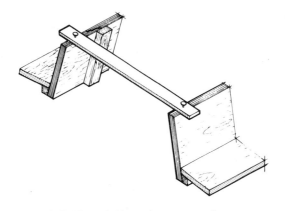

Fig. 143 Holding cabsides at the correct angle

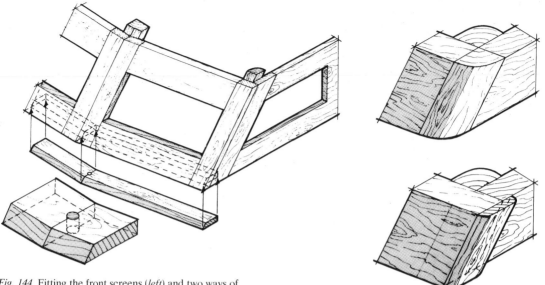

Fig. 144 Fitting the front screens (*left*) and two ways of finishing off the side screens (*right*)

down and screwed to 'grounds'. These are mitred at the joints with a 'stopwater' drilled into the mitre (see fig. 144). If it is a two-piece screen then a centre post must be fitted, making sure that the corner and centre posts are long enough. Normal practice is to let them run at least 2in above the roof height, which makes them easier to cut and fair in. Another point to watch is the beam that screws to the screen which, as it is on a rake, needs to be thicker.

The cab-sides need to be well bedded-in when finally fixed, and a deck quadrant fitted on the outside—which must also be well bedded. When the roof is on and the windows all in, finish off the cab-side with a nice varnished coaming.

The cabin roof beams can be halved into the coach roof shelf which is itself glued and screwed to the cab-side. Alternatively, the roof shelf can be fitted the thickness of the beams lower, and the beams cut to sit on the shelf.

Put a strongback of about 3in $\times$ 2in underneath the beams down the centre of the cabin, and shore it up. This strongback should be as straight as possible so that the roof will not get any bumps or sag in it. When the ply roof is laid and fixed, the strongback can be removed.

Ports and windows

Now on to types of windows. If the vessel is intended to be a sea boat, the first choice would be portholes. One way to finish off around portholes is to make a little box which will act as a condensation- or water-trap.

To do this, you make a box approximately 2in larger all round that your porthole opening and about 2½in to 3in deep. The joints are two-in-one inasmuch as there is a mitre on the face and a halving joint hidden behind (see fig. 145). This is so that you can get a good screw into the halving

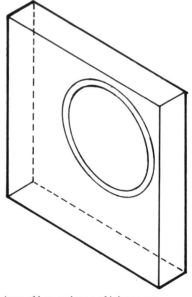

Fig. 145 Area of box and type of joint to use

140

Photo 43 Fairing in laminated cabin beams

Photo 44 Hardwood frame around the porthole also secures the ends of the linings

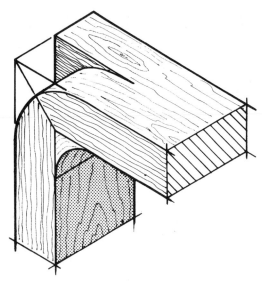

Fig. 146 Finishing off corners

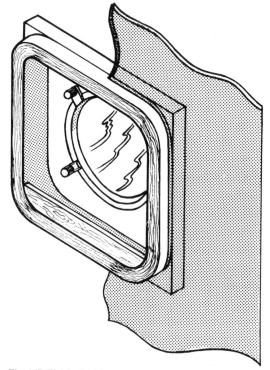

Fig. 147 Finished with water trap

box, and round-off all the facing edges. Offer the box to the port hole, and draw around the inside and outside of the box onto the cab-side.

Take the box down, drill screw holes, put bedding onto the box face to be screwed, and fix it in place. Fit and glue a small fillet on the inside of the window box to stop water dripping over the edge (fig. 147).

If the craft is only going to be used on a river, then you can use the rubber extrusion type of window, which is very popular, or you can have aluminium frames made up, which are very expensive, or you can use any of the following types of construction.

Static pane

This type of window construction is not very elegant to look at, and its shape is also limited to straight lines. If the cab-side is thick enough to stand being rebated, then the cover fillet can be either wood or aluminium. If it is wood, make sure that the fillet has a radiused surface so that the water drains and does not get trapped. Also, make sure that the fillet does not stick over the rebated section and cause a capillary action.

Use plenty of bedding or soft putty between the glass or perspex and the timber. If you are using aluminium, which is generally better looking for the finished job, make sure that your screw-heads are flush or below the surface of the aluminium, so that there are no sharp edges.

Open down

This type of window is more complicated to make because it is an opening window. The principal idea of this type is not to make it watertight when closed, but to concentrate on draining the water out again. These windows do tend to rattle, but it's a small price to pay for a dry boat! What happens is that the water drains into the box and back out through drain holes in the cab-sides. This type of window is only used where the wheelhouse or saloon is above deck and straight, as on a fishing boat or Grandbanks. The box should be made watertight and painted inside. The drawing (fig. 149) illustrates the rubber stoppers, leather strap, cab front and drain holes.

Open in

This is a type of window used on river cruisers— not recommended for coastal boats. But for an

joint and this will strengthen the mitre. You can only really do this if the boat is lined out as the halving joint will be hidden behind the lining.

When the box is made you fit in corner wedges on the inside, and glue them. When these are dry, you can round off the outside of the box, to take away the very square look. Clean up the

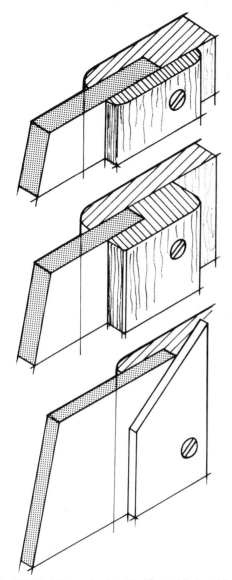

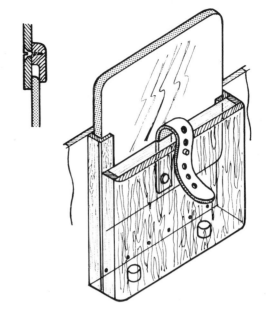

Fig. 149 Train-type windows

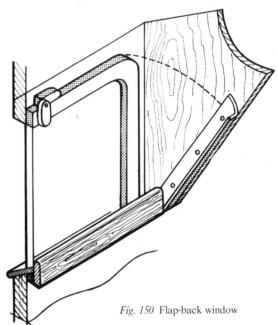

Fig. 150 Flap-back window

Fig. 148 (**Top**) Rebated cabinside, (**Centre**) Rebated frame,
(**Bottom**) Rebated cabinside with aluminium strip

opening window it can at least be radiused on the
corners, and does look quite nice from inside
and out. It can be made draught-proof by
sticking some thin foam rubber around the edge,
where the glass touches the cab-sides.

The knees which stick inboard can be shaped,
to lessen the bulky look, and the sill must have a
fall on it, and overhang the cab-side. Two thin
fillets are screwed onto the inside of the knees
and fitted over the sill. These act as jambs when
the window is open, and there is a turn-button at
the top to hold it in the closed position against
the foam rubber and cab-side.

Slide open

This type, again, is not recommended for boats
which go to sea, as it cannot be watertight. This
window can look very nice if concealed behind
panelling. The window aperture is cut in the hull
or cab-side first, then the watertight box is made
up. This is then fitted to the hull or cab-side, and
marked all around it. Take it off and drill drain
holes in the two bottom corners.

143

Photo 45 Window of the type often fitted in river craft opens inwards and is not suitable for sea-going vessels

The glass can be cut about 1in larger all round than the aperture and placed into the box. Bed the box down to the hull, and screw from the outside. Fit a small hook at one end, to slip over the window knob to keep it closed (see fig. 151). This type of window does tend to rattle, so a pretty good fit is needed, but when finished it is a very nice looking job.

Open out

This window is usually a front screen window and opens out and up. It is made like a normal sash window, and the glass can be held in by either putty or beading.

The only thing to be careful about is if the window is on a rake of any kind. If so, the bottom of the window rebate should be bevelled to allow the water to drain off. The underside of the window frame should have a groove down it to stop the water working back. The window is hinged on the outside, and the batten to which it is hinged is bedded down. A fillet is fitted all around the opening on the inside to form a rebate, and the sill must be on a slope for the water to run off (see fig. 152).

Now that the boat should be watertight, we can think of fitting out the interior, a bit more, and so the next chapter is going to deal with insulation and lighting.

Fig. 151 Side-opening window

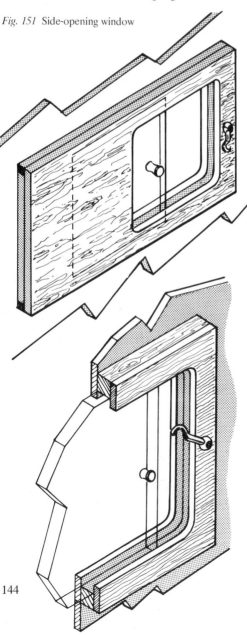

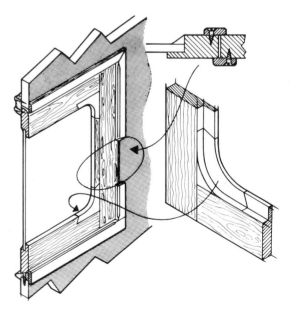

Fig. 152 Timber-framed opening window

144

Chapter 32
Why shiver? Why peer?

If you are cold on your boat you can always add another layer of sweaters until you reach Michelin Man proportions. If it is too dark to see your way into your bunk you can always stick a candle in a bottle, and if you want to read the chart you can always strike a match, or flash a torch. But there are better ways to keep warm when it gets cold and to see once daylight fails, so let us examine what is available to make small boating more pleasant.

The more comfortable you can make things on board, the more you will enjoy sailing, and with a cabin which is both warm and well-lit to retire into at the end of the day you are more likely to get afloat earlier in the season and go on longer. This means more sailing and very probably better sailing, simply because at the end of the season fewer people are out, and most of us prefer the sport when there is less overcrowding of anchorages and harbours.

There are a number of factors to be considered. Most of the many different forms of heating and lighting sold for use on boats are reasonably efficient; it doesn't matter if they sound old-fashioned, like oil lamps and solid fuel fires. The first thing to consider is what forms of energy conversion you have on board already, because all that heating and lighting appliances do is to convert one form of energy into another, and it is nice if you can just extend an existing system.

If you have a diesel engine which incorporates a dynamo or rectifier, as they almost always do, it makes sense to try to use the diesel fuel which you already have on board to provide the heating and the dynamo the lighting, simply because to do so obviates the necessity to have a second form of fuel, with the attendant duplication of storage facilities and having to top up with different fuels.

There are several heaters available which burn diesel oil, and you can use low voltage electricity from the engine battery to provide cabin lighting. The navigation lights almost certainly are powered by electricity in this way, so some of the circuitry may already be in existence, plus fuse boxes and junction boxes.

The disadvantage of this scheme is that you may incorporate so much accommodation lighting that you drain the battery in a very short time, and this means that you will have to run the engine frequently to charge up the battery. You can be in trouble if the battery which supplies the lighting also turns the engine to start it. The way to avoid this is to have two batteries, one for engine starting only, which is 'topped up' first by means of a split diode, so that the second, lighting, battery receives nothing until the first is fully charged. When the engine is running it is obvious when the drain on the engine battery imposed by starting has been replaced. With an alternator this is a very short time: just a few minutes.

A further refinement is a slightly sophisticated trickle charger incorporated in the system in such a way that when a source of mains power is available it can be plugged in to it, thus permanently maintaining the charge in the battery. A voltage regulator and cut-out in the trickle charger ensures that the battery cannot be overcharged, and damaged. If your boat has a petrol engine you can certainly use the engine to charge the battery, but I do not believe that anyone has yet marketed a petrol catalytic heater of the type we will discuss when we get to propane and butane appliances.

The engine can be used to heat the cabin while it is running, by making a heat exchanger of some kind. There is real scope here for ingenuity, because it can be used to heat water for making tea and so on, as well.

Basically, a heat exchanger works by passing hot exhaust water through a chamber through which a completely separate water system is pumped, so that the heat from the one is absorbed by the other. Sophisticated engines make use of this principle, with a sealed fresh water system circulating round the engine while raw sea water is pumped through the chamber to take away the heat.

If hot exhaust water is circulated into the cabin through a pipe with fins on it, then the air in the cabin will be heated, for nothing, because otherwise the heat goes to waste.

If you don't want the cabin heated, in the summer, a by-pass circuit can take the exhaust water straight into the sea just by the operation of a valve.

There is a wide variety of appliances for heating and lighting and often the same source of energy can be used for both. Paraffin, for example, can be used in convector and radiator type heaters as well as for lighting in conventional old-fashioned oil lamps, or in pressure oil lamps of which the Tilley and Optimus makes are the best known. The old-fashioned paraffin lamp creates a surprising amount of heat when it burns as well as giving an attractive soft light. The light from the pressure type is much harsher, though the heat is enough to provide all the warmth you need in the saloon on a smaller boat. Like the free heat from the engine with the heat exchanger, getting something for nothing in this way is always interesting, but of course you also get the heat in the summer.

There may be a temptation to fit your boat with a paraffin heater which was designed for domestic or caravan use, perhaps because it is no longer required at home. These are quite unsuitable in boats and can be dangerous, so it is a temptation to be resisted.

There is a lot to be said for paraffin. It is easily obtainable, and a can which is easily carried will contain enough fuel to heat and light a boat for a week-end.

There is something faintly boaty about the smell of warm paraffin in the old-fashioned type of lamp and their very appearance does add to the nautical atmosphere aboard.

The pressure type of lamp can be taken outside the saloon and used to provide light for working on deck, hoisted as a riding-light, or brought on deck to draw the attention of another craft to your presence while you are under way if you are fearful that they haven't seen your navigation lights.

The trouble with paraffin heaters and lighting is that as the fuel burns so it creates moisture. In a steel or GRP boat there will be condensation anyway from the atmosphere on the inside of the

hull whenever the difference in temperature between the air outside and the air inside is great enough. The paraffin will greatly increase it. Wood does not 'sweat' like glass or steel, but the moisture from paraffin will be noticeable.

One answer to this problem is to insulate the inside of the accommodation in some way. The whole of the inside of a boat can have mineral wool, sandwiched between two layers of foil for ease of handling, stuck directly on to the hull, with an impact adhesive, after painting. This is 100% effective, and as a bonus keeps the warmth inside, where it belongs.

Other materials which can be used for this purpose include polystyrene—make sure you get the type which has been treated to be flame-retardant and GRP wrap of the kind used domestically in lofts.

Butane and Propane (LPG) also create moisture when they burn, although many of the heaters which employ this fuel are designed so that it is vented outside the boat up the flue.

Some LPG heaters use their fuel by chemical action and not by burning.

From the safety point of view there is much to be said for these catalytic heaters. They cannot set fire to anything, are usually attractive to look at and do not occupy much space, always at a premium in a boat. They do not create smoke, soot, or flame, and do not require a flue, which eliminates the need to cut a hole in the deck.

LPG gas can also be used to provide lighting, and here again we have the advantage in cold weather of creating heat with the corresponding disadvantage of producing moisture. The mantles of some of the units on the market are prone to damage, a feature they share with the mantles on pressure paraffin lighting units, and where glass shades are incorporated in the design they are liable to be broken, especially if someone lurches into one in bad weather. But electric leaks are dangerous too.

The manufacturers of the very small LPG containers have developed interesting ranges of appliances, largely for camping and caravanning, but many of them are eminently suitable for small boats where there is no room for more permanent devices.

The small the gas container, the more the gas costs, *pro rata*, but such applicances do not require the careful plumbing which is so important on permanently installed LPG systems,

Photo 46 The lining and joinery hide the insulating material —provided to combat condensation: inside the chain locker the insulating material can still be seen

Photo 47 This caravan type heater can be used in boats but the casters must be removed so that it cannot charge about —and additional securing is essential

because of the safety aspect. This includes stowing the cylinder on deck or in a vented air-tight compartment.

LPG gas is heavier than air, so that leaks collect in the bilge and can create a highly inflammable mixture which can be ignited by a spark with devastating results.

For heating, if there is space for both fuel and applicance, there is really nothing to touch a solid fuel fire. These are rapidly becoming as scarce as hen's teeth, in sizes and shapes which are suitable for installing in yachts, but they can still be obtained if you search hard enough.

A solid fuel fire, whether it burns charcoal, like the 'Pansy', or domestic solid fuel, like the Teddesley 'Queen' and 'Classic Cooker' or the Shipmate 'Skippy', spreads warmth throughout the boat, brings no problems of condensation, and with a little thought can be installed so that the flue runs through a cupboard which can double as an airing cupboard. The fire can even be used to heat kettles, or cook on.

Unfortunately, these assets have to be paid for in terms of dirt, ashes, and a heavy fuel to be brought on board and stored on board, and they really only have a place on larger yachts.

The fuel can be used for no other purpose, so the yachtsman can find himself having diesel oil for his engine, paraffin for his lamps, butane for his cooker and coal for his heater, all in one boat!

The choice of electric fittings is not quite so straightforward as it might appear at first. There are many low voltage strip light units on the market, which have the advantage of low battery consumption, and a low cost, but which interfere with radios and D/F, when they are switched on. Some of the cheaper ones are manufactured to a budget, and are not right for use in a marine environment.

Again, there are several manufacturers of conventional light fittings for incandescent bulbs, but some have been designed for caravan use, and corrode easily. Often the fittings are made of plastic, painted over silver, which does not corrode but does scratch, especially when dirty hands grab them to switch them on by rotating the cover. If the bulb is too near the base it can scorch the head lining.

Diesel fuel can be used in several different types of heater, of which the simplest and one of the most effective is the Danish-make Refleks stove. This is basically a stainless steel cylinder

147

with a carburettor to control the gravity fed flow of fuel, and the unit has been designed so that exhaust gases—and all smells—are vented outside the boat. Meths, or meths pills, are used to light the heater, and from my experience with one I can vouch for their efficiency.

Diesel oil can also be used in heaters which blow hot air throughout the boats in ducts, and they are similar to the type of heaters used in coaches and ambulances. They are effective, but are expensive to buy and to install compared with the simpler diesel-fired heaters on the market, and they do require electric power to run the fans and pumps.

If your boat is large enough, it is worth looking at the range of larger diesel-fired units manufactured by Perkins Boilers of Derby (no direct relation to the engine manufacturers). They specialise in a unit called the 'Gallipak', which combines heating and cooking capabilities with the provision of running hot water for shower and galley as well as central heating, all in one unit. This model has a small brother called the 'Midi Mate', which is a stainless steel cooker with a small back boiler from which water can be obtained for domestic or central heating purposes.

This is really where we came in; if at all possible, use the minimum number of fuels and make any appliance you have on board serve more than one function, to get maximum efficiency. You can spend all your time servicing the different installations, topping up all the different types of fuel, and find that half the storage space on the boat is taken up. All the different systems have their advantages and disadvantages. It is almost inevitable that you will wind up with two different fuels, simply because there is no one fuel which will serve all functions. What you can do is to turn this to advantage by having a certain amount of duplication, so that if one system breaks down or runs out of fuel you can use the alternative.

Photo 48 Four different and commonly used lighting fittings

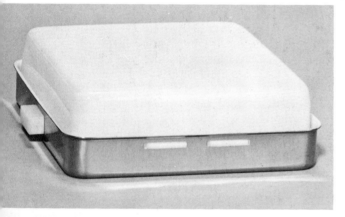

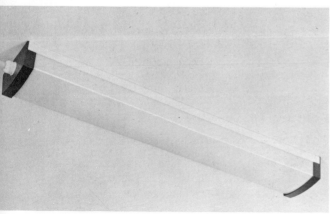
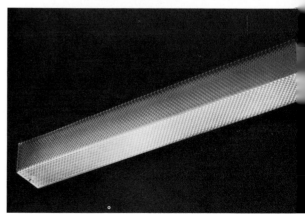

Chapter 33
Saloon and galley in larger boats

With a boat of about 30ft the galley is usually part of the saloon, so care must be taken not to let one encroach onto the other, or else you may have a 12ft galley and a 2ft saloon!

We are constantly on about planning, so that soon you will be fed up with the word, but it will save you a lot of problems. One point to remember is to try to leave as much floor space as possible; it's no good having a 3ft wide settee with yards of storage underneath, and 1ft floor—you will end up walking over the settee, which won't last long.

In the galley, one space which is often missed is under the side decks. This is sometimes a good place to put a plate and cup rack so as to leave a little extra space in the cupboards. Here is one easy method of making a plate rack.

Take one of your cups, one saucer, one plate. Lay them alongside each other with a piece of $^3/_{16}$in plywood between each one, and measure the length (A, fig. 153). Next measure the width or diameter of the largest plate. Now you need two bits of ply the length of A and sufficient width to accommodate the largest plate. Draw the partitions on the ply which is to be your base, and also mark on it the position of the backs for the cup and saucers (B).

Then all you do is box up the base by glueing and pinning the sides and partitions together (C). Fix your top on and last of all the front should be laid on the box, but don't fit it quite yet.

Take your cup and draw around it on the top of the front piece of ply with a thin slit just wide enough for the cup handle to stick out. Do the same for the saucer and plate. When this is done, sandpaper the rough edges and fix the front onto the box (D). Your cups and plates should now sit on top of each other and not swing wildly about when the boat rolls.

Doors are another headache to the boat-builder, as they are hardly ever of a standard house size, but are made to suit any opening in a boat from 9in to 28in wide, with lengths varying from 9in to 6ft 2in. So here is the method to use,

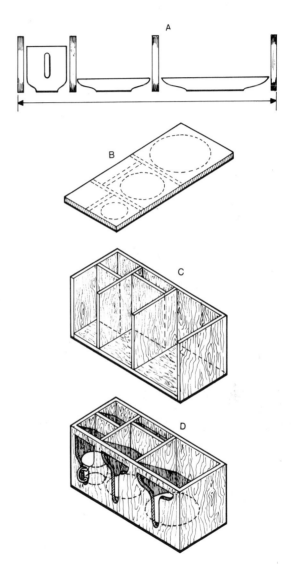

Fig. 153 **A** Set out cups and plates, **B** Base set out, **C** Plate box set up, **D** Front cut out

taking as our example a door just a little out of the standard size range—5ft 2¾in high by 17⅝in wide and 1¼in thick.

Get a sheet of 8 × 4ft 6mm plywood and cut out two panels 16⅞in × 5ft 2in. Lay one panel

149

Photo 49 Three stages in designing and constructing a galley. Note the unusual shaped work surface

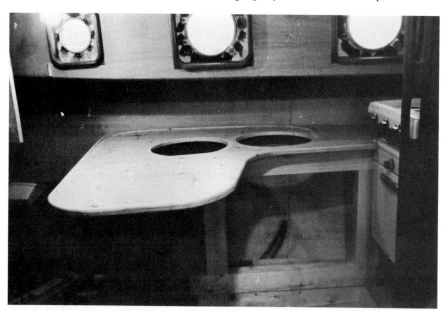

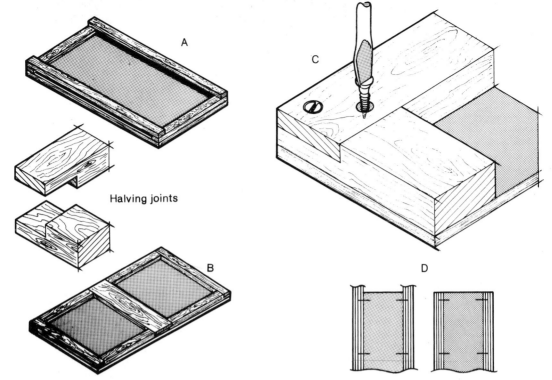

Fig. 154 **A** Set out size of door, **B** Cut joints, **C** Glue and screw, **D** Plane down edges

down on the bench and cut some 2in × ¾in softwood battens to go around the edge (A, fig. 154). Next cut halving joints on each corner.

When this is done, cramp them all together on the door panel. Then decide where the lock would go (if any) and put a wide enough rail across (B). If there is not going to be a lock, just put a rail across the centre the same width as the framing.

When all the joints are done, draw around the inside of the battens and remove them. Now you can glue all the joints and the parts where the framework touches the panel. Then cramp one outside batten to the panel and nail them together with panel pins. Do this to them all and screw the halving joints (C).

Now glue the top surface of the battens and nail down the top ply panel. When it is all nailed together plane down the edges so that they are square and flat (D). The door now needs a hardwood strip around the edges. You could put a 1½in × ⅜in mahogany fillet, mitred at the corners, around the door (fig. 155). The fillets are glued and pinned as illustrated—parallel at the ends and offset along the length. The edges should be cleaned off when the glue is dry. Several coats of varnish finish it off nicely, and the door is ready for hanging.

Usually somewhere on the boat a mirror is fixed to a door, so to prevent the mirror from cracking due to the movement and flexing of the door, fit small rubber washers behind the mirror, and tighten up the mirror screws, so that the washers are just tightly gripped.

Fig. 155 Hardwood edging

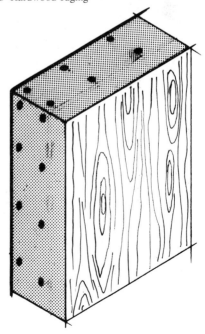

151

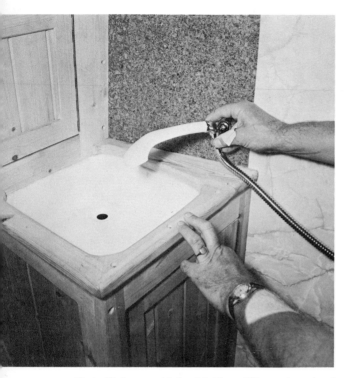

Photo 50 above, and below left Three different views showing the joinery in a finished shower
Photo 51 below right This shot shows the home comforts which can be built into the galley in a large vessel

Chapter 34
Deckwork on larger boats

Let's go outside on the boat now, and do some work on the deck.

It's dreadful how badly some stanchions are fitted. Many, of course, have been fitted by owners not quite sure what the job involves, but some fitted by boat manufacturers or boatyards are almost as poorly done.

One of the important points is, of course, the manner in which they are fitted to the craft. But perhaps more important is the angle they assume once they are fitted. All too often people do not compensate for the camber of the deck, and so the stanchions lean outwards. This not only makes the stanchions and rails vulnerable when the boat rolls towards another boat or a wharf, but it does not provide the safe support for which the rail is intended. Apart from that they don't look very nice, and are dangerous to a person leaning over the side whose point of balance becomes too far outboard for easy recovery.

So, when your stanchions go up they should be fitted onto a timber pad which has been fixed to the deck at a slight fall or slope going inboard, or they can be plumb (fig. 156).

Take one of your stanchions and stand it on a piece of cardboard. Draw around the stanchion onto the cardboard, and then add a border of about ½in as in the drawing (fig. 157). Then cut out your cardboard template, which will serve for all your stanchions. The pads should be at least ¾in thick. Assuming we decide to put the stanchions plumb, cut out a pad and place it in position on the deck, get a small boat-level and lay it on top of the pad. Now, by lifting one end of the level off the pad, until the level becomes level, measure the gap between the level and the pad. Mark this measurement on the pad where the level is touching (fig. 158).

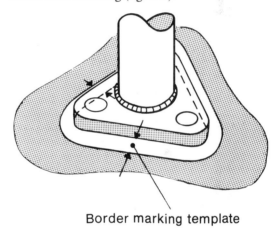

Border marking template

Fig. 157 Border marking template

Fig. 158 Fitting stanchion pad. A amount of plane off a B

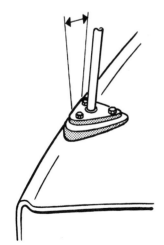

Fig. 156 Declivity of stanchion

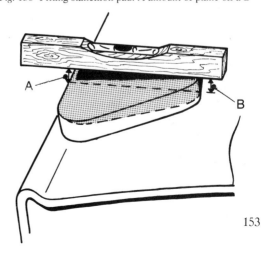

You will see now that the area represented by the shaded portion in fig. 158 should be cut away, leaving the white area on which the foot of the stanchion will stand. This provides the angle that compensates for the camber on the deck, and the stanchion will stand plumb, or inboard if you cut the angle more acutely.

It is a good idea to radius the top edges of the pad all around. Then the pad should of course be sanded smooth and properly painted or varnished as appropriate.

Once your stanchion sits in the plumb position athwartships, how do you want it to look fore and aft? Climb off the boat and walk back a good 50 or 60ft and look at the boat. Try to line your stanchions up with a window post or some vertical line on the boat. If you need to take anything off the pad to make the stanchion sit nicely, be careful not to alter the thwartships line.

When you come to bolt down the stanchions, make sure there is plenty of bedding under the pad. Make sure also to put a cotton grommet around each bolt head. Try to get at least one bolt in each stanchion.

This method with the pads should be done with all deck fittings: fairleads, winches, cleats, vents and so on. While we are on the subject of deck fittings, always make sure that every bolt that goes through the deck or superstructure is bedded, and has a cotton grommet.

If the bolt is having a grommet on the head, take the bolt in the left hand and, with your thumb, hold one end of the strand of caulking cotton to the head. Give about three turns around the head with the cotton and break off the thread.

Fig. 159 Cotton grommet

To stop the cotton unwinding run your finger around the cotton with a bit of bedding on it. If the grommet is to go onto the nut's end, under the washer, twist the thread of cotton around your finger (or on a bolt the same size) about three times, and then thread the tail end of cotton through itself about three or four times as in the drawing. Then slip the grommet over the bolt and put the washer and nut on. It is, incidentally, much neater and nicer to cut off a bolt's thread sticking past the nut than to leave it proud. Apart from anything else, they can be brutal to scalps if someone happens to catch an exposed bolt in the deckhead.

If you decide to put a timber hand rail along the top of the stanchions, make the joints double lip scraphs and put them over stanchions (fig. 160). At the stern you can either mitre the joint with a quarter knee on the inside, or use a mitre on top with a halving joint under—or just a halving joint on its own.

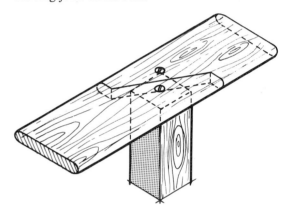

Fig. 160 Handrail scarph

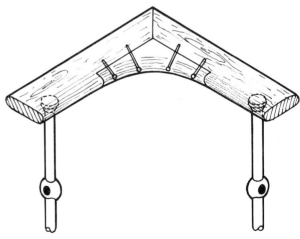

Fig. 161 Quarter knee on handrail

Rubbing bands

These are always being damaged, or even rotting through damage, and if they are left (which they nearly always are) rot gets into the deck planking at the sheer and on into the gunwale. This then becomes a major repair. So look after the rubbers.

Rubbers are essentially there to protect the boat from knocking or rubbing in cases such as berthing or coming alongside the jetty, and are not put on for structural strength. Here are a few different ways of attaching them (see fig. 162):

1 In this one the rubber is through-bolted into the gunwale about every 30in, and screwed every 9in. The gunwale rubber is fitted just below the covering board (fig. 162, top left).

2 The rubber is again fitted just below the covering board, but this time is just screwed into every frame or timber, staggering the screws in a zigzag line (top right).

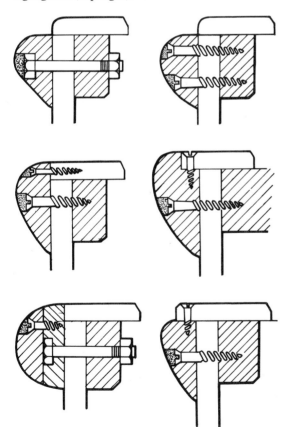

Fig. 162 Six type of gunwale rubbers

3 Here the rubber comes flush with the top of the covering board, and is screwed into the covering board and planking in zigzag fashion.

4 The rubber here is rebated to take the covering board, and is screwed into the planking and frames. The covering board is then screwed into the rubber.

5 This is a double rubber, where the inner one is through-bolted into the gunwale and comes flush with the top of the covering board. Then another piece is screwed onto the face of the bolted piece (bottom left).

6 This is like No2, but the covering board runs over the top of the rubber and screws down into it (bottom right).

Well, which ones do you think are best? Let's have an analysis.

1 This is not a good method because if it gets a very heavy knock or bang it will rip up the top plank and split the gunwale. Also, there is a through-joint for water to creep in under the covering board which cannot be very heavily caulked as it will simply lift at the end.

2 This is a bit better, but there is still the bad seam on the covering board. To make this perfect the rubber should cover the seam.

3 This is a good one as it protects the covering board seam, and also one can stagger the screws better. These will still rip out if heavily knocked.

4 This one is a lot of work, and not very good as it will create further work if damaged.

5 This one is quite a good method, as it covers the covering board, and can be ripped off quite easily without causing too much damage—although there is still the possibility of it taking the top plank with it.

6 This is as bad as No4, but there would be less work in repairing than No4. Still, there's that covering board seam to watch.

All in all, No2 is probably the ideal fitting of a gunwale rubber, but with the rubber lifted up a bit to cover the seam on the covering board.

Fibreglass hulls have rubber around the sheer which eventually stretches or sags. One way of making a nice rubbing band, instead of that rubber, is to cap it in timber, and it is worth describing how to do it.

Glass hulls and decks are usually fitted together by one of two methods: one is to overlap

Photo 52 Cleaning off the dowels after fixing the rubbing band

showing the raw edge of the hull (see fig. 163). This is filled with a timber fillet which is glued in, and later the whole rubber is planed into a nice round shape (fig. 164).

If there are stanchions to go on, then make a pad and span the stanchion over onto the rubber, which will add a little more side deck. The stanchion should be bolted down through the rubber and pad (see fig. 165).

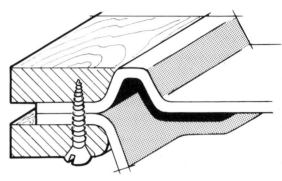

Fig. 163 Fixing into flange and top timber

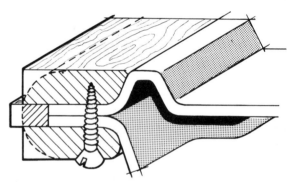

Fig. 164 Shaping up the rubber

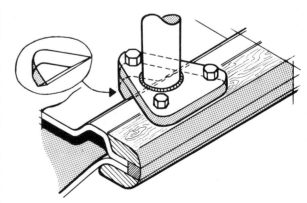

Fig. 165 Fitting a small stanchion pad

the deck onto the hull, and the other is a flange joint. This latter is the harder one to cap so I will deal with this one.

The top capping should be about 2in wide by ¾in. Round off the inside bottom edge to fit the toe rail on the deck. This can be done to the bottom piece of capping as well, and then you can seal them with varnish where they will be hidden. With most glass boats the deck line is very bluff, not a nice easy curve as in most timber boats—hence the rubber extrusion gunwales.

So, the fore end will have to be cut out of a wide piece of wood. A template should be made of this curve to save any excessive strain on the timber. It is best to start from the stem first and work your way aft. Where the timber joins make a splice-scarph with the outside feather edge aft.

Fix as you go, making sure that you spring the timber in gently. Screw up through the flange into the top timber first, then screw up through the bottom timber in to the top piece, which should leave you with a gap in the middle

Chapter 35
Waterline scribing, boarding ladder and boarding platform

How often have you seen wavy waterlines and boot tops? Well, if you have suffered from a wandering paint brush, here is the correct way to put in a waterline and a boot top, but first a word of explanation.

A boot top is a wide, or deep waterline, which is done that way as it is very difficult to keep a boat at its correct waterline—and nothing looks worse than a boat floating too low or too high from a thin line.

To scribe in the waterline you will need: a spirit level; a good long length of chalk line (at least as long as the boat); two straight-edges (of which more later); a few nails; a hammer; a pencil or scribe.

Let us assume we are going to put a boot top on a 25ft boat which is on a trailer. The first and very important step is to get the boat level fore and aft and athwartships. To do this, take your level and put it against the main bulkhead in the vertical (plumb) position. You can raise or lower the trailer on blocks and wedges until it is plumb. Then put the level on the door frame to get the boat level athwartships (see fig. 166). Then go

back and check the level in the first position again to make sure it has not altered. When you are satisfied that the boat is level all round you can set up your straight-edges.

If the boat has been in the water long it will have made its own tidemark around the hull which you can use as a guide when setting up your straight-edges. Set your straight-edge about 2in lower than the tidemark and this will give you a bit of leeway. To set them up use a couple of trestles or some form of framework, one at the stem and the same at the aft end, making sure that the trestles are wider than the beam of the boat (see fig. 167).

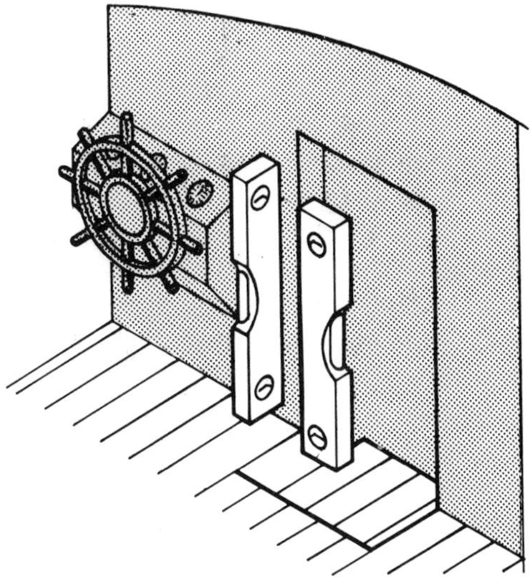

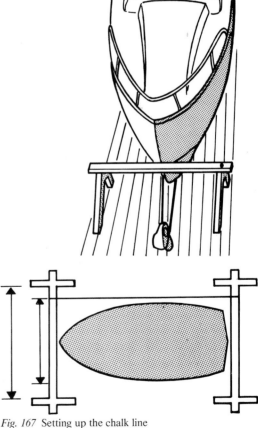

Fig. 166 Levelling up the boat

Fig. 167 Setting up the chalk line

Now stretch your chalk line between the tops of the straight-edges, as tight as you can. This is to take the sag out of the line. Bring the chalk line in as close as you can to the side of the hull but without it touching. Take your level and, starting from the centre, work aft (or forward). Put the spirit level under the chalk line and get it level, then make a chalk mark on the hull about every foot or less (fig. 168).

When all this is done, join the marks up with a wooden batten. Make the batten at least 6ft long, and preferably get others to hold it along the chalk marks.

That takes care of the waterline, so now let's put in the boot top. Let us say we are going to put in a 4in boot top midships, rising to a 6in boot top at both stem and transom. This extra 2in at each end helps the looks of the waterline as this is where the trim of the craft alters the most.

Here is how it is done. You need two 4in high blocks and two 2in high blocks, both about 6in to 9in long (see fig. 169). Slip the 4in blocks under the chalk line at each end, which gives you your 4in high boot top. Get your level and mark across to the hull this new line above the first one. Do this for about 2ft each side of midships.

Then take out one 4in block, let's say the rear one, and replace it with a 2in block and put the other 2in block on top of your 4in block which is still up forward. Using your level, and working along the rising line, put your level marks onto the hull (as in fig. 168). When you are putting in the rising boot top line you must keep the level square to the line at all times as you transfer the marks over, otherwise you will not get a fair line.

Then do the same towards the other end by changing the blocks, so that you get a 4in and a 2in block on top of each other on the high end, and just a 2in block at the bow end. Repeat the same procedure as you did before and then join up the chalk marks with your batten and this should give you a nice true boot top.

All you have to do now is to cut in your paint properly with the aid of masking tape. Run the tape along each line and then you can paint over the area between the two tapes. But do take the tape off before the paint dries or it may take flakes of paint off with it.

Sheer legs

Some round bilge boats could benefit from the addition of sheer legs. These are fitted to a clamp, or through the gunwale itself. So, if you

Photo 53 This Breton fishing boat takes the mud at every tide and has been fitted with sheerlegs to prevent her falling over

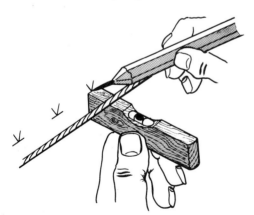

Fig. 168 Transferring the line to hull

Fig. 169 Setting up the boot top

prefer these to bilge keels (see Chapter 16) then this is one way to go about making them.

First you need to know the height from the keel up to the sheer where the sheer legs are going. They should go where the beam is widest. Fit a clamp inside the boat underneath the gunwale. The clamp should be roughly 3ft long by 6in × 3in for a 30ft boat. Bolt it through the hull; if it runs across any frames bolt through them. Now drill a hole through the clamp and hull to take a metal sleeve which should be big enough to pass a bolt through (see fig. 170).

The sheer leg can be about 4in × 4in hardwood with a hole drilled through it to take a sleeve. The sheer leg needs to lie out from the boat at the bottom to give it more beam than the boat, but don't make the boat lean over 5° or the sheer leg takes too much dead weight of the boat.

So, before drilling the hole in the sheer leg, plane off about 1¼in at the top down to nothing over the length of a foot. Try the sheer leg for angle, and if more needs to come off then take more off until it is right; then drill your hole for the bolt square off the planed side (see fig. 170).

Drill a hole about 1ft up from the bottom of the leg to take a rope. This rope is tied to the stem and stern, so as to prevent the leg twisting up when bolted in position. When the legs are not in use, have a bolt with a rubber washer on it fitted to the hole in the hull to make the hole watertight.

Now, consider how you are going to clamber in and out of the boat. Here are two ways which are safe, and making them yourself can save a lot of money.

Boarding ladder

A traditionally-built boarding ladder is always a bit of one-upmanship, especially if you have made it yourself and it's all varnished and shimmering (fig. 171). First decide what timber you are going to use; preferably a hardwood like mahogany or teak. It can be made of softwood, but choose carefully—there should be no knots, splits or faults.

Fig. 171 Finished ladder

The ladder sides in this example will be 4in × 1in × 4ft long. The four treads are again 4in × 1in, by 18in long. So, first of all sharpen up your smoothing plane and set it very fine, and plane over every bit of the timber to get out the grooves left by the planer.

When this is done, lay the ladder sides together and lightly clamp them, and then mark out your treads (see fig. 172). Square off the ends, using a square, and then measure 12in inwards, and

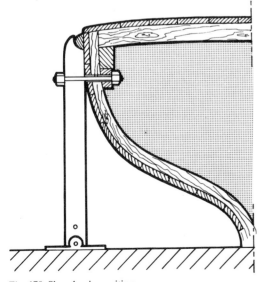

Fig. 170 Sheerleg in position

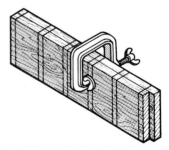

Fig. 172 Marking out treads on the sides

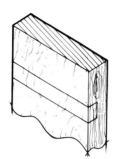

Fig. 173 Side marked ready to cut

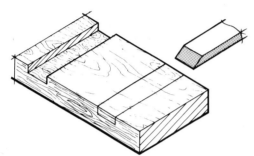

Fig. 174 Cutting out sides

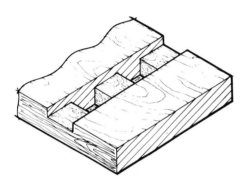

Fig. 175 Cutting out mortise in sides

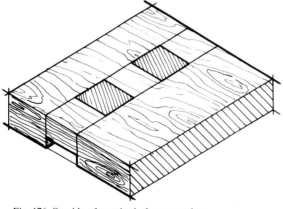

Fig. 176 Outside of mortise before recutting

mark the thickness of the tread. Measure 10in and another tread, and so on. When you have squared all around you can take the clamp off. Now get your marking gauge and set it ⅜in and gauge each tread end (see fig. 173).

Cut on the inside of each line where the tread goes with your tenon saw, down to the gauge marks. Then cut out the unwanted wood with a sharp chisel (see fig. 174). When you have cut out all the tread housings, measure in on each housing ¾in and then another ¾in. This will become a mortise and tenon joint (see fig. 175). You must be very careful when you do this as it will be seen when finished, so take your square and square round the tread to the outside of the ladder. Then measure in again the ¾in and square across, then your next ¾in and again square over. Do this on both sides (fig. 176).

The shaded areas on fig. 176 are to be cut out. Before you start wielding your mallet and chisel, take a marking knife and mark around the spot to which you intend to cut. This will help you not to split the wood and leave a jagged edge.

When you have cut out the holes, scribe across the top and bottom of the holes with your marking knife about 1mm from the edge, and bevel this through to nothing on the inside edge (see fig. 177). This way you will have a smaller hole on the inside.

Now we come to cutting the treads out. Take your four treads and clamp them together, then square them around at one end, measure 18in and square around the other end. Keep them clamped together and cut them to length, making sure that they are nice and square all round (fig. 178). When this is done measure in ¾in and square all around. Release the clamps and finish off squaring all around each tread.

Now take tread No1 and place it into the groove or housing. Making sure the sides are flush, and without moving anything, with your sharp pencil mark around the two holes—and before you forget, mark on it 'left side No1' (fig. 179). Repeat the same process at the right hand side. Now square down the lines. You can then cut off the waste and have a test run to make sure it is done correctly. It should be a nice tight fit on the sides and have a gap on the top and bottom of 1mm.

If you are happy with the fit, then take it apart and cut a slot down the centre of each tenon. Repeat the same procedure with each tread,

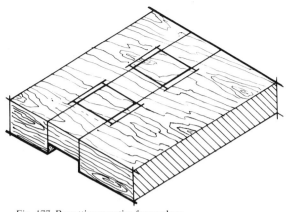

Fig. 177 Recutting mortise for wedges

Fig. 178 Marking out treads

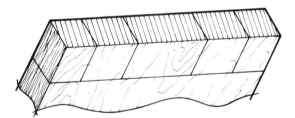

Fig. 179 Tenons marked for cutting

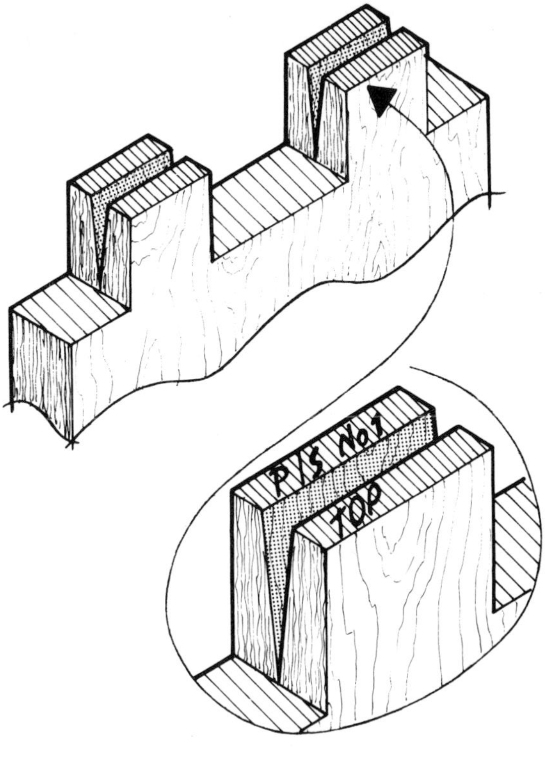

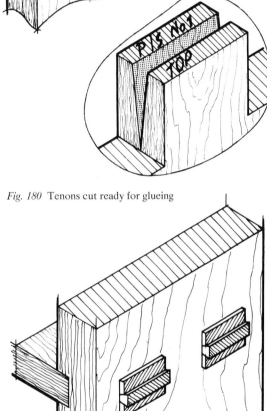

Fig. 180 Tenons cut ready for glueing

making sure that you mark each one so that you know where it goes. It is a good idea to mark them on the end of the tenons (as in fig. 180) for then you can sandpaper everything to get rid of all the pencil marks which would otherwise show—using a sanding block. After this you can glue up the joints, for which we would recommend Cascamite glue.

When you are all glued up and everything looks square, cut up some very fine wedges 1in long by 3mm, and tap them into the slots you cut in the tenons with a bit of glue (fig. 181). Wipe off the surplus glue with a wet rag and after checking it for squareness put away to dry.

While it is drying there are two brackets to make. These should be made to suit wherever you are going to hang the ladder, but they usually look something like the drawing (fig. 182), being the width of the gunwale to the toe

Fig. 181 Ladder glued and wedges home

rail, and being about 6in. Use 3in 12g. screws to fix the brackets. They are cut into the top of the ladder and screwed, once the ladder is cleaned up and nicely varnished.

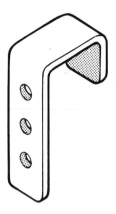

Fig. 182 Bracket for ladder

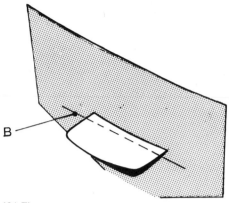

Fig. 184 Fit to transom

Boarding platform

Also called a 'Marlin' platform (fig. 183), these are great for swimming from, useful for getting into and out of a small dinghy, for skin-diving and for inspecting outdrive props, not to mention the protection that they can provide for the outboard or outdrive leg from accidental impact.

Don't be put off by the fact that numbers of the older traditional platforms were intricate constructions where almost every joint was cross-halved. There is a much simpler way of doing it, and the result will be just as robust for pleasure-cruiser use.

The first thing to do is make up a template, which can be of a piece of hardboard. Make sure the bit which touches the transom fits well (see fig. 184). Measure 2in along each edge from the transom, and draw a straight line—which is

where it will hinge up. On your template draw a 3in border, and up the centre a 2in strip (see fig. 185). Now, working from line B measure ½in spacings until you come to the end, and draw parallel lines (see fig. 186). The next step is to shade in every other space. These will be strips of white wood (pine) 1½in × ½in, and the all black patches will be mahogany blocks of 3in × ½in for the outsides, and 2in × ½in down the centre. Thus you will get the effect of a grating.

The strips are glued and pinned. When you get to this stage, glue your block and nail it in

Fig. 183 Boarding platform. As it should be

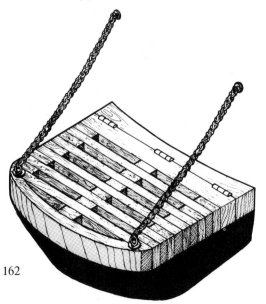

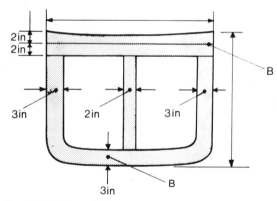

Fig. 185 Mark out platform

Fig. 186 Template all marked out

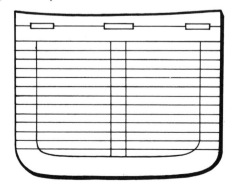

162

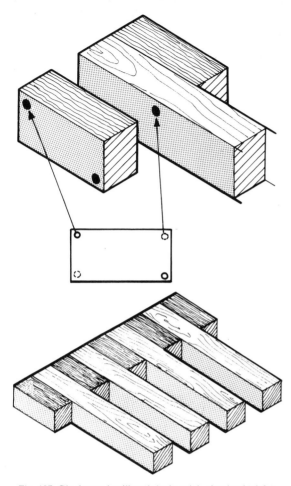

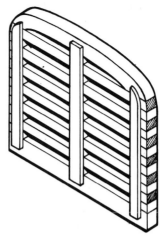

Fig. 188 Glued and screwed batons

Fig. 187 Glueing and nailing (*left*); how it looks glued (*right*)

diagonal corners to the 2in × 1½in piece of mahogany. Then, when you nail in the strip, the nails go in opposite corners. This way you should not nail on top of any other nails, and chance splitting the wood. When the glue has dried, plane the top and bottom level. Then clean off any glue which is stuck in the corners, to improve the look of the finished article.

Now you need three pieces of hardwood 2in × 14in, the length of the platform. These need to be chamfered on all the edges, and then screwed on the underneath of the platform as in the drawing (fig. 188).

Next you have the hinges to fit to the platform, and to the transom piece, which should be at least 2in wide, and the same thickness as the platform. You should use three hinges, one in the centre, and the other two about 2in in from the edge each side. The piece of wood which you have shaped to the transom can be screwed from the inside of the transom if it is GRP, or bolted if

it is a timber transom. Fit the platform about 6in above the waterline.

The final job is to fit two ring bolts on the outboard corners of the platform and run a chain up to the transom. This can then be unhooked and drawn in when not in use. The hooks on the transom can be screwed into the rubber if it is a wooden boat. If it is a glass hull it is a good idea to put a timber pad inside and out and the hook can be bolted on (see fig. 189). The pads can be about 5in × 3in × 1in thick, nicely chamfered on all corners. The bolts which go through the transom to hold the platform on can be galvanised coach bolts, and don't forget to use bedding and cotton around each bolt head.

When you come to varnish it make sure that you get in between the slats, and start off with the first coat 50/50 varnish and white spirit. Give at least three coats of varnish, for the platform will be constantly in and out of the water.

Fig. 189 Hooks to take chains

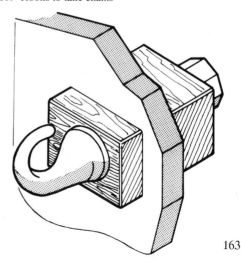

163

Chapter 36
Restoration is a labour of love

Restoration of a boat is a labour of love and devotion, and can take much longer to do than you ever dreamed.

However, if you have found the boat 'just right for you' and it is in need of a great deal of restoring to its former beauty, take heart, because if it is done properly it can become an asset.

Restoring an old boat obviously has to be done out of the water, so try to get the boat in a yard or a field as near to home as possible so that too much of your time isn't taken up in travelling.

When the boat comes out of the water get it chocked up in the level position. This can be done by using a spirit level laid along the waterline amidships, or if there is not one there and there is still some flooring or floor bearers in the boat use them to put your level on. If there is a bulkhead in the boat this can also be used to level up on. When the boat is level make sure that the keel is chocked up properly; try to keep the chocks about 6-8ft apart. The boat should have 'squats' put under the bilges as well as shores along the sheer (see fig. 190 B).

If the boat needs a big restoration job then it should be tackled in the same stages as when it was being built. So after the boat has been set up, check over the whole boat looking for defects and write them down as you go. You can get a surveyor to do this if it has not been surveyed in your purchasing.

When you have your list of repairs start on the hull first. The construction could be carvel round bilge, carvel hard chine, double diagonal, or single diagonal—these are about the commonest. So to replace a plank and a frame in each here is how to go about it.

1. Carvel

After the plank or planks have been marked for replacement, if their butt ends are not on a frame then put the butt in between the frames so that a butt block can be fitted. Drill a small hole and cut across the plank at the butt ends. This will stop you chopping past the marks when you become involved in chopping out the planks. If you cut across the plank in between the frames it is easier to split the plank out with a chisel across the fastenings (see fig. 191).

If there are a lot of planks to be replaced,

Photo 54 This lovely old lady will amply repay all the hard work which is going into her

Photo 55 A batten has been extended to produce the plank line to get the widths of the new planks correctly

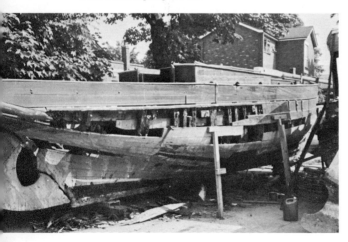

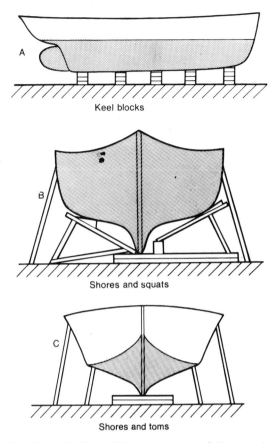

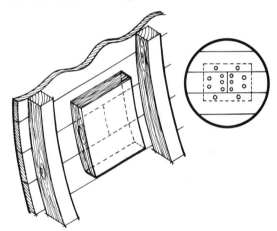

Fig. 190 **A** Keel blocks **B** Shores and squats **C** Shores and toms

stagger the butt joints—never have them all together or they will become a weak spot. Try to have at least two planks between each butt on the same line.

Next fit your butt blocks; they can be the same thickness as the planks, or thicker if you want. They should be fitted to the hull with the grain of the wood running downwards or at right angles to the planks' grain. The butt block should overlap the plank above and below by about one inch (see fig. 192).

Now we're ready for the plank. Get a strip of ply about 3in or 4in wide and tack it to the frames where the plank will be. Let it run where it wants to as you pin it to the frames (see fig. 193). Now you can either dumbstick the top edge of the old plank onto the spiling batten which will then be the bottom of the new plank, or you can take pitch measurements at each frame and mark them onto your batten. This is done by measuring up from the plank's edge on to the batten a chosen measurement, but when the batten is

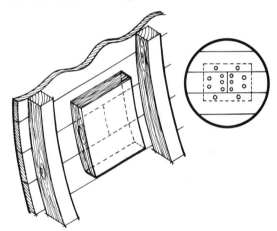

Fig. 192 Butt block and nailing pattern

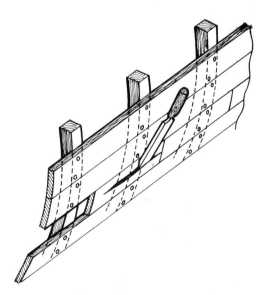

Fig. 191 Chopping out planks

Fig. 193 Spiling batten

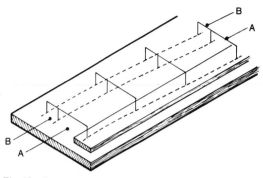

Fig. 194 Transferring measurements

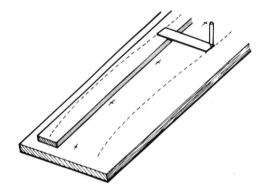

Fig. 195 Using a dumbstick

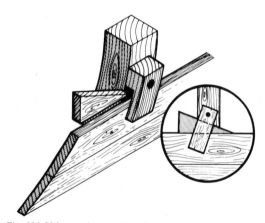

Fig. 196 Using wedges and hutches

being used to transfer the shape of the new plank the pitch measurement used must be transferred back at the same point (see fig. 194).

If you can, use the dumbstick on the batten for your new plank and pitch marks at set spacings along the length of the batten, this will give you the plank's width at those points, and it not so confusing.

If the planking being replaced spans several planks over the same frames so that you lose the

width of the planks, what you should do is measure the gap and divide it by the number of planks to go in; this will give you the plank's width at that point.

With carvel planking you must put a caulking seam on the planks. The seam is planed onto the ends of the planks and only on the bottom edge of the plank, the top edge being left square so that if hutches are used the wedges won't twist off (fig. 196).

2. Chine carvel

To replace chine carvel the method is the same as round bilge but there is little shape in the planks compared to round bilge.

3. Double diagonal

Double diagonal planking is one of the most expensive forms of planking to repair. Yet it can also be one of the quickest ways of planking up a new hull, and the wastage is practically nil. Another advantage is that the hull can be thinner, and this leads to a lighter displacement.

First, look over the inside and mark with a pencil how much is to come out. Then with a drill you drill right through to the outside at the part where each new butt joint will be, so that you can then see on the outside how much of the outer skin must be removed to fit the new inner skin.

When every plank is marked then you have the job of cutting off all the heads or rivet ends of the nails. This plays havoc with your chisel, but the job must be done and all the nails punched clear and withdrawn.

When we come to planking the inner skin, planks must run in line with the old ones, which makes it easier to rivet up. Once the inner skin is planked, calico is then stretched over the whole surface on the outside and tacked on, then covered with boiled linseed oil. This will prevent water getting between the seams where they cross over one another.

The outside skin is then put on, and again planked in the same line as the old skin. As each plank goes up you have to draw every plank seam frame and stringer onto the outer skin. You must do this, otherwise you will never know where to drill the nail holes to pull the planks together.

Photo 56 The first skin in a double diagonal repair is being laid

Fig. 197, showing how it is assembled, also shows one type of nail pattern, which pulls all the seams together. All the nails and screws should be well countersunk. If this is done properly your plane iron will not get damaged, for every inch of the new planking must be planed before painting or filling.

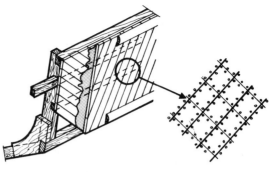

Fig. 197 Double diagonal construction showing type of nail pattern

4. Single skin diagonal

This looks like double diagonal but at every seam there runs a diagonal stringer which is notched into the frames, and the planks are either screwed or riveted to them. The planks are spiled the same way as carvel except that again there is little shape in them.

Double and single diagonal planking are not caulked in the seams, so the plank edges must be left square.

Where all the planks touch the chine or the gunwale in single or double diagonal, and even in chine carvel, they must be fixed with a bedding compound between the planks and the chine or gunwale.

Photo 57 Single skin diagonal under repair showing the seam battens to which the planking is fixed

Chapter 37
Frames, stopwaters and the stem

In most old carvel boats the frames are grown frames, i.e. cut out of solid timber. These are generally made up in three or four pieces. The joints are known as futtocks and these futtocks are staggered every other frame so that a weak spot does not occur. If you can remove the frame or section in one piece it will give you the plank bevel. If not, make a template of the frame and mark off every second plank the bevel of the hull to the frame (see fig. 198). This will give you the running bevel which must be planed off the frame to make it sit square and in line with the rest of the frames. If the frame has to be cut out and its new futtock is in line with the next frame's futtock, then fit a biscuit each side of the joint (see fig. 199).

Chine carvel frames are usually cut out in one and butt-jointed at the chine with a biscuit each side to hold the joint. The planks are usually screwed into the frames.

Double and single diagonal frames are similar to the chine frames, except that they have stringers housed into them which makes it a little harder to fit a new frame. Also you will not be able to get all the fastenings out of the double diagonal as the outer skin will prevent this, so just cut the fastenings flush with the planking.

With old boats the keel and garboards take quite a hammering, and if the boat is going to be out of the water for quite a while then the timber will shrink, leaving the keel bolts loose. So it might be a good idea either to rebolt or at least tighten them up. I would recommend you at least to drift one bolt out and inspect it for corrosion.

The garboards might need re-caulking and even re-fastening as they take a lot of punishment if the boat 'works', and when the boat is out of water the keel garboards take a lot of unaccustomed weight.

Another point to think about is the stopwaters. A stopwater is a wooden dowel rod made out of softwood, preferably pine, and is usually ⅜in to ¾in diameter, according to the size of the vessel.

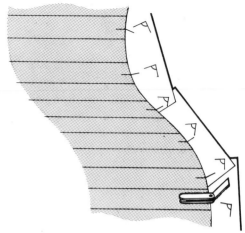

Fig. 198 Taking bevels for new frame

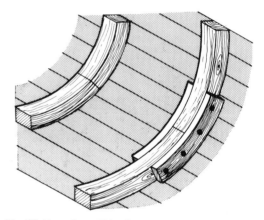

Fig. 199 Futtocks and biscuit

It is found at the rebate line where the keel's scarph joint runs past the planking line (fig. 200). Its purpose is to swell up and form a natural block for the water travelling up the scarph joint when it is working. It is situated from port to starboard the scarph joint through.

Sometimes, when the ship or boat's keel bolts move and the scarph joints work open the stopwater can become too small to serve its purpose. Even if the keel bolts are re-tightened it is too late to prevent the scarph joint from parting company. So, to make doubly sure the vessel will not keep leaking, you can either replace the stopwater, or put another one alongside it. It is not as easy as it sounds, as you have to make sure the stopwater does run down the joint of the scarph.

First you have to locate the run of the scarph behind the planking. This is done by projecting the line of the scarph up or along the plank end.

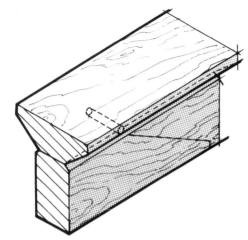

Fig. 200 Stopwater in keel

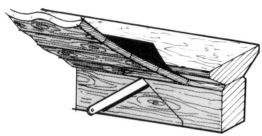

Fig. 201 Finding bevel

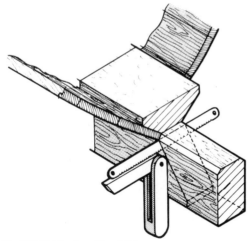

Fig. 202 Taking bevel for drilling

Also try to locate the back rebate or beading line on the hog. When this mark is found, that is where the old stopwater should be.

To make sure that your new stopwater hole will run squarely through the scarph joint you will have to use a square or a bevel as a drilling guide. Let's say that the scarph joint is slightly

Fig. 203 Where stopwater should go

open, by $\frac{1}{16}$in. Slip a hacksaw blade through the scarph, and slide it up to the edge of the plank. This will give you a guide as to the centre of the scarph joint.

Place a bevel off the keel and along the hacksaw blade's edge. Take the bevel and reproduce it onto a piece of plywood. This will be your drilling guide to give you the same height up the scarph both sides, and the hacksaw blade will give you the line of direction when drilling.

Obviously, when putting in a new stopwater you don't want to remove the garboard or stem plank, whichever the case may be. So you will have to drill through the plank. Don't worry though, the stopwater will protrude past the plank and you can trim it off flush with the planking after the job is done.

One word of warning: the stopwater should not be painted, primed, varnished, sealed or otherwise prevented from getting wet and swelling—which is the whole object of the exercise. You can, however, paint the end grain where it pokes through the planks, to prevent infestation.

To make the stopwater itself, for example with a hole $\frac{1}{2}$in in diameter, you will need to cut a length of softwood $\frac{5}{8}$in square, and long enough to poke out both ends of the hole you have drilled. The grain should be as straight as possible, with no knots or any blemishes which could cause the stopwater to snap when being driven home.

Get your chisel and taper the square to six sides at one end (see fig. 204). With the bit you used to drill for the new stopwater drill another hole into a piece of scrap wood. Now tap your stopwater-to-be into the hole in the scrap wood for about $\frac{3}{8}$in to $\frac{1}{2}$in. Withdraw it, and use the marks made by the scrap wood hole as a guide to plane your stopwater to a smooth cylindrical shape, keeping in mind that it must be a reasonably tight fit, which should need to be

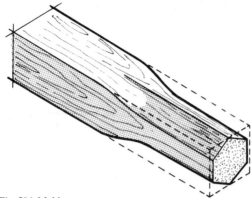

Fig. 204 Making stopwater

hammered home—but not with a 14lb sledge.

Your boat, of course, could be made of plywood, and if so and the hull is damaged then you can either fit in a new sheet or cut out a patch. If it is a new panel, try to take the old one off and use it as a template; if this is not possible make up a template of the panel out of thin ply. If it is just a hole, cut out the torn or ragged bits; you can cut out your patch first and offer it up to the hull and draw around it. Then cut out the hole. When this is done fit seam battens around the ply edges to form a rebate (see fig. 205). Glue and screw, or even nail the seam battens in place. Then in goes the patch, and fix.

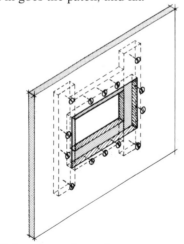

Fig. 205 Seam battens for patch

Stem

It might pay to put in a new leading edge on the stem if it has been knocked about. Run a straight line down the stem both sides and mark off the scarph (see fig. 206). Then find where the stem bolts are and cut on each side of them down to the line across the stem. Do this every 6in and

then chop out the wood (see fig. 207). You can then cut the stem bolts off and drift them back. You will then be able to get a plane onto the wood to make sure that the surface is flat.

If the bolts are in a good condition then just cut them behind the nuts and rethread them with a stock and die. Next comes the template marking, and mark each bolt if it is not being replaced.

Cut out your new stem and mark your bolt holes onto it and drill them with a clearance hole so that the stem can slide on and off for fitting. When the fit is satisfactory slip off the stem and put plenty of bedding between the timber, making sure that there is a cotton grommet behind each bolt washer when the stem is fixed. Put a good screw in at the scarph end and then fair in the whole stem with your plane.

Staying at the sharp end, the forefoot also could be suspect. If it is, the method or repair is the same as the stem, except that you might want to laminate it as the curve of the forefoot may be rather sharp.

If you are going to laminate, the first thing is to make your template to the shape of the forefoot with your scarph joints cut on it so that it is the correct shape for the boat. When that is done you must make up a glueing jig. This can be done

Photo 58 Makeshift glueing jig for a new forefoot. Oh that the weather was always like this!

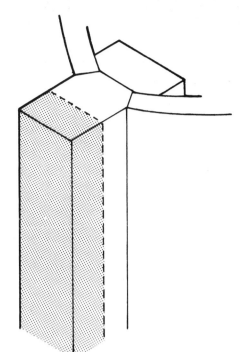

Fig. 206 Marking out where to cut

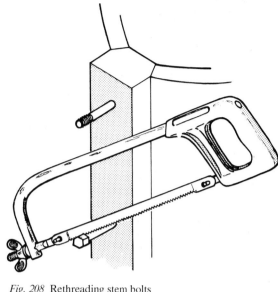

Fig. 208 Rethreading stem bolts

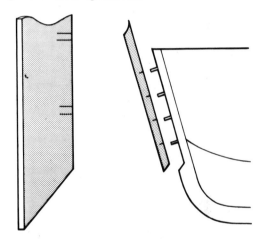

Fig. 209 Template of stem and bolts

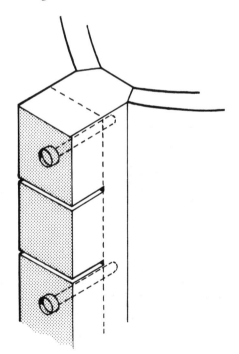

Fig. 207 Saw cuts to help chopping out

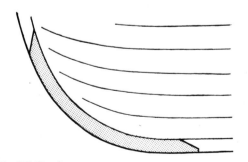

Fig. 210 Forefoot

on the bench or an old door (or even a sheet of ply) but it must not be flexible, because if it is your laminating will get a twist in it.

Now place your template on the jig's base (the

door or whatever you're using) and draw around it. Then cut up some wooden blocks to be screwed about 10in apart along the inside of the curve. Some more blocks will need to be screwed

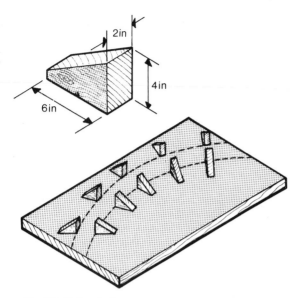

Fig. 211 Jig for glueing

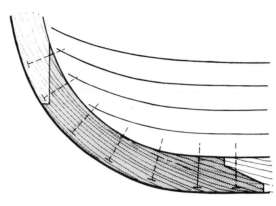

Fig. 213 Scarphs and bolting forefoot

Fig. 212 Glueing up forefoot

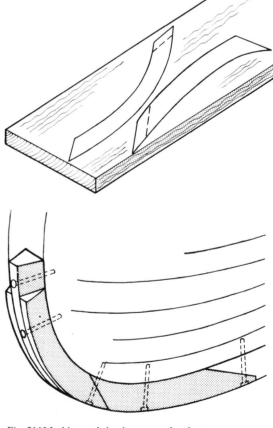

Fig. 214 Marking and shaping grown forefoot

opposite the ones on the inside of the curve, and the blocks on the outside of the curve should be about 1in off the line (see fig. 211). This is to make it possible to wrap the laminations around the jig and tap home wedges against the blocks to close up the laminations (see fig. 212). Cramps can be used between the blocks to make sure that the laminations close up and glue.

One important thing to remember is to put newspaper over the jig so that the laminations sit on the paper and don't come into contact with the wood of the jig, or you will never release the job from the jig. Let the glue dry and cure for a few days before releasing it from the jig.

Place your pattern on the laminations and mark off the scarph joints and shape it up to suit the boat. When re-fixing it put plenty of bedding between the forefoot and the hull. If you have a piece of wood to use instead of laminating, make sure that you don't get too much short grain— so you might have to put in an extra joint to lose the short grain.

Chapter 38
Caulking and paying

One of the biggest mysteries of the shipwright's craft is caulking—but it need not be so. The most obvious evidence of caulking is between the planks of wooden decks, but in certain constructions it is also found between hull planks, in superstructure, at the keel and elsewhere. Generally speaking, the method of tackling the re-caulking remains much the same wherever it is found.

The first part of the job is raking out, and to do this you will need to make up your own seam rake. This is a piece of steel about 10in long by about ¼in to ⅜in diameter. It can be an old file, heated and bent. About 4in from the end you bend this to a right-angle. Then grind or file this to a chisel-like point. As with all such hand tools, a handle is essential. File handles can be bought from ironmongers.

With the rake in the seam, pull towards you with one hand, pressing down with the other hand to make the rake dig into the pitch. Care must be taken to prevent the rake skidding out and across the plank surface. The rake chips out old pitch (or if hull planking, stopping) and can even pull out old cotton or oakum which needs replacing.

Rake out only about 5ft to 10ft at one go, or just enough for you to replace easily at one session.

If the caulking looks in good order after the seam has been raked out, it may only need hardening up. That's where one just goes along the seam with a caulking iron, hardening down the cotton or oakum.

The size of caulking iron to use depends on the width of the seam. Normally they are about ³⁄₁₆in wide, so your iron will be a single seam or a blunt iron. The method of making the caulking irons is described a bit further on.

When you start using the irons, try to make every hit the same pressure, and get a constant rhythm which helps to regularise the pressure. To harden down you travel along the seam with the iron, moving about 1½in after every hit. When you have completed this you repay the seam with new pitch (see below).

Re-caulking is required if the caulking comes out with the seam rake and looks a bit rotten, or with oakum if it is very dry. If it is cotton, look to see how many strands there are. If, for example, there are three, put three-strand cotton back. If you put back more you are likely to open up the rest of the seam where you start and finish.

Caulking cotton is made up of eight or ten stands. Cut off and unravel three strands about one and a third times the length of the seam you are going to caulk. Tie one end of the three strands to a rail or post and the other end to a bent nail in a wheel-brace or slow-speed drill. Spin the nail until the cotton has rewound itself like a piece of loose rope. This is, surprisingly enough, called 'spinning cotton'. Untie the ends and roll it up like a ball of wool; your cotton is now ready to caulk with.

Caulking is rather more difficult than it looks. It's not just a matter of belting in the cotton—you have to drive it home evenly. This is done by using a very thin caulking iron which is almost knife-sharp, and the cotton is put in in tucks. These are when the cotton is pinned in small loops along the seam before caulking proper. The tucks are then hit home into the seam with a constant rhythmic hitting, rocking the iron

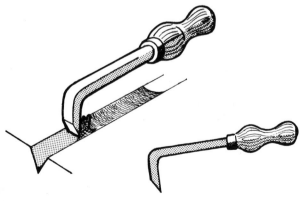

Fig. 215 Seam rake

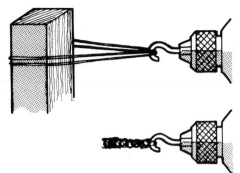

Fig. 216 Spinning cotton

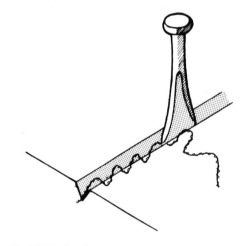

Fig. 217 Tucks of cotton

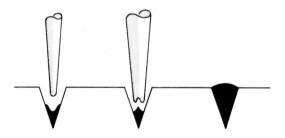

Fig. 218 Caulking (*left*), hardening (*centre*),
seam payed (*right*)

slightly as it is moved along. The rocking motion helps to prevent you jamming the iron into the seam.

After you have done the initial part of the job with the thin caulking iron, you go over the whole seam again with a single seam iron which hardens down the cotton, following which you can re-pay your seam with pitch. One thing to remember is when you start and finish your

caulking, caulk lightly so as not to open up the old seams any further.

If caulking with oakum, the method is much the same except the spinning. Instead of using a wheelbrace the oakum has to be picked and rolled. It comes in small bales, about 5lb each, and has to be picked and thinned out to the thickness you need. Picking entails getting out all the bits of twig and stalks, and then you stretch and roll the oakum on your thigh to the thickness and diameter required. This is then coiled, ready for caulking. A hint for caulking with oakum: dip the iron tips in paraffin to stop them sticking.

Paying the seams means pouring in the pitch or, if you prefer, Jefferies Marine Glue. The two important points to remember are: (a) never let it boil, which lets in too much air and breaks down the properties; and (b) always let it overflow as it shrinks down a lot. When you have scraped off the excess with your deck scraper, iron out the seams with your home-made smoothing seam iron which will smooth and shine the seam like a new yacht's deck. Heat up the seam iron so that when you run it over the pitch it will just melt the top to smooth out the seam.

You may well have to make your own caulking irons as they are almost impossible to buy. First of all, make a fire—a hot fire, like a blacksmith's forge. Use coke if possible, and you can give it a blow from a vacuum cleaner to make it hotter. Take a length of ¾in diameter iron rod, about 3ft long, a 2lb hammer and a 20lb to 30lb ballast block or iron weight. Heat about 3in of your rod until it is a nice bright yellow. Move it swiftly to your anvil (the weight or block) and beat out the end of the rod (see fig. 219). It will take five or six heatings to do it properly. Do not hit the metal when it gets too cool or it will split and be ruined. When you are hammering, work from the centre outwards, trying to keep it even.

Having beaten out the iron to your satisfaction, clean it up with a flat file. File out the hammer marks and clean up the edge. If you are making a seam iron cut the groove last of all.

Incidentally, the smoothing iron is the only one which is used hot— the other caulking irons described below are all used unheated.

Starting with the cleaned up hammered rod, you will then file or grind it back to the approximate area shown by the dotted line in the illustration (fig. 220), which means that your ¾in

Fig. 219 Hammering out

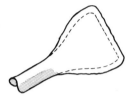

Fig. 220 Shape to grind to

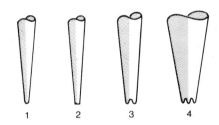

Fig. 221 Types of points end on

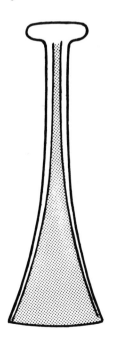

Fig. 222 Iron face on

Fig. 223 Smoothing iron

Fig. 224 Deck scraper

bar will finish in the form of a blade about 2½in wide and 5in to 6in long.

No1 (fig. 221) is a knife-edge seam iron. No2 is a blunt iron, with an edge $\frac{3}{32}$in wide. No3 is a single seam iron on which the edge has a total width of $\frac{1}{8}$in and a 'V' slot $\frac{1}{16}$in deep. No4 is a double seam iron with a total edge width of $\frac{3}{16}$in and twin 'V' slots $\frac{3}{32}$in deep.

Now to the smoothing iron—the one that is used hot. This must be a bit wider than the seam. The steel to make the smoothing iron starts as flat 1in × ¾in metal. It is cranked half way along its length, and the outer end tapered to take a stout handle. The working end is slightly curved with a file and/or sander.

The deck scraper to be used to remove excess pitch is also wider than the seam. It is a flat file, heated and bent like your seam rake, and sharpened to a chisel edge. This completes a set of caulking irons.

Chapter 39
Sealing decks and checking fastenings

When all the caulking is done and the boat still tends to leak through the deck, it might not be the deck seams but the timber itself. When the timber starts to get old it begins to break down in the pores and then it splits.

One way out of this problem without having to re-deck the boat is to wash the whole deck over with raw linseed oil. Brush it on with a broom and let it dry, and then give it another coat. It might need three coats, but it will do the job. The way it works is to fill up all the splits and cracks and pores with oil, forming a skin which seals the wood. Water then cannot get past the oil.

Of course you can paint the deck as well, but there's nothing a nice as a bare laid deck.

Graving pieces, mentioned in Chapter 15 earlier, are the best way of dealing with a small area of rot on a wooden deck, or in a handrail or part of the superstructure.

Graving pieces are generally put in where rot has just begun, so all the work you are doing with new and old timber needs to be protected, otherwise it will probably rot rather more quickly than expected. The processes for dealing with wet rot, dry rot or woodworm in old timber is set out in Chapter 1.

Photo 59 A new coach roof has been fitted to this working boat and the deck is ready for paying

Fastenings

When you are looking at the hull it's a good idea to check all the fastenings on inlets and outlets, and even chainplates if it is a sail boat. With old boats they are bound to have either corroded or broken down through electrolysis.

So, take out the bolts and replace them. If they look good to you then take one and put it in a vice and hammer it over; if it breaks and shows a bright gold in the centre with a definite change to dull as though there were two separate metals, then that is a sign of electrolysis. Another way is to tap the bolt with a hammer and if it flakes off in chips the bolt has had it.

It's really not worth saying that they are O.K. for a couple more years—if you are not sure change them anyway.

Hull fastenings should be looked at also, especially with double diagonal chine construction, as in a choppy sea they tend to pound and the forward end takes a lot of strain. If the screws into the frames and stringers are corroded. or even broken you can replace them with a bigger gauge screw or rescrew alongside the old fastening. Another way is to fit in extra frames over the stringers between the existing frames, and screw up through the hull.

Chapter 40
On deck again

On to the deck now. There are several ways of laying decking; firstly, the laid deck comprises planks nailed into the deck beams and caulked just like carvel planking on the hull, except that the decking is composed of parallel planks. The butt joints always end on a beam and are staggered the same as hull planks. The usual method for deck planks is as shown in the illustration; the shift of butts, as it is called, is spread over 6ft, whereas the decking can be over a 3ft span. The king plank is usually twice as wide as the decking and this runs down the centre line of the boat. The outside plank around the deck is called the covering board and again is usually twice the width of the decking.

In very old boats the bulwark posts run through the covering board. Although this is a very strong method it leads to a lot of rot around the covering board.

The second method of decking is ply, and this is much cheaper than a laid deck. The ply can be scarphed together or butt-jointed on seam battens. One usually has stringers chopped into the deck beams running parallel off the centre line, and the ply is glued and screwed onto the beams and stringers (fig. 227). Another way is to lay ply and then lay a thin teak decking on top which is glued to the ply to look like a laid teak deck. This is not caulked but the deck seams are payed to look realistic (fig. 228).

Where do the decks leak? The commonest places are around the cabin sides, along the covering board, around hatches and deck-fitting bolts and, if it is a laid deck, through the deck seams themselves. So what is the remedy?

Cabin side leaks usually occur when the deck quadrant has been broken or the bedding between the quadrant and the deck has dried out and cracked; so remove the quadrant and re-bed it back onto the deck. The covering board with a laid deck tends to curl a little, breaking the bedding joint. Some boats have the bulwark posts coming through the covering board and this leads to a weakness around the covering

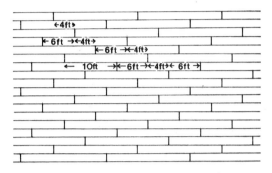

Fig. 225 Shift of butts

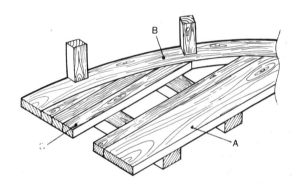

Fig. 226 **A** King plank, **B** Covering board, **C** decking

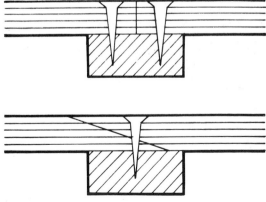

Fig. 227 Ply decks

177

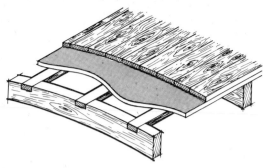

Fig. 228 Laid deck on ply

board, making it tend to split and move when the boat bangs against something. The seams around the post should be re-payed and the post itself checked for rot. The deck fittings tend to be pulled and lifted, also breaking what bedding joint there was, and sometimes the water gets down the bolts. This calls for the bolts to be drifted out and new cotton grommets to be fitted, and at the same time for the fitting to be re-bedded.

While we are on the subject of leaking decks, the gunwale rubbing strake should be looked at as this can sometimes prevent the water getting under the covering board, although the main purpose is to protect.

Cabin sides

Most old boats' cabin sides and coamings are made from solid timber and are either jointed or glued together.

Let us look at a motor cruiser's cab-side and see how it is made, and consider its weak spots. The sketch is of a 40ft cabin side made out of mahogany. It has a top rail and a bottom rail with posts mortised and tenoned in to the rails to form window apertures. The posts generally run up alongside a bulkhead where a fastening can be made through the cab-side into the bulkhead. At the after end where the side runs down to form a coaming, the mahogany can be jointed by halflap joints or butt joints with a glued spline down the centre. The halflap should be done so that the seam of the joint is on the bottom outside, as fig. 229 shows; the water then cannot run into the joint and coaming.

Carlings

As I'm sure some readers who have wooden boats with timber cab-sides find, they have a tendency to leak along the carlings. Usually they just need new bedding under the quadrant, that is if the construction has a quadrant.

Let's look at three methods of fixing a cab-side to the side deck and treat each one for possible leaks. Fig. 231 shows probably the most common method. The bedding compound usually dries

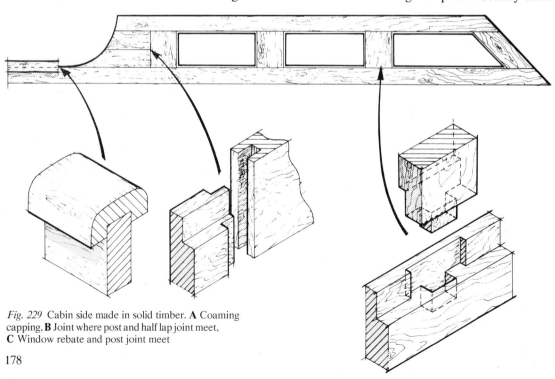

Fig. 229 Cabin side made in solid timber. **A** Coaming capping, **B** Joint where post and half lap joint meet, **C** Window rebate and post joint meet

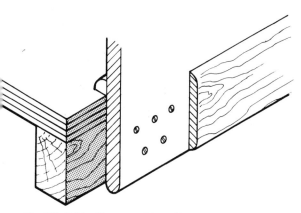

Fig. 230 Cabin side screwed to carlings

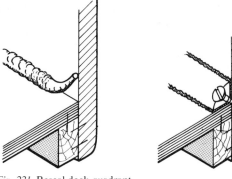

Fig. 231 Reseal deck quadrant

up and cracks under the quadrant and between the carling and cab-side, so the water can then find its way down. What must be done is to remove the quadrant and scrape off all the dried bedding, then very lightly, with only one or maybe two strands of caulking cotton, caulk down between the deck and cab-side, making sure that you don't force the cab-side away from the carling.

Mix up some bedding compound and run it along the corner, then put back the quadrant and re-screw it. Make sure that the quadrant has plenty of bedding behind it, and that it oozes out over the edges. This should do the trick.

The next method of fixing the cab-side to the deck is not as strong as the first but is commonly used (see fig. 232). The cab-side sits on the deck and is screwed to the coaming, which in turn is screwed to the carling. The cab-side is set down on bedding and a run of caulking cotton. If the cab-side leaks, all you can do is re-bed the quadrant.

One other method sometimes used is the next one. There is a moulding, for example 2in by 1¼in, glued and screwed to the deck. The cab-side sits on top of the moulding, bedded down and through-bolted to the carling (see fig. 233).

The cab-side is thinner than the top of the moulding, which leaves about a ¼in lip on the inside. A coaming is fitted to the inside of the carling, which forms a channel or gutter which catches any water from the windows, etc. Drain holes are drilled at various places such as bulkheads or corner posts.

This method is a lot more work but is virtually leakproof. As an extreme example, if the cab-side parted company with the moulding, the gutter would still drain the water back out.

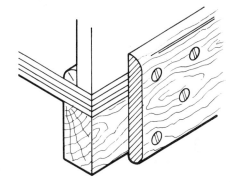

Fig. 232 Cab-side sits on deck and screwed to coaming

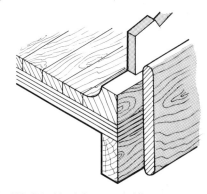

Fig. 233 Cab-side sitting on moulding

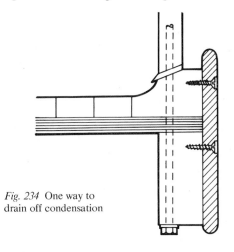

Fig. 234 One way to drain off condensation

179

Chapter 41
Covering coach roofs, bulwarks, spars and rigging

Most old boats had their coach roofs canvassed, which is a very effective method of waterproofing if done properly. To re-canvas a coachroof you must strip off all the old canvas, and take all the beadings and quadrants off as well where the canvas ends. It is best to start right at the beginning, so get the sanding disc working and sand off all the paint under the old canvas, then prime the roof with at least three coats of a good quality primer paint.

Now fit the canvas to the roof. Use about 10oz material rather than one that is too heavy, otherwise it becomes too hard to work when the fitting and tacking starts. The canvas should overlap where the beadings go and one edge can be tacked down with copper tacks spaced about ½in apart (see fig. 235).

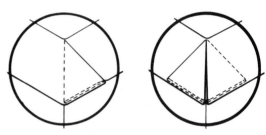

Fig. 236 Stretching canvas

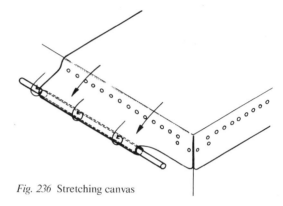

Fig. 237 Way to fix corners

and wrap a small piece of timber up in the end of the canvas and use it as a lever to stretch out the canvas (see fig. 236).

Stretch and tack as you go, and when you come to a corner don't cut it but fold it around (see fig. 237). Where the seam comes across the roof the method of jointing the next strip of canvas is as shown in fig. 238, and tack down. Then start again on the next strip.

You must paint over the canvas with primer before the paint under the canvas goes off; this bonds the two coats of paint together.

When all the roof is covered and the paint dried, you can fit the beading and quadrants, then last of all cut off all the canvas below the beadings with a very sharp knife or chisel. The canvas can be painted over with undercoat and gloss to finish off.

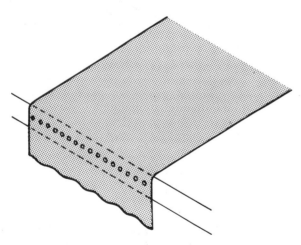

Fig. 235 Tacking down sides

Only do one strip at a time, otherwise you will end up the same colour as the roof. In the old days the canvas was painted with red lead paint, but with modern health regulations red lead paint is not manufactured, so use an oxide primer. Give the area you are going to cover first another coat of primer and straight away lay over the canvas. Get on the other side of the roof

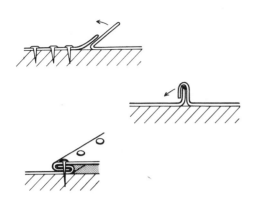

Fig. 238 How to do seams

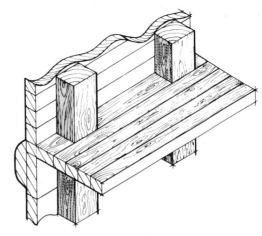

Fig. 239 Covering board fitted between posts

Bulwarks

Before we leave the deck area, bulwarks can be a bit of a problem where they cut through the deck. So, as new ones might need to go in, here is how to do it. Let us say that five or six need doing, some together and some spaced out between old ones. Remove the bulwark capping first and if the bulwark planking is no good remove that as well.

Now cut off all the old post or posts at deck level, and if the covering board is fitted in between the posts as in fig. 239, then just chop it out so that you can chop or split out the rest of the post. However, if the covering board is much wider (as in fig. 240) than the posts, then chopping out the posts must be done carefully. Use a drill and drill down into the post as much as possible to make it easier to chop out (see fig. 241).

There should be a bolt running through the planking and shelf pinning the bulwark post, but if the post is a continuation of the frames then there might not be. What you will have to do here is cut the frame about three planks down and chop out. Try to stagger the joints if the posts are all next to each other; one way is to run a scarph joint over the frame instead of a futtock joint (see fig. 243).

Returning to the posts, if they are separate from the frames, when you come to fit them try to get them to follow the hull's shape one or two planks down from the shelf. Bolt them lightly through the shelf and planking, allowing them to wobble a bit.

Run a fairing-in batten along the bulwarks and sight them in. If they need to lean outboard or

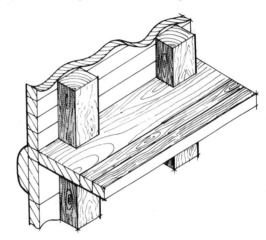

Fig. 240 Wide covering board

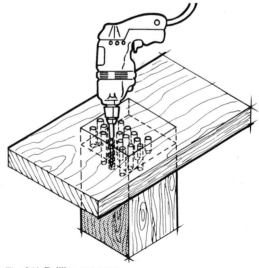

Fig. 241 Drilling out posts

181

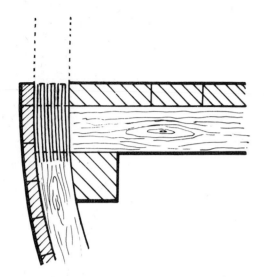

Fig. 242 How far to drill

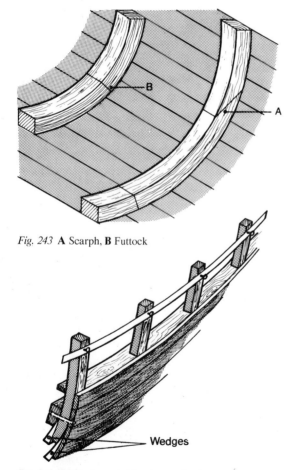

Fig. 243 **A** Scarph, **B** Futtock

Wedges

Fig. 244 Fairing in posts (showing wedges)

inboard as the case may be to fair in, cut some nice wedges and tap them home either between the hull and post or the shelf and post (see fig. 244). When the posts are faired in you can tighten up the bolts and screw the wedges so that nothing will move.

If the posts are part of the frames then you must be much more accurate in your cutting out of the post. It is still a good idea to bolt through the shelf.

Depending on how many bulwark posts are replaced, you can lose the fair line along the top. If this is so run a long batten along the top and stand back and sight it in. When it looks nice and fair mark it in on the posts and cut them off.

Again, if you are going to put new bulwark capping around, you can either scarph them or 'bird's-beak' them together (see fig. 245).

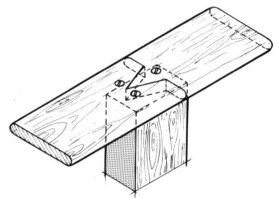

Fig. 245 Bird's-beaking a handrail

Spars

When restoring a sailing or motor yacht the mast and spars should not be overlooked; they are a very costly item to replace, so check over the one you have or the ones you are going to buy and alter to suit your boat.

If the mast has any splits in it which are not too wide and you think they won't close up again then you can fit a brass or copper band around it. First cut two pieces of wood about 3in × 2in thick, and cut a hollow in them. Now cramp them together as close as possible to the widest part of the split and try to close up the split (see fig. 246). You can pour in some glue if you like.

The band can be about 3in wide; punch nail holes about every ½in apart, about ¼in from the edge. Using copper nails, nail the end of the strip

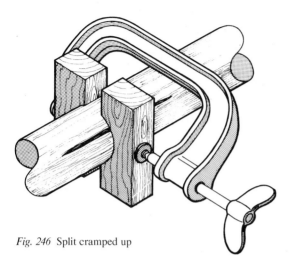

Fig. 246 Split cramped up

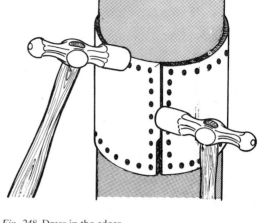

Fig. 248 Dress in the edges

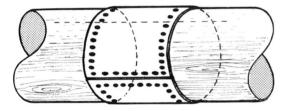

Fig. 247 Fitting brass or copper band

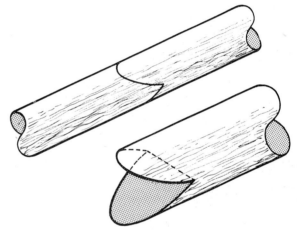

Fig. 249 Glueing a splay on a boom

at the opposite end to the split, and as you wrap the strip around keep it tight and square and nail it as you go (see fig. 247). If you come to the end or the beginning and it is a bit too long, trim it off with a file or tin-snips and nail it.

When it is all nailed, go around the edge of the brass and dress it into the wood very lightly (see fig. 248).

To lengthen or repair a broken spar or mast you can scarph the new piece on, and to play safe, if you are not confident with the scarph joint, fit a band around it as well. The scarph should be at least six times the diameter of the spar and the scarph should be a 'splay'.

Before glueing a splay, or lip scarph, fit it dry and put a screw at each end, because when you come to glue and cramp it, it will slide all over the place. You can screw it together and then cramp up, and when it is all dry take out the screws and clean up with a plane and fill or stop up the screw holes before varnishing.

If you want you can join a spar together by doing a splay on each side of the spar and screw and cramp (see fig. 249).

One point to bear in mind with the mast is whether to use a tabernacle, or whether to step the mast through the deck. We rather like tabernacles as they enable you to go further inland, and if you wish just to motor and not roll about all you have to do is to drop the mast and this gets rid of a lot of the pendulum motion.

The tabernacle needs to be strong enough to take the strains, and tall enough to allow the mast when pivoting to clear the cab top. The tabernacle should be through-bolted and not screwed, and if it can sit over a beam all the better. If it is sitting where the mast once went through the deck you should either reinforce the deck area with a bulkhead or fit a mast support

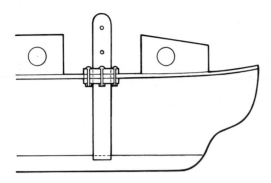

Fig. 250 Tabernacle on a old boat

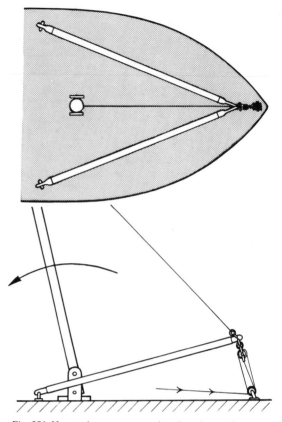

Fig. 251 How to lower a mast, using sheer-legs and a purchase from stem to forestay, taken to a winch

as though the mast still ran down to the keel. As you see in the illustration (fig. 250) this is what was done to an old sailing boat once, and it was very successful.

If you fit a tabernacle, how are you going to get the mast up or down without injuring yourself? There are lots of ways, but one of the best is to use two sheer legs which are bolted to the deck at the bulwarks and meet at the stem. They are shackled to the forestay, and a block and tackle is connected to the stem head and the forestay; the forestay is then unshackled from the stem head and the mast is lowered aft while the sheer legs rise up.

If you are altering the rig, make sure that the chain plates are well fastened and if possible into a frame or timber in the hull. Never just fasten into the planking—at least fit a pad on the inside to spread the load. On some motor sailers the chain plates are fixed onto the cabin sides or wheelhouse roof; all you can do here is make sure that the fastenings are man enough and sound.

Rigging

This is a major subject in its own right, and there are good books available which deal with nothing else. If you are going to re-rig I suggest you study one or two.

The important things to remember are, firstly, to study the projected re-rig on paper before you do anything, and make sure that the centres of effort look like being in the right places for all the sails before you commit yourself to anything, and secondly, to try to ensure that if anything does not work out as you had hoped you can still adapt your first ideas.

As far as the standing rigging is concerned, make sure that the masts are stayed adequately forward, backwards, and sideways, with as wide an angle as possible at the point where the shrouds meet the mast. You need at least two side shrouds, one slightly forward of the mast and one abaft it, each side. The strains on a tall mast may be such that topmast stays are needed as well as lower shrouds, and probably spreaders as well.

Shrouds can be attached to the mast either by a spider band or by having soft eyes which slip over the mast, suitably laced one to the other, and pulled down to sit on cheeks through-bolted to the mast or over the spreaders.

Wire rigging of a suitable weight and lay—1 × 19 is usually accepted as being the right one for standing rigging—should be set up with rigging screws (sometimes called bottlescrews) and shackles, and there is no sense in having any one part of the chain—mast, eye, shackle, wire, rigging screw, shackle, eye, chainplate—any weaker or stronger than the rest.

It is a rule of thumb that a boat should be capable of being lifted out of the water by the mast, relying on the strength of the standing rigging to support the entire weight.

Blocks can be hung from the mast on wire grommets or pendants, or shackled on to the spider band. It is important to try to keep the weight of mast fittings down as much as possible, because weight high up has a leverage effect as the boat rolls, and to save a little weight can make an appreciable difference to stability and motion.

Setting up topmasts, rigging topsails, organising bowsprits and bumkins, are all part of the fun of renovating old boats, but the ramifications are too wide to enable us to discuss it all here. Sufficient to repeat the advice given earlier— read it up in as many books as possible, and try to find a real expert to help. But *then* do as much as you can yourself.

Appendix
Extracts from the *International Regulations for Preventing Collisions at Sea,* 1972

Rule 21 *Definitions*

(a) "Masthead light" means a white light placed over the fore and aft centreline of the vessel showing an unbroken light over an arc of the horizon of 225° and so fixed as to show the light from right ahead to 22.5° abaft the beam on either side of the vessel.

(b) "Sidelights" means a green light on the starboard side and a red light on the port side each showing an unbroken light over an arc of the horizon of 112.5° and so fixed as to show the light from right ahead to 22.5° abaft the beam on its respective side. In a vessel of less than 20 metres in length the sidelights may be combined in one lantern carried on the fore and aft centreline of the vessel.

(c) "Sternlight" means a white light placed as nearly as practicable at the stern showing an unbroken light over an arc of the horizon of 135° and so fixed as to show the light 67.5° degrees from right aft on each side of the vessel.

(d) "Towing light" means a yellow light having the same characteristics as the "sternlight" defined in paragraph (c) of this Rule.

(e) "All-round light" means a light showing an unbroken light over an arc of the horizon of 360°.

(f) "Flashing light" means a light flashing at regular intervals at a frequency of 120 flashes or more per minute.

Rule 22 *Visibility of Lights*

The lights prescribed in these Rules shall have an intensity as specified in Section 8 of Annex I to these Regulations so as to be visible at the following minimum ranges:

(a) In vessels of 50 metres or more in length:

— a masthead light, 6 miles;
— a sidelight, 3 miles;
— a sternlight, 3 miles;

— a towing light, 3 miles;
— a white, red, green or yellow all-round light, 3 miles.

(b) In vessels of 12 metres or more in length but less than 50 metres in length:

— a masthead light, 5 miles; except that where the length of the vessel is less than 20 metres, 3 miles;
— a sidelight, 2 miles;
— a sternlight, 2 miles;
— a towing light, 2 miles;
— a white, red, green or yellow all-round light, 2 miles.

(c) In vessels of less than 12 metres in length:

— a masthead light, 2 miles;
— a sidelight, 1 mile;
— a sternlight, 2 miles;
— a towing light, 2 miles;
— a white, red, green or yellow all-round light, 2 miles.

Rule 23 *Power-driven Vessels underway*

(a) A power-driven vessel underway shall exhibit:

(i) a masthead light forward;

(ii) a second masthead light abaft of and higher than the forward one; except that a vessel of less than 50 metres in length shall not be obliged to exhibit such light but may do so;

(iii) sidelights;

(iv) a sternlight.

(b) An air-cushion vessel when operating in the non-displacement mode shall, in addition to the lights prescribed in paragraph (a) of this Rule, exhibit an all-round flashing yellow light.

(c) A power-driven vessel of less than 7 metres in length and whose maximum speed does not exceed 7 knots may, in lieu of the lights prescribed in paragraph (a) of this Rule, exhibit an all-round white light. Such vessel shall, if practicable, also exhibit sidelights.

Rule 25 *Sailing Vessels underway and Vessels under Oars*

(a) A sailing vessel underway shall exhibit:

(i) sidelights;

(ii) a sternlight.

(b) In a sailing vessel of less than 12 metres in length the lights prescribed in paragraph (a) of this Rule may be combined in one lantern carried at or near the top of the mast where it can best be seen.

(c) A sailing vessel underway may, in addition to the lights prescribed in paragraph (a) of this Rule, exhibit at or near the top of the mast, where they can best be seen, two all-round lights in a vertical line, the upper being red and the lower green, but these lights shall not be exhibited in conjunction with the combined lantern permitted by paragraph (b) of this Rule.

(d) (i) A sailing vessel of less than 7 metres in length shall, if practicable, exhibit the lights prescribed in paragraph (a) or (b) of this Rule, but if she does not, she shall have ready at hand an electric torch or lighted lantern showing a white light which shall be exhibited in sufficient time to prevent collison.

(ii) A vessel under oars may exhibit the lights prescribed in the Rule for sailing vessels, but if she does not, she shall have ready at hand an electric torch or lighted lantern showing a white light which shall be exhibited in sufficient time to prevent collision.

(e) A vessel proceeding under sail when also being propelled by machinery shall exhibit forward where it can best be seen a conical shape, apex downwards.

Annex 1
Positioning and technical details of lights and shapes

1 *Definition*

The term "height above the hull" means height above the uppermost continuous deck.

2 *Vertical positioning and spacing of lights*

(a) On a power-driven vessel of 20 metres or more in length the masthead lights shall be placed as follows:

(i) the forward masthead light, or if only one masthead light is carried, then that light, at a height above the hull of not less than 6 metres, and, if the breadth of the vessel exceeds 6 metres, then at a height above the hull not less than such breadth, so however that the light need not be placed at a greater height above the hull than 12 metres;

(ii) when two masthead lights are carried the after one shall be at least 4.5 metres vertically higher than the forward one.

(b) The vertical separation of masthead lights of power-driven vessels shall be such that in all normal conditions of trim the after light will be seen over and separate from the forward light at a distance of 1,000 metres from the stem when viewed from sea level.

(c) The masthead light of a power-driven vessel of 12 metres but less than 20 metres in length shall be placed at a height above the gunwale of not less then 2.5 metres.

(d) A power-driven vessel of less than 12 metres in length may carry the uppermost light at a height of less than 2.5 metres above the gunwale. When however a masthead light is carried in addition to sidelights and a sternlight, then such masthead light shall be carried at least 1 metre higher than the sidelights.

(e) One of the two or three masthead lights prescribed for a power-driven vessel when engaged in towing or pushing another vessel shall be placed in the same position as the forward masthead light of a power-driven vessel.

(f) In all circumstances the masthead light or lights shall be so placed as to be above and clear of all other lights and obstructions.

(g) The sidelights of a power-driven vessel shall be placed at a height above the hull not greater than three quarters of that of the forward masthead light. They shall not be so low as to be interfered with by deck lights.

(h) The sidelights, if in a combined lantern and carried on a power-driven vessel of less than 20 metres in length, shall be placed not less than 1 metre below the masthead light.

3 *Horizontal position and spacing of lights*

(a) When two masthead lights are prescribed for

a power-driven vessel, the horizontal distance between them shall not be less than one half of the length of the vessel but need not be more than 100 metres. The forward lights shall be placed not more than one quarter length of the vessel from the stem.

(b) On a vessel of 20 metres or more in length the sidelights shall not be placed in front of the forward masthead lights. They shall be placed on or near the side of the vessel.

5 *Screens for sidelights*

The sidelights shall be fitted with inboard screens painted matt black, and meeting the requirements of Section 9 of this Annex. With a combined lantern, using a single vertical filament and a very narrow division between the green and red sections, external screens need not be fitted.

9 *Horizontal sectors*

(a) (i) In the forward direction, sidelights as fitted on the vessel must show the minimum required intensities. The intensities must decrease to reach practical cut-off between 1° and 3° outside the prescribed sectors.

(ii) For sternlights and masthead lights and at 22.5° abaft the beam for sidelights, the minimum required intensities shall be maintained over the arc of the horizon up to 5° within the limits of the sectors prescribed in Rule 21. From 5° within the prescribed sectors the intensity may decrease by 50 per cent up to the prescribed limits; it shall decrease steadily to reach practical cut-off at not more than 5° outside the prescribed limits.

(b) All-round lights shall be so located as not to be obscured by masts, topmasts or structures within angular sectors of more than 6°, except anchor lights, which need not be placed at an impracticable height above the hull.

10 *Vertical sectors*

(a) The vertical sectors of electric lights, with the exception of lights on sailing vessels shall ensure that:

(i) at least the required minimum intensity is maintained at all angles from 5° above to 5° below the horizontal;

(ii) at least 60 per cent of the required minimum intensity is maintained from 7.5° degrees above to 7.5° below the horizontal.

(b) In the case of sailing vessels the vertical sectors of electric lights shall ensure that:

(i) at least the required minimum intensity is maintained at all angles from 5° above to 5° below the horizontal;

(ii) at least 50 per cent of the required minimum intensity is maintained from 25° above to 25° below the horizontal.

(c) In the case of lights other than electric these specifications shall be met as closely as possible.

Index